THE BOX OFFICE POISON STORY

(Pioneers of Pop Noir)

By

RUSSELL C. BRENNAN

DECEMBER BOOKS UK

Published by December Books UK

Cover Photo by Anne Bygrave

Website: http://dedicated-follower.co.uk/December-Books.html

Email: december.books@yahoo.com

Author website: http://dedicated-follower.co.uk/rcb.html

Website for Music in book http://futurelegendrecords.com

Special thanks to Annie Bygrave who took many of the photos in this book and Dieter Marsoner for designing some of the record sleeves.

LIMITED EDITON

FOREWARD

Many bands made a big splash, had one or two hits then disappeared and their CD/vinyl usually resided in a charity shop or boot fairs not long after. Bands with multiple hits would prevail. However, music pioneers live just below the surface in a shadowy corner marked *'Influencing from the sidelines*'. They often have much longer shelve life, selling consistently over many years, never going out of fashion like so much of the mainstream. It's usually music lovers that live and breathe creative music and latch onto such bands. Only occasionally will such a band venture out above the parapet to breath some mainstream air and get spotted. These one-off appearances, be it on radio, in the press and occasionally on TV do in fact reach quite a lot of people. Some people are excited to discover such acts but most mainstream people forget about them within a few days but unknowingly something sticks, They then buy mainstream acts music who have often taken the basics of what these innovators have done but watered it down grabbing some success with it. Amongst the pioneers, one such act was Box Office Poison.

Although to the outside world, or least those that were paying attention, Box Office Poison made a splash in music in 1993. However, it's important to know the embryonic evolution of this band that would pioneer the new music genre of POP NOIR, which had a Punk/Jazz attitude, a classical ambience, gritty or sexy lyrics and a filmic feel.

I was the person behind the band but the embryo actually came about during my first big music success with my ex-wife, pop singer Eleanor Rigby, who is still a massive cult figure with many sales behind her even though she is no longer around. Her biography explained a lot and one thing very briefly touched on was that she was feeling a lot of pressure as a solo artist and felt she would cope better as the lead singer of a band. I was already writing and producing her songs and played on them occasionally but didn't become a band member due to management duties but once I ditched those she said we should now be in a band together. We discussed the fact that we had taken her music as far as it could go without repeating itself. She was very much like a combination of Debbie Harry fronting the 60s sounding Kinks although she also had a very distinctive and versatile voice and was as hot as Debbie looks-wise. Although we had added harpsichord & organ to the guitar-based sound and incorporated some Motown as well we were both looking to grow as artists.

One day I saw my favourite artist David Bowie on TV doing a cover of *Sorrow* from his 'Pin-Ups' album. Although he was very guitar/piano rock-based he was always progressing musically and the instruments dominating this cover were sax (of which he was an excellent player) & violin, no guitars. So I said to Eleanor it would be great to have two different instruments as the leads instead of guitar or piano and I liked this combination but preferred cello to violin and thought we could keep the harpsichord we had started to incorporate and ditch the guitars. Also after discovering the koto, (Used to good effect when producing her No.1 hit *You Only Live Twice*,) I wanted to feature that as well. It was also a little known fact (although it was exposed in her biog) that she played the sax. So a blueprint was forming and I decided to test it out on the original release of 'Themes from the 60s Vol.1' covering *Man in a Suitcase & Mission Impossible* in this new style. All I needed was a new band name and came up with Ministry of Defiance, which featured random musicians along with myself. (Eleanor was out of practice sax wise so didn't play on it). A limited edition of this album came out in 1988, sold fast and was quickly deleted but those tracks in particular proved popular. The cult themes albums would go on to be very influential when launched properly in 1993 and I produced and arranged over 100 tracks over 7 albums in the end. With the themes production style I had also added to the feel & sound of what Pop Noir would be about, which was a filmic feel even though we would be song-based. The other big influence on Pop Noir, although I didn't know it at the time were the big hits by Dave Dee Dozy, Beaky, Mick & Titch. They did three-minute film type scenarios in songs such as *Last Night in Soho, The Legend Of Xanadu, Don Juan & Wreck of the Antoinette*. These were fantastic sounding records and pulled you into the story in both words, atmosphere and musically. Ironically I also became really good friends with the producer of these influential DDDBM&T tracks, one Steve Rowland who had surfaced as a gig promoter and put on one of Eleanor's early concerts.

My songs and production were more Film Noir than mainstream hence the Noir tag, although having previously written catchy pop songs this added the pop element and the phase 'Pop Noir' was born to hang this genre on. However, Eleanor's new manager Dick Crippen wanted us to stick with a winning formula and he had managed to pull together a band of people from other famous bands like The Mission, The Piranhas & Peter & the Test Tube Babies to back her but they insisted on being more than a backing band and as she wanted to be part of a band she agreed and it was then supposed to go out under the name of The Eleanor Rigby Band. So I continued writing songs in the Eleanor Rigby style of Mod/Britpop and had about half a dozen new songs. Then all hell broke loose and as those who read 'The Definitive Eleanor Rigby Story' will know she had a nervous breakdown and couldn't go on tour and a doppelganger was found to replace her for the tour. Eleanor then up and disappeared and the band became The Psychomatics with them still doing a few of my songs, both new and old but they then imploded. With my career & marriage on the rocks, music was the last thing on my mind and like Eleanor, the mental & physical strain took its toll and I too left the building for a while.

I returned to music the following year but it wasn't with my new formula but another music love of mine, Ska and I put out what was effectively a solo single, *Skankin with The Toreadors,* under the name of Ministry of Ska. It proved popular with 50,000 sales on an album called 'Ska Beats'. I was then offered a few record deals. I accepted one with Big Wave Records who had earned a lot of money from no.1 hits by Jive Bunny. They gave me a £3,000 advance to do a 12" version of my hit track and then I bumped into Dick, who also wanted to do Ska, so we became a duo and so my alternative 'Pop Noir' musical journey was put on hold to concentrate on Ska for a year or so. Big Wave then went bust before releasing our 12" single and paying us some promised advance money for our album, so we turned to other labels who had shown a lot of interest but they ended up messing us around and with both of us in demand as record producers we decided to shelve Ministry of Ska but not before achieving some modicum of success playing a massive concert in Belgium and appearing at the Diamond Record awards (Which is an interesting story I itself and in my full biography). We later released what is now considered a classic album 'Rarin To Go' on Future Legend Records)

CHAPTER ONE

BOX OFFICE POISON ARE BORN

A new decade seemed like the right time for a new band but things stalled initially. There was some spill over with Ministry of Ska and then Eleanor decided to return from the wilderness and we got back together again. Music took a back seat and things went well with me & Eleanor for 9 months but then she up and disappeared again. Unlike last time where I couldn't bring myself to do anything I decided to throw myself into my new music project and made a big decision. For others not to let me down, I had to be in the band this time. I had already written many new songs which Eleanor had been very keen on and I was hoping she would be the lead singer in the new band but she made it clear music was the past for her now and nursing was probably what she wanted to do, although I never knew what she ended up doing as she disappeared again. So at that point, I was a band of just one.

I had decided the musical line up would be cello, sax, harpsichord, vocals and drums but was in two minds about adding a bass guitar. I had managed to persuade Eleanor's harpsichord player Avril to fill that spot and I was going to concentrate on drums & percussion. I also decided I wanted it to be an all-girl band except for me as I usually related to and got on better with girls. I wanted them to be top of the range musicians, so put an advert in the music papers and thought I'd quickly found the perfect line up. Sadly, I don't remember the sax players name but the cellist name was Catherine. Aurora, who stood out from the crowd, as she was bald was the vocalist. However, after a few rehearsals, it was clear the girls didn't get on at all and disliked each other.

After this false start, I was in Dicks recording studio producing other acts to get some money in and afterwards started recording some demos of new songs I'd written and in walked his current girlfriend Katie, who was quite sexy but very young. She started saying I like those songs what are they for? I filled her in and she imparted to me that she had ambitions to be a singer but Dick wouldn't take her seriously. Since she was keen and scrubbed up very well I said I'd give her a chance, she then added that she knew a great musician who could play many instruments and was looking to join a band so I enlisted her friend James and this looked like the prototype line up and some good demos were recorded. However, James started to become unreliable and after I told him off for the 5th time he quit. At this point, Katie had split up with Dick and was going out with James so followed him out the door not wishing to stay unless he was kept in the band.

At the time, I was also going out with a sexy dancer called Jane, when I told her what happened, she said she'd always fancied being a singer and was willing to step into Katie's shoes.

Jane was also pretty and not a bad singer, so I decided to record a few more songs with her then hit the record labels. But after almost finishing all the demos, Jane informed me she had been offered a very big dance job in Japan for 9 months and was taking it. I understood completely, as dancing was her first love and paid her rent. If the job had been in the UK she may have been able to juggle both. So it was back to square one but not for long as I bumped into another girl, Solfreid whilst at a music exhibition and she was looking to be a singer. So another round of recording demos were done but I had a few reservations about her singing but the matter resolved itself when she split up with her husband and decided she wanted to become an airhostess.

Above SOLFREID

CHAPTER TWO

MUSICAL CHAIRS

As well as producing other bands I had returned to DJing to pay the rent and one gig involved supporting a covers band called 'Pin Ups'. They had a sexy blonde girl singer, Nikki, so you can imagine what I was thinking but I soon discovered she came attached to the guitarist in the band and the keyboard player was also keen on her in an unrequited love type way and the bizarre thing was they all lived together. I hit off with the keyboard player Paul in particular. But I was still looking to blag the singer for my band. So after they invited me around for dinner I got to work but she wasn't interested and happy being in 'Pin Ups'. Then fate played a hand. A contact that used to be with the now-defunct Big Wave Records contacted me about producing a track but he didn't have a band to do it. I was already getting a small rep for being the new Joe Meek and so he chose me because the track they wanted to cover was the Heinz hit *Just Like Eddie,* originally produced by Joe but the deal breaker was I had to find a band to do it. So I turned to my newfound friends in Pin-Ups and produced it for them. The record was released but very little promotion or money was spent on it and it flopped. I ended up getting the best result from this episode. On reflecton I felt Nikki wasn't quite right for an experimental band like my new outfit so good she turned it down. Paul on the other hand was just right for the band. So at least now I had one new person (Avril had just left to go to University). I had already come up with a name by this point. I decided Ministry of Defiance wasn't quite right and because I had big ambitions for the band and have a bit of a sense of humour, I thought wouldn't it be funny to be number one with a name like Box Office Poison so that became the band's name. Well you have to aim high, Don't You?

(Pin-Ups are below & Paul is on the left)

The next turning point had its roots in something that had come along previously. I had written a book called 'Music Business Bastards (How to do well in the music business without getting ripped off) earlier in the year and it was put out by Martin Breese Publishing and it had done very well, with me doing mainstream interviews on Channel 4, Radio One & Capital Radio. The launch party for it was at Martins place and I was introduced to a music manager called Phil Simmonds. His son was in one of the TV soaps and he had managed hit bands Siouxsie & The Banshees and The Real Thing plus Mike Stock before he became part of the famous Stock Aiken & Waterman hit team. He was no longer managing any of them but he still had the contacts and was looking for new talent, so he gave me his card. I thought now would be a good time to get a manager (Although I knew record label people myself I was sure he would carry more clout)
I now had Paul so was looking for a new vocalist, sax & cello player. Only this time I wouldn't go for the best just the most compatible. The sax player came first. Sadly very few applied and I decided to give a novice, Dave a chance. He was a painter & decorator by trade and stood on the football terraces at Millwall at the weekends so didn't seem the usual musco type. What I wanted from the sax was an improvised jazzy type part not just solos like *Baker Street.* Dave was perfect for this as I would suggest riffs on occasion but mostly just get him to play and take the best parts from the recordings. Since he was still learning his trade a few interesting things popped out. Getting a singer proved trickier. After working with the calibre of Eleanor for so long it was hard to find anyone anywhere near that level, so I set my sights lower but the girls I auditioned either sung well but looked terrible or looked very good but couldn't sing very well, then along came Louise and it was her back story as much as her voice that won me over. Lou had been a singer since the age of 13 and between 14 & 15 had been in a popular outfit from Bath called The Graduate. They were offered a record deal but because she was underage her mother had to sign the deal and refused, saying her daughter was far too young to be in a band. So the rest of the band signed the deal without her and the songwriters became the singers and after one record changed their name to Tears for Fears who went on to have big worldwide hits with tracks such as *Mad World* and *Everybody Wants to Rule the World* (I think they had a thing about the word '*World*'). Louise was gutted and went off the rails finding herself pregnant before turning 16 and being forced to quit school (Not that she went much anyway). She was devoted to her daughter for a while but as her daughter got older she decided she still wanted to fulfil her music dream and moved to London and that's where I came in. Louise was a very good singer and in some small way reminiscent of Eleanor especially when I produced her but not as distinctive. Looks-wise she wasn't ugly but neither was she a stunner, she could look hot on occasion but whether she had that star quality I was never convinced in that department but she was dedicated and enthusiastic and with other options thin on the ground I decided she was worth giving a shot to. he cello position proved the most problematic, however. Every single cello player auditioned said they were classically trained and could only read music and play that way and couldn't improvise.

So with my vision for B.O.P and this new Pop Noir idea faltering I decided the quickest way to get what I wanted was for me to learn to play the cello. So I took 6 lessons from a guy called Igor. (With his Eastern European accent he sounded like someone from a horror film but looked more conventional). He wanted me to try and read music like all the other cello players but I instilled in him, I just want to learn the basics, where the notes were and how to play them and I was going to write my own songs.

He said he would be interested to hear these, as he was sceptical that someone who couldn't read music could write it (I believe Lennon & McCartney didn't do too badly)

However, when I returned with some recordings some months later he announced this is the sort of thing Mozart would have done had he been around today and was impressed. (I didn't dwell on this as it may have scrambled my brain, as that would be a lot to live up to). I then developed the punk cello (more about punk cello in its own chapter). Another thing that gave me a smile from this episode was, as I was still learning he put red tape on the cello neck so that I could remember where the notes were. I could have taken it off as got the hang of the cello but left them on purposely to make it look amateurish but to me, it was a funny & rebellious to do. Later Mouse (who will feature eventually) designed a netting Jacket for the cello to wear. It was supposed to be for it at home but I kept it like that for gigs and it made the cello very distinctive and eventually famous. So finally Box Office Poison's line up was complete.

CHAPTER THREE

WHAT's IN A NAME?

Many pop stars have had made up names and I feel this adds colour to proceedings.. Although Louise surname became a famous name when Jess Ennis won gold at the Olympics I didn't think it had a pop star ring about it, so re-christened her Debbie Detroit. Dave likewise needed a name. He would often turn up to rehearsals wearing a bowler hat (this was more a of a nod to Clockwork Orange than the gents in the city), so I christened him Bowler. I was still trying to think of a name for Paul but nicknamed him Keys for the time being. Strangely, I wasn't going to change my name but the others all ganged up on me and said, if they had to change theirs I had to change mine. My argument was, my name was known because of my success with Eleanor and would add value to our PR but the band weren't having it. So because I was first and foremost a writer, I changed my name to Russell Writer and produced under that as well or R C Writer. I later reverted to my real name with my current band Psykick Holiday and made my name in many arts. With the music done it was time for an image and some photos. My initial idea had been to make us a mystery group and put out a rumour that we were someone famous. To go with the film and mystery angle I dressed as Zorro and Dave as a Highwayman. I then came up with lacy Victorian underwear that looked quite distinctive for Louise. Since I was in the group I got another photographer to take the shots but directed the photographer in what we wanted. Both Dave and Louise were very nice people and I got on well with them but neither were the brightest people in the world. One of the looks I wanted was us walking out of the mist and I had brought some smoke pellets along to get this effect. However, strangely on the day of the shoot, it happened to be foggy outside so I gave both Dave and Louise a carrier bag each and asked them to go and capture some fog for the shoot. They only went and did it, then came back saying. It's impossible; the fog kept escaping from the carrier bags. I then said I had another idea. I had brought an old stereo speaker with me, which Louise had seen but Dave hadn't. Dave was looking around the photographer's office before the shoot and commented on what a good stereo system he had. I then took a few photos of Dave and Louise myself but suddenly stopped, saying the background looks too boring. The photographer had gone out to get something to eat at this point and I went into his office and then came back with my speaker making out it was the photographers. I took one photo with Dave by it and then said it still looked boring. I then produced some matches and set light to the speaker. Dave went white as a sheet saying' You're crazy, the geezer will do his nut when he comes back and finds his speaker on fire. But it had served its purpose, I got a great picture of the expression on Dave's face with a speaker on fire nearby. Sadly I can't locate this photo anymore only one of the speaker still smouldering,

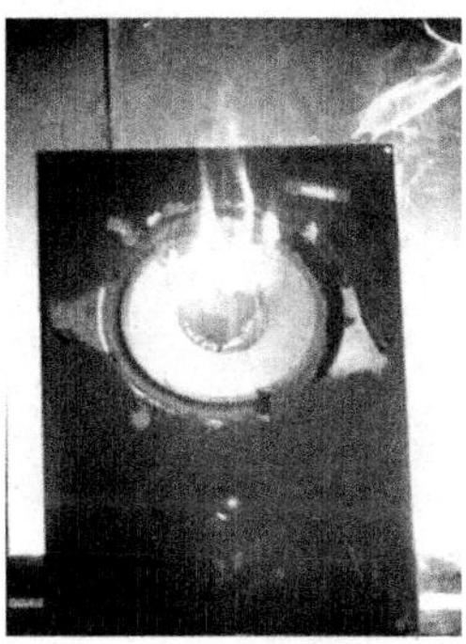

Our first photo session and image turned out quite good so we were good to go.

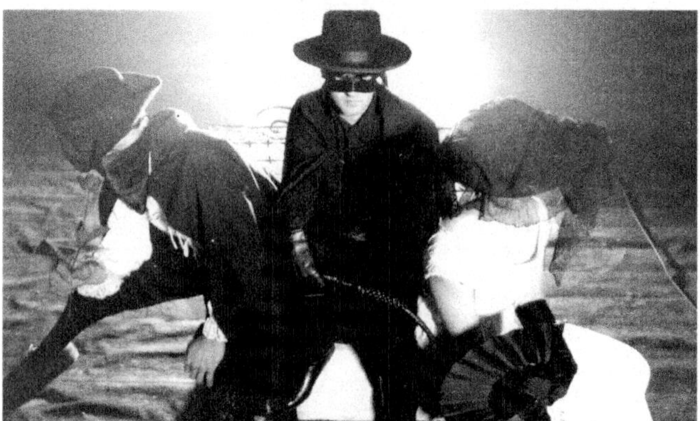

Talking of Zorro. I made good use of my outfit at a fancy-dress party at a hotel that Xmas, but ended up taking things too far and nearly crippled myself. I was trying to impress a waitress I had chatted up and was on the first-floor balcony that went around in a square and in the middle was a chandelier. I had a whip and whipped it around the top bit of the chandelier and tried to swing from one side of the balcony to the other but the whip came loose and I went hurtling onto a table below along with part of the chandelier. I was lucky not to break any bones. I was battered and bruised but despite the embarrassment, I still got the girl, a very sexy French waitress. In the morning I got the bill for the chandelier repair though. Ouch!

Although I had written new songs I was always good at thinking up new song arrangements and sounds for cover versions to make them more distinctive and one track I thought would suit our style was *Laser Love,* a very minor T-Rex hit. The original had 2 distinctive guitar riffs and like a call and answer approach as they call it in the trade. I wanted one to be played by cello & one by sax to dominate the track. I also started experimenting with sounds like a tree branch being whipped through the wind & also cracking a whip in a high pitched way and I had also made it sound like a bass drum sound (Something similar turned up in Prodigy's no.1 hit *Breath* many years later). I also added extra percussion, mostly tambourine and Paul played the harpsichord on it as he did on the next track *1995.* Back in the Eleanor Rigby days, many fans said my song *1995* should have been an A-side, not a B-side so I decided I would make this our first single. I had the basic bare bones of what I wanted from James backing track then added Bowlers sax and then some cello.

With a Box Office Poison package ready I started seeing record labels and sending them out to others but I was finding things tough. Phil had also found the same problem and given up and commented that many new kids in A &R wouldn't take him seriously as he was old. So he decided to retire but said I could call on him for advice any time. Most A&R people thought the music was too innovative and the general public wouldn't get it. Some even offered me large sums of money to just go and re-create another Eleanor Rigby and repeat myself. They couldn't understand that it wasn't about the money, as an artist I needed to grow and achieve new goals. I knew when I thought up a totally new genre of music there would be resistance and it wouldn't be easy but I was willing to persevere with it. Also, there could only ever been one Eleanor.

Being ahead of your time and an innovator can often be a lonely road to travel. Most people lack visions and people in positions of power often have mediocre minds which leads to massive resistance to change. But if you look at music history it is the people who came up with something different that had a lot of resistance or struggled that hit very big when the public finally heard them. The Beatles, Elvis, The Sex Pistols, Abba to name but a few.

I finally got one or two breakthroughs. At SBK, (an E.M.I subsidiary that had Cher and a few other big selling acts on its label). The A&R person got excited by the music but wanted to hear more material and advanced me some money to record a couple of new tracks. I recorded *Cry Out the Pain* and *Sad World* and he recommended we be signed up. However, his boss was frightened by the innovation and we were blown out. Island Records were also quite keen on us but it was a similar story, the A&R person had some vision but his boss didn't.

My favourite track written for Eleanor was *Think For Yourself* and I set about reconstructing this with cello being the dominant feature. Two new tracks, *Sad World & 16 Year Old* were then added to a limited edition vinyl white label and I persuaded Phil to give one last go at getting us a deal as I was definitely not keen to be the manager. Labels reactions were mixed, mostly about Louise. Some thought she was hot others called her ugly. Many said go and find yourself another Eleanor Rigby and do what would become Britpop, some didn't get the new concept saying it was too Avant-Garde. Others thought it had possibilities. But the overall opinion was Phil was finding it hard. His solution was as follows. He would continue to try but felt the easiest deal to get was for dance music (His son had just got one) and so we should consider doing a few dance tracks.

I wasn't keen to be lumbered as a dance act and although I said guitars were out I didn't have anything against dance music and quite liked it on occasion. Some weeks later a great idea dropped into my head. I always liked the hit *Popcorn* and I could see a dance version of this might do very well, so I got together with Paul and did a dance version of this classic with Louise doing atmospheric backing vocals & Bowler Jazzy sax. I did percussion, cello & production. It came out extremely well and whilst on a roll, I also came up with an original dance track called *Checkmate.* (Sometimes songs take years some times they can be done in ten minutes and this was the case with this one). This session went so well I was keen to carry on but we couldn't get any more time so Paul and I decamped back to my house where I recorded on my own home set up. Paul had come up with a fairly hypnotic backing track with a few bits of music floating along in it. I loved the feel of the track. So I just switched off all the lights played the track and sung along with the track the first thing that came into my head and that became the first draft of *Mysteries*. Later I added quite a bit to the music and created a part 2 that would feature Louise at a later date.

Phil got a few bits of interest in us, which then fizzled out. We then had a band meeting and the rest of the band said Phil was not only too old but too old school to get us a deal and we should get a younger manager. He was happy to finally retire, so there were no hard feelings.

The problem was we had no replacement, which would mean muggings would have to become the manager. Not at all what I wanted but then fate played a hand. As stated before, I had written a popular book, Music Business Bastards and this was responsible for a few results. I had said to my publisher, why not sell advertising space in the back of the book, as the adverts would reach their exact target audience (the music industry). He said it had never been done before. I said that's not a reason not to try it. He didn't think anyone would advertise but I managed to get quite a few music biz places to advertise in it shocking him. He was over the moon about the money he earned from it saying, it was the first book he ever put out that made a profit before it was even released and it helped me pay a few of my bills too. Anyway, one of the advertisers was a guy called Mike, a very edgy character from New York, now living in London who ran a record pressing plant. He was also in a semi-famous band called The Cannibals and after hearing some of my previous releases with Eleanor, he hired me to produce a few singles for them. They were very much a cult garage band and he was the singer. They'd had albums out and were a big live draw but wanted their shot at stardom and some hit singles. They identified that I was very good at breathing new life into classic songs and doing interesting classy and catchy song arrangements & productions.

Mike had said 'Censorship' by Eleanor Rigby was one of his favourite albums and he was blown away by the production of it and in particular the cover of the Stones song, *Play with Fire* and it was also a Stones song he wanted to cover, *Get Off My Cloud.* He wanted it done in the new 'Baggy' style (This was a phase attached to bands like the Stone Roses, Happy Mondays & Primal Scream). So that's just what I did but I had reservations about doing such a famous song as it was always going to get compared to the original especially with a male vocal, so he said as a back up he would do a less famous cover and wanted to do a version of The Doors *Soul Kitchen.* (This was just a Doors album track on their 1st album but it had possibilities).He said he also knew I was a very good percussionist and asked me to play on the track, so I did and this exposed the big difference between a record producer & arranger and a studio engineer. Many studio engineers are technically good but have zero imagination when it comes to arrangements and production, that's why most but not all don't make great record producers. They always seem to make bland clear sounding records. A good example of this was when engineers were freaked out by my EQ frequencies on a mix. I asked why they didn't like it and many replied, I had not done it according to what's in the manual, which is how they did all their mixing. I pointed out that if he wanted to be a producer he should use his ears not put all the eq's the same on every recording just because it was some sort of technical specification. (Joe Meek used to get the same argument from engineers as me and he didn't do badly).
Anyway, at The Cannibals session, I was playing a tambourine and shaker but instead of playing it on the OFF or ON beat which is the bog-standard way to do it, I was using it to punctuate the bass line in the song. The bass would play a line and then stop and a gap would appear and I filled it with an interesting rhythm with one of the percussion instruments. This particular engineer's kept saying it's wrong; it isn't on the beat or off the beat. As a producer, I hear the finished product in my head even before I've done it and although I like to leave room for improvisation, I know exactly what I'm going for. I told Mike & the engineer to trust me, as I knew what I was doing. To them, it seemed I'd jus play all of a sudden for no reason and with only the bare bones of the track done and unmixed I could see why they were getting concerned. But come the final mix both were raving about what a big difference it made to the track and it helped grab people's attention. I knew Mike had a record pressing plant but he surprised me at this session by telling me he also had a record label and it was doing well. So I got talking to him about Box Office Poison. He said he was so happy with what I had done producing his tracks he was willing to give me a record deal for B.O.P as a bonus. There would be no advance but he would pay for a 7" & 12" vinyl on any release and video & plugger. It was tempting but I had already made an appointment with a music business legend about getting a deal. (Mike pictured below)

CHAPTER FOUR

THE LEGEND & ME

Mickie Most had produced a string of big hit singles like *House of The Rising Sun* for The Animals, all Herman's Hermits hits including the No. 1 hit *I'm Into Something Good*, also the American No.1 *To Sir With Love* for Lulu and *Hi Ho Silver Lining* for Jeff Beck. There were many others in the 60s but come the 70s he went to an even higher level if that were possible and launched his own record label, 'Rak', who were the most successful label in the 70s beating even the major labels when it came to hit rate. They had numerous numbers one hits by Suzi Quatro, Mud, Hot Chocolate & Smokie to name but a few. Nicky Chinn and Mike Chapman had written many of these hits along with others for bands not on Rak like Sweet. Mike also went on to produce many of Blondie's biggest hits at the tail end of the 70s. But this showed that not only was Mickie a legendary record producer but a top A & R man, discovering the acts & songwriters and putting the right ones together. Although the 70s were Rak's golden period they still had lots of hits in the 80s as well with Kim Wilde being another success story & the reissue of *You Sexy Thing* by Hot Chocolate that also just kept on giving.

As many will know Eleanor Rigby got offered a few major record deals at the start of her career but the likes of Virgin & E M I but they wanted her to ditch her Mod image and fans and do twee cover versions. So we turned them down. CBS initially wanted Eleanor but chose Altered Images instead with Claire Grogan as their flagship pop girl on the label and saw a great future for her but they got it wrong as Altered Images success was short-lived and besides, Claire was more of an actress. Eleanor proved more influential and successful than Claire in the long run. I doubt her records sell much these days and if you do see them it's in a charity shop. Then there was the ill-fated £100,000 offer from Warner Brothers that Eleanor turned down while cracking up. Pye Records would have been a good home for her and to be on the same label as The Kinks would have been some sort of poetry but Pye were now on their way out and had become PRT. For some reason I found it easier to get in-person appointments with the majors than with smaller companies, the Indie label boom had only just started but there were these mid-level companies like Rak around and most of these wouldn't see me, so I had to send them stuff. They blew us out but I did meet Mickie at the music business party after Eleanor had just disappeared. I pointed out that I had sent him Eleanor's stuff and thought he would have gone for it. He said he didn't recall getting anything and said he was impressed with the splash she had made with *I Want to Sleep with You* and thought the condom idea was genius. So he even went and bought the record and loved it. His summation was, even had I addressed the package to him (which I did) it would automatically go to the A&R department and someone there would check it out first and only if they were really sold on the act would it go to him. He also thought that even if the act was good if they had a similar act IE: Kim Wilde this would have been a reason to turn it down. He concluded you win some you lose some but I had got it right with Eleanor and should I have something else in the future to come and see him personally.

Anyway, it had taken a while but here I was in his office in the upmarket London area of St Johns Wood up close and personal and the thing that sticks in my mind most was he was wearing the smartest pair of red shoes I'd ever seen. As I drank my complimentary coffee and he listened to the 5 Box Office Poison tracks. (One of which was the cover of *Lazer Love*),

He then got all animated when discussing one song in particular, saying, *Think for Yourself* was one of the best songs he had heard in years. I was thinking where do I sign. Then he said have you got any more like that? I said I was writing more but maybe that would make a great first single although I thought he might have gone for 1995. He then went quiet for a moment and said with publishing it's all about the songs. I was puzzled and explained I came to him because of Rak's great track record. He then gave me some unexpected news. Rak records were no longer going and he had sold his back catalogue to E M I. and he was now concentrating on music publishing only, plus keeping his hand in producing the odd act. I was gutted as I was after a record deal, not a publishing deal so there seemed to be a few cross wires. I had also been advised to hold onto my publishing rights but Mickie was an influential person so maybe signing to his publishing company might be a good move so asked him about it. His reply was *Think for Yourself* is definitely a winner and I love it but sadly I wasn't blown away by any of the other tracks. He concluded the meeting by saying if your write anymore like *Think for Yourself* come back and see me but in publishing, we only sign songwriters who have at least a handful of great songs, not one-off songs. I had seen Rak as my ideal home for record releases but it was yet another disappointment and with Phil also now giving up for good and only Mikes definite offer on the table I signed with his Hit records label to move things forward and keep the band together as the troops were becoming restless.(Mickie below)

Think For Yourself

What are we hear for, what's it all about. Who are we bluffing, I want to scream and shout

Cigarette perfume litters your breath. Time to get going, to the house on the corner, Drink yourself to death

Chorus

Think for yourself don't be a fool, Think for yourself you can be cool, think for yourself, think for yourself

Living in a catalogue world, buy and sell my life, Unfaithful husbands looking for someone else's wife

Adverts sound as sweet as honey but all the really want is your money

Say no to people ruling your life, from when you're a daughter to when you're a wife

Stay individual and do what is right,Think For yourself, yeh, Think for Yourself

CHAPTER FIVE

FROM HIT TO SHIT

With the Mickie Most deal being a dead-end we signed with Mike's label, ironically called 'Hit Records' (Not that they had had any) However, it was too late to save one band member. The best musician in the band by far was Paul but after I told him the good news about the record deal he shocked me by quitting, not quite what I was expecting! I could tell something was badly wrong so I jumped into the car and drove down to see him in Portsmouth. When I arrived Paul was in a bad way as his story started to unfold. First, he was at pains to point out his decision to quit had nothing to do with B.O.P or me. I knew he always had a thing for the lead singer in his band, Nikki but the other band member was the boyfriend. As well as being in the band together they also shared a house. The whole thing had come tumbling down like the walls of Jericho. Something had happened to make Nikki suddenly feel uncomfortable (whether he had suddenly seen her naked in the bath or something I don't know). It may have been a case of the couple's relationship going up a notch and them wanting their own place and Paul had read too much into the situation. The end result was, that not only did they want to move out but also dissolve the band as well. Although Paul had a lowly paid council job it was the earnings from the covers band that brought in the lions share of the money and Paul was the person who had fronted the mortgage for the house and the others were just renting and sharing the bills. He also had a company car and this was taken off him due to council cuts around the same time. He felt like his world was collapsing around him and was hit by severe depression and found it hard to get out of bed for weeks and hadn't paid any bills and a repossession order was made on his house. He had to be out by the following week. For some strange reason, he blamed music for everything. If he hadn't done the band he wouldn't have met Nikki and not found himself doing what he considered he was born to do, be a musician, harbouring big ambitions that were now dead. I pointed out B.O.P could be his musical outlet but he said it wouldn't pay the bills. I managed to cheer him up a bit but couldn't change his mind to stay with B.O.P. So I left and asked him to call me if ever he needed me. I did see him a few years later when he came back to do Department-S for B.O.P on a Cult Themes album and he said he ended up having a mental breakdown but had recovered and now lived a sedate 9-5 existence with a new girl he thought he might marry. Next up I met my other band members who were a lot happier and it seemed I had just got the deal in time as far as Bowler was concerned. He was getting fed up with the rejections and thinking about quitting.

Straight after I signed the deal with Mike, he wanted to move quickly and thought *Popcorn* was a winner and we should go with that as the first single before the original tracks but we needed a B-side and 12" mix of Popcorn. I met up with Louise & Dave and we recorded the B-side for *Popcorn*, *Getting thru the Day*, which was a popular song I'd written for Eleanor but I now did a dance version of it. (Mostly to keep Louise happy as she loved dance music and she had lived the lyric). It came out well and I then did the 12" mix of *Popcorn* and alternative 7" mix. I gave the tapes to Mike and he quickly pressed up some white/yellow label promos and gave them to a plugger. The plugger said he had got a mixed reaction and asked for another mix (which was common back then) so I did a new mix of *Popcorn* that I considered far superior to the original and that was chosen for the release and another white label pressed up for radio where it started to get a good reaction.

Next up, I did a psychedelic photo of a popcorn box that people into Acid House would like as that music style was just breaking through. Then the ball started rolling for the single to be pressed but just before that Mike had offered to pay for a promo video for the track and Dick had recommended a director. I saw his work and a shoot was arranged for the next weekend as some of the band members were working.

(Black & white version of colour sleeve)

But when I turned up to see the video director the day before about the script for the video he informed me Mike's deposit cheque had bounced. What was going on? The director said he would only shoot the video the next day if we brought cash. So I tried to reach Mike but he proved elusive and didn't answer his phone, so the video shoot was shelved. A few days later I decided to just turn up at Mikes factory and sure enough, he was there and looking very despondent. At first, he was surprised and a little embarrassed to see me but after a coffee, he unburdened himself to me and felt better for it.

All record labels need distributors and Mike's was the famous Rough Trade company and they had just gone bust. Although he could look for another distributor things were a lot worse for him because not only had Rough Trade been his distributor they also used his pressing plant for many releases and when they went bust they had owed him tens of thousands of pounds. So this in turn made him bankrupt as well and that's why the cheque to the video director had bounced. Luckily or unluckily depending on how you look at it, he hadn't quite started pressing our single up when he got the news about Rough Trade so no copies were made to even take away and try and sell or get a deal for elsewhere. So Mike voided our contact and our debut single was now no more.

I'm not one to give up easily and I'd recently had a call from my mate Steve Rowland who I name checked at the start of the book. He was a legendary record producer with many number one hits including *The Legend of Xanadu* for Dave Dee Dozy Beaky Mick & Titch & *I Lost My Heart to a Starship Trooper* for Sarah Brightman & Hot Gossip to name but a few. He had also put on Eleanor's first ever gig at Le Beatroute in Soho. He told me he was now an in house producer at the famous Britannia Row recording studios (used by New Order U2, Asward and many others) but was also A & R consultant at Arista Records. When I'd last seen him he was doing dance music and had just produced a big dance hit called *Monkey See, Monkey Do* for a dance label he was working for.

I had of course seen him about B.O.P's original music and he said it was too Avant-Garde for the majors and not dance music, so couldn't help in his position at the time. So as *Popcorn* was a dance track I called him back and went to see him. He thought it was a winner and recommended it to Arista but they said they couldn't see it getting anywhere. Yet 6 months later a novelty dance version not as good as our version of *Popcorn* hit number one by the Crazy Frog. It showed I was on the ball as usual but also as usual the major labels had no vision. I'm also someone who just carries on to keep the momentum going rather than give up and I knew the other band members would be down about us losing our record deal and *Popcorn* not coming out, so I booked some recording time at Dicks studio to record a few more tracks as he owed me a favour for producing some acts for his small Indie label.

Although I'm usually ahead of my time I am also aware of what was going on. Acid House was the big thing and I had thought *Popcorn* could cross over to that market (Hence the sleeve for it) but I was also a fan of a Rolling Stones song called *We Love You* and had thought up a new original arrangement for it that was very Acid House. So wanted to record that. But it was also important to keep writing original material and I had written a song called *Nightmares* and wanted to record this as well. It was a very experimental song, I even played the drums on bits of paper and rustled up crisp packets and scraped the walls on it, harpsichord and punk cello along with Bowler's sax made up the rest of the song apart from the vocals. As soon as we recorded it Bowler said, it sounds like it should be in the film Nightmare on Elm Street. I agreed so added a few Freddy references to it and before our next session to do *We Love You* I found out a guy called Robert Shay of Nu-Line was in charge of the Elm Street films so sent him a copy of the track.

NIGHTMARES

(Knick Knack paddy whack…Freddie's back, Freddie's back)

Creeping through the twilight hours, Drifting through he morning showers

I will see you in your Nightmares, In your Nightmares., In your Nightmares

I will steal your mind in the blackness of night

I will send you images that will give it a fright

I will leave you sweating in the cold light of day

About lots of demons that will take you away

I will see you in your Nightmares In your Nightmares. In your Nightmares

Skulking around the corners of your deepest fears, I will be with you for years and years

I will see you in your Nightmares In your Nightmares. In your Nightmares

We returned a few days later to the studio to do *We Love You*. With Paul having left the band, keyboards were often down to me but I was only barely competent on them (Our previous singer Jane had taught me how to play) At the time, working on computers gave you a lot of scope to try out new ideas without having to hire lots of musicians, or if a band member had left this helped me fine-tune the keyboard and organ parts, so I started recording in this manner. We had almost finished recording the track after 2 days when the computer crashed and according to the engineer Howard, who had been helping us, all the work was lost. Louise was then off on holiday and after she was due back the studio was fully booked for 3 months with an album project. So I had to shelve the idea, which wasn't good news as Rave music was at its height and a big hit at that time was *Strawberry Fields Forever* by Candy Flip which hit number 3 and my version of *We Love You* was not a million miles away from both style and vibe. It was so annoying. But it was about to get beyond annoying.
Dick and I had been friends for quite a while. It started when he managed Eleanor and we experienced the doppelganger affair together then continued our friendship when we joined forces for Ministry of Ska. Although we didn't always see eye to eye in Ministry of Ska we did still get on as friends and he says the Diamond Record Awards escapade he experienced with me was still a career highlight for him (even though he has toured around the world and had many hits with Tenpole Tudor) So he was the last person I thought would stab me in the back. So what happened? Well, three months after our *We Love You* recording session he had gotten a record deal for a young Acid House band called Sun doing an identical version of *We Love You* to what we had done. I wasn't happy. He protested his innocence and tried to blame it all on the engineer Howard (who definitely wasn't innocent) He claimed Howard had played him this arrangement claiming to have done it himself. (So the computer hadn't crashed it was a ploy to steal this arrangement) Furthermore, Howard introduced Dick to Sun. He saw the hit potential for an Acid House Rave record. To add insult to injury he had contacted a music company in Germany that had wanted to sign me to a publishing deal (which later fell apart when Eleanor was no longer here to sing the songs). The thing was they initially wanted to sign me because I wrote good songs but Dick pointed out it was Eleanor that was an important part of the package and so the publishing company waited for Eleanor to return but she never did so it fizzled out, or so Dick said. Anyway, he got ten grand advance money from this contact that my talent had attracted in the first place and got a hit in Germany for *We Love You* and the track also hit the lower region of the charts in the UK, so he earned a fair bit from it. I pointed out we had done it first and he'd ripped us off. He said he didn't know we had done it. I pointed out that he had come into the recording studio briefly when we were actually recording it. He claims it didn't register with him. I did have a very rough mix of it before the computer crashed on cassette but it did need more work and played it to him. He went bright red and said yes does sound very similar but then said he thought it was Howard's idea and he had paid him some money out of the advance and he had since had a row with Howard and sacked him. I told Dick I thought he should pay me some of the advance money. Dick refused, saying, you can't copyright an arrangement of a cover and I had no legal grounds to claim anything, which would have been a different case had it been an original song by me and added the best he could do was offer me a months recording time for free as compensation. At the time the money was much needed and I had no plans to record for a while so wasn't happy.

However, we made up in the end when we recorded more Ministry of Ska tracks for a Cult Themes album and that is when the free recording time did come in handy so it wasn't so bad in the end.
I decided not to tell the rest of the band, as they were not as good at dealing with setbacks as I was and fortunately such are the ups and downs of the music industry that some good news was just around the corner. Robert Shay at Nu-Line pictures got back to me saying he loved the Theme for Nightmare on Elm Street and wanted it to be the theme for the final Freddy film 'Nightmare on Elm Street Pt 6'. So this kept the band happy for a short while but we were still lacking that all-important record deal.

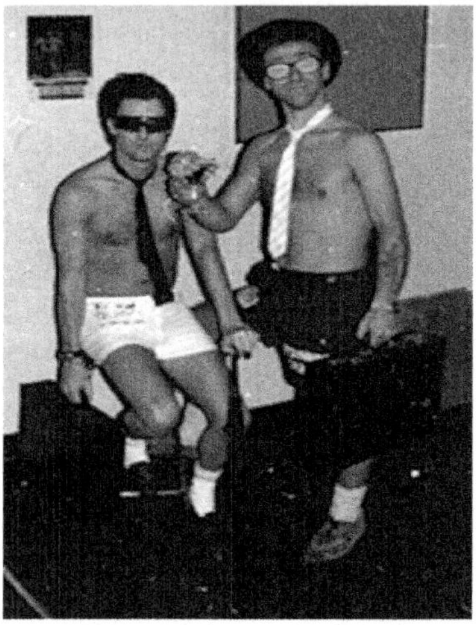

Ministry of Ska (Russ & Dick)

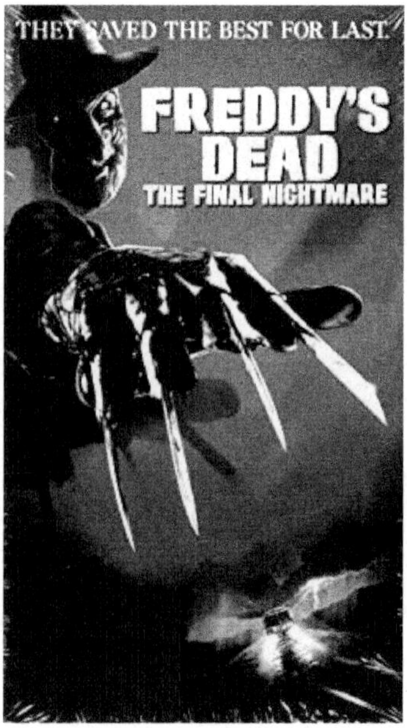

CHAPTER SIX

LEGACY & INFLUENCE

Although I felt the mystery image for the band was good and based on famous characters it hadn't quite worked and it was time for a new image for the band and me in particular. Although I was still a Mod at heart I was also an individual and my own style was always a priority and it's doubly important to stand out from the crowd when in a band. I had spied what could be best described as a futuristic bullfighters jacket. It was a one-off and definitely made me stand out. I added trousers tied at the sides and high collar or zip shirts. I had also designed my own Parka which was black with various patches on the sleeve (related to my life more than Mod bands) and it had a padded inside with a map of the world which I later changed to books. Dave/Bowler was less inclined to go for anything that stood out too much apart from his bowler hat, so I lent him my coat for the new photo shoot. Sod's law, Dave only forgot to bring his bowler hat on the day of the shoot. He nearly always wore it but had a quick painting job on before the shoot and didn't want to get paint on it so left it at home and running late he just jumped in his van and came straight to the shoot. He lived a bit too far away to go back and get it so we sorted out a different hat for him. The Victorian underwear image I had devised for Louie/Debbie Detroit still looked good and stood out so we kept that and it influenced many other singers in later years. My coat was much sort after and I had many offers for it over the years but something not too unsimilar turned up in the film The Matrix a few years later. Also because of my traumatic experience with Eleanor I had let my hair grow long but ever one to be distinctive I did what I called a double Samaria look. (Two ponytails at the back of my head, one near the top and one at the bottom) Music industry types including Eddie Pillar started to copy me but with just one at the bottom and it became a trend and so I cut mine off. So not only was I pioneering a new style of music but to some degree new fashions. *(Louise, Russell & Dave below)*

Most people in life, if successful have one thing that makes their name. I'm lucky in having multiple things I'm known for (I must be a freak) Publishers found it hard reading my biography (not yet published) not because it wasn't any good (JK Rowling's agent said I was one of the best raconteurs he had come across) It was because my multiple achievements showed up other biographies. As I said other biographies centred around one notable achievement and the rest of the book was padding. They couldn't get their head around the multiple talent/achievement thing and especially as they were all in different fields to some degree.

Eleanor Rigby's legacy lives on and her music still sells daily 30 years after she disappeared. Other labels always want to licence the notorious single *I Want to Sleep With You* for compilations such as Millions Like Us, (Mod comp) Sharon Signs (Iconic Indie Girls) and even on a number one hits comp (featuring Dusty Springfield, The Supremes & Fleetwood Mac) but in that case, it was *You Only Live Twice*. But not a year goes by without meeting someone from the music biz who still remembers the 'free condom' promotion for Eleanor's debut single. So that idea most definitely gave Eleanor's story a splash from the start (Her biog sold out in just a few weeks backing up that she had made an impact and I was 50% of the reason for that, which she always acknowledged)

The reason I'm bringing up this subject is because the next big splash I had was with my debut book release Music Business Bastards (how to do well in the music business without getting ripped off) mentioned earlier. The title got it noticed and I did mainstream interviews on Channel 4, Radio One & Capital Radio and it also featured in The Stage magazine. One of the first people to read this book, Tim London (original bass player with Eleanor Rigby) used it as a blueprint to get success. He formed his own band, Soho and had an international top 3 hit with *Hippy Chick*. But this book just kept on giving and influencing people, Other spins offs were, I was hired by the BBC to advise on Rogue Traders spin off show, 'The Worst', exposing a rip off record producer. This led to me bumping into Chris Cowey, who I had encountered when he was one of the producers on The Tube TV show and wanted to feature Eleanor. He was now in charge of Top Of The Pops 2, so we grabbed a coffee to catch up. We were both big Bowie fans and I tipped him off to the fact that some rare BBC video recordings had not been shown on Top of the Pops and one was a Bowie & Pete Frampton one of *Day In Day Out* and *Gene Genie* from an earlier show. He was very excited. Because I have a photographic memory for pop trivia and am a big record collector it comes in handy (More recently with my books 'Memories Are Made of This (The Ultimate Retro Pop Trivia Quiz. Vol.1 & 2'). I was aware that TOTP often recorded performances of singles that were popular in what was known as the midweek charts and most got featured in the show but if the record had dropped down the charts or run out of steam before the official chart those clips were never played and Bowie's was one of these. (I had seen 2 on a bootleg clip video I acquired) So Chris got on the case and tracked them down and showed them on TOTP 2 and got a lot of kudos for it, so he called me and bought me a meal as a thank you and asked if I'd be interested in using my knowledge in return for the odd gift or meal and in rare cases a cash bonus as he wasn't keen to put me officially on the books at the Beeb because of financial restraints but I could see, if it got out that I was doing what I was doing he would get a lot less kudos but I was happy to help. I agreed but only did it for a few months as I was busy with other things but I'd opened the door on a new world for Chris and he was more than capable of doing what I had done as time went on.

Also after MBB came out I was much sought after as a stylist and adviser for band images, names and photos (But don't mention this much) I finally get to why I brought up this subject and why it's relevant to Box Office Poison. An ITV show Motormouth had also noticed the book, got a copy and asked me to come and see them. The idea was for me to take an obscure band and turn them into a successful pop group using all the tips in my book and featuring a chapter each week. Now, I had to practice what I preached. They put an advert in the music press and got a sack load of tapes. I thought about going through them all but decided in the end to pick one at random as it would save time and be more of a challenge for me as well. The lucky band were 'Gold Against the Grain' (Yes folks bands do have such crap names). The band had been going 5 years and had only got as far as recording a demo and packing out their local youth club. It would definitely be a challenge. The band consisted of 3 guys and 2 girls. Their idea of image was still wearing their bank clerk clothes and standing outside a nondescript building in the city. The 2 girls were quite good looking as was the male lead singer and their voices were not too bad either. The material however wasn't very strong and the demo that I heard had no real arrangement and bland production. (Yes it may have been done in a 24-track studio and sounded clear but it didn't jump out at you or have much atmosphere and it travelled along all at one level)

So, first I came up with a name and an image and got a photo session done. The name I came up with was 'Perestroika'. It was a name featured in the news a lot at the time and a name people were noticing. With a Russian name, it made sense to go for a Russian image and I fashioned a Russian peasant image for them. My girlfriend Anne had long wanted to become a photographer and had been getting good at the technical side of things and had cut her teeth on doing the last B.O.P photos, so I asked her to do the photo session with some composition stylising help from me. We shot the pictures in Highgate Cemetery at Karl Marx Tomb. (It saved on a trip to Russian)

Let me tell you, just this small step alone, a name that stood out and a striking set of photos was enough to get people excited in the band even before we had recorded a note. As I felt only one of their tracks had any commercial potential I worked on the arrangement for this making it more catchy, dynamic and interesting and suggested a cover version as a second track to include on the demo. They had a similar vibe to Simple Minds so I chose a more obscure Simple Minds track called *Love Song*. (Never a hit but one of their best I always thought)

According to T.V people, it was a stunning and exciting transformation and it was like a totally different group. With the package now ready, it was time to send some out to industry people to get management and a record deal. Within 2 weeks after 5 years of struggle, they got a manager. The manager in turn then had 6 record companies chomping at the bit and interested in signing them after the obligation of seeing them live first of course. It was all going so well but then came the usual problems. At the recording session, the drummer quit halfway through and I had to finish off the drum track myself. (Apparently, his wife had once been in the band and had recently been sacked and was looking for revenge and forced him to quit to stall their big chance) While we were actively looking at getting a replacement it became apparent that the guitarist was freaking out and wanting to leave. Apparently he had felt great about being a local guitar hero, but now the big time beckoned he thought he couldn't handle going up a league and quit. It shocked me as I thought the reason to quit would have been not getting anywhere. Not long after that, the keyboard player Jane's boyfriend put pressure on her to leave. He was happy with things while the band was going nowhere, but now things were getting serious he thought Jane would meet someone else or he would hardly see her, so he offered to marry her if she left the band and since she had wanted this all along she left. Finally, Sophie the other female in the band had only joined the band because her mate Jane was in it and once she left Sophie didn't want to stay.

So that left Perestroika to become a one-person outfit of Kevin the vocalist and bass player. Not good news since the record companies were all dying to see the band live. But this was now not possible. To cut a long story short, they missed their chance and to add to this the T.V. documentary being filmed was scrapped after Thames lost their I.T.V. franchise to Carlton. Although this was bad news for Kevin & Perestroika it was looking like good news for me. As well as bass Kevin also played keyboards and as I needed a keyboard player I asked if he would like to salvage things by joining B.O.P. He was still a bit down about his missed opportunity but said one area he thought he was weak in was songwriting and asked me to teach him how to write better songs and he would then consider joining B.O.P and I agreed. (below The blonde is Sophie, Jane is the other girl & Kev is the one on his own)

I set about giving Kevin some pointers about songwriting. Not that I was any sort of expert because nearly every time I would write a song I did it differently. It was just that I'm good at spotting the catchiest part of any song and bringing it out whereas Kevin couldn't see this and his songs just meandered along with no variety. I was also known to be very good at lyrics and although his were not terrible he felt they could be better. We got 2 songs from these sessions that are still 2 of my favourites and they became B.O.P songs (So know you know why I'm mentioning this story)
First, I played a percussion riff using Arabic sounds and I hummed a bit of a melody and played a few Arab/Asian string sounds. Kevin added a few piano chords and then wrote some lyrics for it and added a bit to the melody. The song was originally called *Blood and Sand* about terrorist and hostages. It was O.K. but I thought I could do better so I wrote a song about the downtrodden life of a prostitute and called it *Is It Sex You Seek*. Instead and here it is.

IS IT SEX YOU SEEK

I could be in Casablanca, romance dripping from the walls

But instead I'm on the streets of Soho and I'm the one you call

One thing I've learnt in this life, There's no luck for me at all

Is it sex you seek, or just a peek of my body writhing

Is it sex you seek, Your flesh is weak, see my mind dividing

Is it sex you seek, let me hear you speak Your words of lying.

Is it sex you seek, this old body's weak

From its daily pounding

Is it sex you seek, my whole life is bleak

From my surroundings

Is it sex you seek, hear my body creak

Please stop this hounding

The above song took a while to come out in the end and eventually surface in 1998 a mere 4 years before other pop records started incorporating these sounds and similar riffs into mainstream pop. So I was 10 years ahead with this as usual and although I'm sure there were other influences like Bollywood music, which influenced the Asian Arabic pop music in 2002, I was still ahead of the game by releasing such a track.

The next song was probably 90% written by me as I wrote the words and melody and did the drums and strings on it. Kevin just came up with the piano & bass parts. I think I asked Kevin to think of a title for the song and I'd write a song about it. The song was called *Magic* but the lyrics had nothing to do with magic at all, it was more a case of it being about dreams, Chinese proverbs and some leftover feeling about my marriage. I also like to put messages in my songs that may influence people to improve their lives in some way.

MAGIC

When the night takes your mind away, and teaches it new tricks to play

And your soul begins to glide, and shows you pictures from the other side

Dust the cobwebs from your soul, and you will search and it takes hold

When the night takes your mind away, and teaches it new tricks to play

And your soul begins to glide, and shows you pictures from the other side

The shadow gangsters have come to take control

The shadow gangsters have come to take control

Feel those hands so deep inside holding back the darkest tide like magic

It's like magic, it's magic

Let time lick your wounds away, try to keep the pain at bay

Time to put those memories away

Time to put those memories away

Feel those hands so deep inside holding back that scary ride like magic

It's like magic, it's magic

You look but you do not see

You listen but you do not hear

You touch but you do not feel

Oh, are you real, Oh, are you real

Are you real

Magic made the first B.O.P album but Kevin did not. He worked for a big insurance company and was offered a big promotion and a lot more money and after seeing how quickly things could fall apart in the music industry he decided it wasn't for him. I tried to persuade him to do both and did manage to get one solitary release for Perestroika (Although some might say this to could have gone out under B.O.P) but more of that later.
Footnote. In the new millennium, someone looked at these lyrics and said they were as good as the best poetry and I should enter it for a poetry competition. So as a bit of fun I did and to my surprise won a world Poetry competition where it won best international poem in 2005.
During my Eleanor Rigby period, I was advised to hang on to the publishing rights of my songs so formed my own publishing company but as I wasn't that confident at the start as a songwriter I wanted the best songs possible for Eleanor, so I signed up a few other songwriters for one-off or batches of songs, David Hubbard being the main one. Although we didn't have a record deal the publishing company was active and earned a bit from the first Ministry of Ska single I did on my own.
Like many other publishers, we were listed in the Music Week yearbook and so I often got tapes sent to me by songwriters, singers and bands. I always used to think they must be more desperate when they got to my company as it started with a 'W' I had assumed these wannabees started at A and worked their way through the publisher's list. But that wasn't always the case; some had bought a record release and if they liked the record would look up who the publisher was. Enter one Joanne Sharp, a singer/songwriter who had bought a copy of Eleanor's Censorship album and liked it a lot and tracked down the publisher. I have to say most stuff I got through was a load of dross. Many songwriters think the way to be successful is to see what is number one and try and copy it. I even got people calling me saying I have written a song like Whitney Houston*'s I Will Always Love You* and so you will earn millions from it. How naive, apart from the fact I hate that song it's not all about the money and I had a reputation for credibility. So there was no chance of a deal for this type of person. People can be so green. That's why I wrote the book Music Business Bastards and by coincidence, Joanne had got this book as well as the Censorship album and realised I was connected with both so contacted me.
I have to say her tape blew me away and her voice was reminiscent of Karen Carpenter and her songs were very good. So I asked to see her and ended up signing her to a publishing deal. I was still waiting on many new results myself for B.O.P. But I was now on what's known as an accredited list of music biz types making it easy to get in and see labels instead of sending things in. So I took advantage of this to try and get Jo a deal. She'd been struggling for 10 years and I could see straight away where her problem lay. A combination of music business prejudice mixed with her not making enough of herself. She was plain-looking and wore glasses but I could see she had the potential to look good facially with not much work but her one main drawback as far as a record deal were concern was she was overweight. During our conversation, she concurred the problems I had outlined were the reasons for her not getting on in her career because as a singer she was as perfect as it gets and as a songwriter, she knew how to write great songs. I knew it would be an uphill task but I felt sorry for her and hate any sort of prejudice. So, I tried to get a record deal for her as well. She was over the moon that someone finally believed in her. I contacted half a dozen major record companies that I had a good rapport with and went to see them. Two companies were interested immediately, Arista and Warner Brothers. Nathan at Warner Brothers kept saying, I can't understand why this

girl is not signed she's got one of the best voices I've ever heard and the songs are great. Then he paused and said she doesn't look like Alison Moyet or something does she. I then showed him her picture and he said I thought so. In some ways, Alison Moyet's success didn't do any favours to overweight singers who were not that stunning. This is because whenever you tell a singer they need to lose weight they just say 'Well, Alison Moyet made it and she is overweight, so it is acceptable to look that way and get a deal.' These people were kidding themselves. Anyone who knows anything about the music business would say, Alison Moyet, despite her great voice, had no chance of being signed and had already been turned down by most companies. The only reason she became successful was that ex Depeche Mode man Vince Clark was already successful as the songwriter and had numerous hits and just needed a singer to sing his songs, which were virtually guaranteed to be played and gain hits because it was him. So, when Alison came along she and Vince went out as Yazoo and it became successful. Once she'd had a number one and some big hits with Yazoo it was easy to get airplay and coverage for her when she went solo. So, Alison got in through the back door but people were kidding themselves that they could still get through the front door on talent alone, that's just not the way the music business works. I'm not saying I agree with it because I don't. That's just the way it is. I have to admit I do have some sympathy with record companies because as they pointed out to me they need press and magazine covers and T.V. and there is often prejudiced from the media about featuring overweight people in a glamour business and so if they signed Jo promotion would be hard work with little results. Even DJ's seeing a record cover of her would vie against playing it because they tend to go for safe bets and if they thought a media push was not behind a release they would lose interest in a record. I thought the problem could be overcome by not featuring Jo on the record cover and push the music, then see if the music took off and champion overweight people as an angle. I mentioned this to Nathan but he thought there was an easier way. He said he was so keen to sign her, Warner's would pay for Jo to go to a health farm and get slimmed down and a stylist would then make her good looking as well.
Arista were a bit more brutal, they said she had a brilliant voice and material but come back and see us again when she has lost weight then we will sign her, it's as simple as that. Her career future is in her own hands if she wants to be a singer that badly. Otherwise, at best all she could ever be was a songwriter. I reported back to Jo and she just said she was not prepared to lose weight and people had to take her how she was. So her opportunity to make it as a solo artist vanished. Sometimes it's about timing and this was the wrong period in time for an overweight girl to hit big. Adele proved years later what was possible and Jo (below) was as good as her.

CHAPTER SEVEN

CELEBRITY STATUS

I had high hopes for Box Office Poison, the songs were good, we stood out and looked the part and I felt we had sufficient talent to carry things off but I did know that doing a totally new style of music from scratch with no ready-made audience would be a tall order. As talented as Eleanor was and as good as the material was we had a ready-made following on the Mod scene and she played live so it was a much easier ride. Convention dictated that maybe our next move should have been to do a few gigs but without those extra few musicians it wouldn't work and those people became elusive.

After the *Popcorn* disappointment, we then got the news that my Theme for Nightmare on Elm Street was not now going to be used. Robert Shaye was very apologetic saying he still loved the track but Brian May of Queen had asked to do the theme and soundtrack as he was a fan of the films and since he was a big name that would help the film, it was too good to turn down. He added normally we would put your theme on the next Freddy film but it was already announced it was the last, so that wasn't an option. This disappointment and more record label rejection tipped Dave (Bowler) over the edge. He decided to quit and try out for another band called 'Dog' I heard from him 6 months later and he said despite the band doing very mainstream rock music the same thing kept happening to them. They'd get A & R people not showing up to gigs and those that did claimed they wanted to sign the band only to pull out a few weeks later. He concluded the music business was full of wankers and he was going to concentrate on his painting and decorating business instead. So there I was needing yet another band member.

But as I said the music biz has many ups and downs and some ups were starting to come along but from unexpected corners. I was about to sample some celebrity status despite B.O.P not having a release or a deal. I had actually known what it was like to be a noted celebrity when I was an international DJ in my early years. I went from venues holding a few hundred in the Uk where often a chalkboard with my name partially washed away by rain stood outside to playing to thousands every single night in Scandinavia with my name on a marquee outside with flashing lights. In the smaller towns, I could go into any shop or restaurant and never have to pay for a thing; everything was on the house as long as I gave out an autograph here or a mix-tape of my set there. Plus up until I met Eleanor girls were fighting over me most nights. Yes, this was a definite taste of what it was like to be successful and a celebrity all right. I had even had two blasts of fame as a kid. First being chosen to front a movie campaign for a big Civil War film because I belonged to the American Civil War Society and before that for winning a medal at the Junior Commonwealth games for Wrestling. Both featured photos of me in a national newspaper. *(below news photo of me as junior wrestler with the famous Mick McManas)*

The celebrity status that hit me next was a bit surreal. My former UK agent as a DJ, Allen was an ex-professional footballer who had played for Portsmouth and a writer and photographer, so we had quite a few things in common. Allen had seen me play and his opinion as a professional was, if I had gone for it and not given up after my injury while an apprentice at Watford I would have made the grade of at least as a Championship player. Because he was a showbiz agent and had a football pedigree he was heavily involved with the famous Showbiz Eleven football team. This is something that has been around for many years where celebrities from films, stage, T.V and music plus a few ex-footballers made up a Showbiz team and they would go around the country every month playing matches against traditional league teams to raise money for charity.
With Ministry of Ska getting a reasonable profile and Music Business Bastards book getting some mainstream attention I was considered genuine celebrity material. Although there was some truth in this, not many people knew what authors looked like and if you weren't a Mod or into Ska it was likely nobody else would recognise me. Adding international DJ to the mix did add to me C.V but I was still more of an unseen type celeb. So, I had a bit of apprehension about this venture at first. I needn't have worried; I was to become the star of the show.
A match had been arranged to play Hereford football club, then in the fourth division. As I boarded the team coach at Hammersmith in London I scanned the faces of my fellow team-mates looking for the household names. Apart from Jess Conrad, an early sixties minor popstar turned actor who was about 30 years past his sell-by date (who only came to prominence again via the annual pantomime) I didn't recognise a soul.
I started doing the rounds on board to see who was who. I had to stop myself from laughing. The first guy I spoke to said he'd once had a walk-on part in 'Eastenders', The next person had done a voice over for a Cadbury's flake advert and another said he had been a reserve team player for Everton football club 10 years ago in a cup final. (I later found out this guy was more famous than I thought as he had been banned from football because of a gambling scandal). The calibre of other celebrities was similar. If we were comparing track records I was the superstar of the bus but I just didn't see a recognisable face. Finally, I found a pop star but although he'd just had a number 19 chart hit, he was a keyboard player in a faceless dance act. So, I may have seemed like a nobody to some but I had, as usual, at least dressed the part to stand out from the crowd.
A hilarious scene then unfolded when the coach arrived at Hereford's stadium. Hordes of people were running alongside the coach with autograph books banging on the side with excitement. This soon turned to severe head-scratching and frowns when we alighted from the coach. A number of the team walked past the fans without being bothered. Jess Conrad had his pen in his hand already but it was so funny when people pushed past him and surrounded me asking for autographs. Even though I've been in over 100 magazines, done scores of radio interviews, appeared on half a dozen T.V shows and performed live to lots of people throughout my career I still find it funny signing autographs. I was also prone sometimes to get myself in trouble. I'm quite a flirt and I once signed my book for a girl at a party with the inscription, 'Thanks for last night', even though I'd only spoken to her and nothing else had happened. I met her a second time and she told me her husband who happened to be in a hit band found the book and accused her of having an affair with me. The point I'm trying to make is, I prefer to put a comment rather than just a signature, as I don't see the point of just a signature that hundreds of other people have. But of course, it's not always practical if you have to sign lots of autographs. Anyway, I

doubt that there were more than 2 people who were asking for autographs that knew who I was. It just looked like I was a star and once again this proved my theory on image. As I walked towards the dressing room Jess Conrad gave me a look that told me I had not endeared myself to him. He finally found a use for his pen and signed some autographs for a few old dears (those pantomimes had paid off!) Jess was the captain of the team and the only ever-present member, so had a lot of clout. As I hit the dressing room, finally, I saw a famous face of an actor who played Inspector Munroe in the T.V show 'The Bill'. He had arrived separately by car. Tactics and positions in the team hadn't been discussed on the bus. So I asked Allen where I would be playing. He said as a forward he presumed but it was up to Jess. Jess then turned around to me and said don't worry yourself about positions, you're position is on the subs bench. I wasn't too happy to have come all this way to be a substitute. However, the decision was quickly reversed as a quick headcount revealed that we only had 11 players, so I was in the team like it or not Mr Conrad. He then said that John Leslie the Blue Peter presenter at the time and someone famous for going out with actress Catharine Zetta Jones was expected, as was Tom Watt formerly of 'Eastenders' and we should hang on for them. He delayed the match as much as he could but had to eventually start with the 11 we had. After 10 minutes I scored a goal and within another 10 minutes, I had scored a hat trick. I then passed the ball back to Jess who was in goal and he shouted to me 'Your off'. Tom has arrived he's substituting you. I was substituted and Tom Watt took my place. In football terms, it was a crazy decision since I was clearly an asset to the team but it wasn't about football it was about egos and I had somehow rubbed Jess up the wrong way but I was not alone on that score. As I sat on the sidelines complaining to Allen he said, one reason why there was a lack of household names involved was that Jess liked the limelight and had fallen out with quite a few people in the past and many people more famous than I had had to endure Jess's way of doing things. As is often the case I had the last laugh though.

A nice food spread was put out for the team, which most wolfed down and some free drinks were available at the bar, which also went in double-quick time. As soon as the last drop of the free drins were done and dusted someone mentioned paying for drinks. The celebs were out of the door in Usain Bolt fashion.

The organisers asked about us taking part in many of the fundraising events that were going on throughout the night and Jess told them we'd be back later to do them. We all headed off to a nice hotel to get spruced up.. Expecting to then go back to Hereford football club, I was surprised when many turned around and said 'We're off clubbing'. I thought they meant they were just going off to a club for a few drinks and then going back to the football club, so I joined them. I was then shocked by the majorities' attitude. None wanted to go back to the football club. They came out with comments like, 'I've done my bit; I've shown my face and played football that's me done. Then others said they were only interested in pulling girls and walked around the club giving it the big 'I am'. I said we were expected to take part in some other fundraising but no one was interested. So I got a cab back to Hereford where they were very pleased to see me but very concerned that no one else was with me. A lot of interviews had been lined up with radio and press and I ended up doing all of them. Nice promotion for my book and Ministry of Ska output. I was then roped into every event going including a girl's midnight netball match, which was very interesting and beneficial because I ended up getting off with 2 of my team-mates. About 2am everything finished and I was heartily thanked by the organiser and also told they were not impressed by the others who'd let them down. I then sneaked my 2 netball pals, a nice blonde & brunette back to my room for a threesome. The next morning Allen knocked on my door to see if I was coming to breakfast. I came to the door and told him I wasn't bothered about breakfast but would appreciate it if he could bring me a nice big pot of coffee and 3 cups. He yelped, 'Three', who have you got in there. He walked in and looked at the bed and saw the 2 girls and scuttled out to start the scandal sheet rolling. He brought me the coffee and asked if he could join in with me to which I said no. A while later he knocked again to say the coach was leaving. I then came out of the room with a girl on each arm and walked up to the bus and kissed them both goodbye. I got on the coach and got a round of applause along with some rude comments but a scowl from Jess. It turned out only one person had pulled that night at the dance club. It was in fact Jess, (I wondered why he hadn't return) One celeb then said to me, they didn't remember seeing those girls in the club. I pointed out where I'd met them and that there was a whole netball team of randy girls desperate to bed a celebrity and they'd all missed out. I was half-joking but I hoped that I'd taught them a valuable lesson. I went to one further Showbiz 11 outing but it was obvious Jess had it in for me as I was only down as sub yet again and told I was unlikely to play. Luckily, Allen had advised me to bring down some records and some copies of my book and I spent most of the day signing and selling them, which helped me survive financially. It's a shame really that I didn't do any more Showbiz 11 stuff because there was something I liked about the concept of it. But as long as Jess was involved I'd be wasting my time.

Above unrelated Showbiz 11 Flyer

CHAPTER EIGHT

NEW MEMBERS

Back in the real world, I was still in need of new band members and it was looking like Ministry of Ska was my future rather than B.O.P as we had quite a bit of interest, so started recording some new tracks including one called Condoms (what is it with me and Condoms?) It was to become notorious. Dick had done the music and asked me to put some lyrics and vocal melody to it and I did it in one take complete with a Jamaican accent. Dick had another track that he wanted to keep instrumental that I just played a few bits and pieces on and did a few vocal sounds but not words. He felt it needed a sax and had enlisted the services of one Ron Howe. He had been in the multi-million-selling band The Cure for an album or two and then in The Cure offshoot Fools Dance and played with his cousin Rat Scabies band, Punk legends, The Damned. Anyway, Ron did some fine sax work that impressed me. We got talking and I mentioned B.O.P and played him a few tracks and he said he was blown away by it as he was getting fed up of only doing predictable solos on other peoples work and wanted to improvise more and this new Pop Noir style was what he had been looking for. So I told him we'd lost our sax player and would he like to join the band, he agreed on the spot. Soon after this his finest hour arrived. I still thought Mysteries was our best track and after adding more music and multiple hypnotic percussion & koto to the evocative production I got Ron into the do the sax. I had noticed when doing Ministry of Ska stuff he did some interesting licks when warming up. So as he warmed up, unknown to him I taped it all. Then he asked me what I wanted, so I asked him to improvise but he struggled a bit once the pressure was on so I told him I already had what I wanted and he could go home. Then I just stuck the bits I liked in the track where I wanted them. I had also asked Louise along to meet Ron and they got on and I got her to sing part 2 of Mysteries that I had recently constructed. Although we still needed a keyboard player to really complete the band.

(3 rare photos of Ron below)

CHAPTER NINE

TURNING POINT

In some ways, I had the answer to getting a record deal in my hands all along. It's always hard to get a record deal and ten times harder if you are doing something innovative and different. Even with Eleanor who always had mainstream appeal, it was difficult getting a deal so we went down the route of getting our own Indie label (it also helped keep control over your creativity) I had earned quite a few quid as an International DJ and along with a couple of loans a record label became viable but I was now low on funds so didn't consider this route. However, after yet more rejection from the last few record labels I was very desponded. So to cheer me up Anne took me to dinner. I imparted the latest state of affairs to her and she responded by saying you did well with your previous record label and getting a new label was probably the best way forward, I also still had Eleanor's copyrights and Themes from the 60s Vol.1 which she thought was a winner and although B.O.P was a harder sell she really believed in us and thought the songs excellent. I then said but that takes money, you can't do a label on fresh air. To which she replied if you had the money would you do it? I said of course. She asked how much I would need. I wasn't sure but going on previous experienced and taking into consideration how important pop promos had become, I thought £30-50,000 was probably needed. She said, if you can make it work with £25,000 I will give you the money. I was shocked and asked if it was a loan and if so where had it come from. She told me she had just sold her house and made £50,000 profit and needed half for a deposit on a new place but I could have the other half. She added it was a loan of sorts and if I was successful I could pay her back plus interest but if I wasn't successful it didn't matter and she was willing to lose it and she would rather see me happy and at least try to realise my dream than do nothing and had every confidence in me as I was very good at what I did and by rights should have been very rich from the Eleanor episode if she hadn't disappeared but concurred it wouldn't be easy, especially with B.O.P and I was in for a lot of hard work because it wasn't just a matter of doing B.O.P but running a label as well. I was overwhelmed by the gesture and this secured a special place in my heart with Anne whether we went the distance as a couple or not and we are still best friends today. Such an event is not like winning the lottery so it wasn't about the money so much as someone having that much belief in you that really meant something. (my saviour is pictured below)

CHAPTER TEN

BIRTH OF AN INFLUENTIAL LABEL

Now that I had the funding and most of the new band members plus a decent amount of material it was time to think seriously about the new record label. First, we needed a name. Although it would be a label predominantly to promote Box Office Poison and sell back catalogue I did have ambitions to help break new artists with more volumes of the Cult Themes idea. I thought some of these acts may become future legends of music and so I called the label Future Legend Records.

Many understandably thought I'd got the name from a David Bowie track off Diamond Dogs but that was never the case but I was happy to discover that coincidence being a big Bowie fan.

I already had the first two singles for B.O.P recorded and was mulling over what to do about Eleanor's back catalogue. I also thought The Cult Themes album would be a winner and it did, of course, have two Eleanor tracks on it; *You Only Live Twice & Up the Junction* and because the original vinyl sold out very fast her fans were always keen to get hold of those tracks. So it made sense to reintroduce Eleanor via that album. However, I had put an instrumental track, *4 x 4* by The Reaction on the original album (as they were signed to W.S label) But this was never a theme, it just sounded like one and I wanted to promote them at the time. So I wanted to replace this track with a proper cult theme, then fate took a hand. Kevin of the now-defunct Perestroika contacted me to go for a drink and discuss the songs we had written. I'd always fancied doing *The Adams Family* so put it to him that Perestroika could finally have a release. Of course, he said it wasn't really a band, only him and he'd given up on the idea of having a new band. I then decided to take the plunge and do it with him and so the two of us became Perestroika. But I said I fancied having a female voice speaking some of it and he said his girlfriend would oblige, however, she didn't turn up to the studio so I did what was going to be a trademark of mine, go to the pub across the road from the studio chat up a girl and get them to come and do it and this worked a treat. The track turned out very well indeed. After this, another strange thing happened. A Mod guy called Darren contacted me about his band CBU. As well as being a fan of Eleanor's he had gotten the original cult themes album and asked if there was a chance of his band doing a track for volume two if there was going to be one. The reason this was strange was, the original album had come out 5 years before and he contacted me now of all times, not knowing that I was about to revive it. I saw this as a sign and met up with him.

I thought CBU were the best Mod band I'd seen in ages so asked them to learn 2 Gerry Anderson themes, *Stingray* and *Joe 90* and if they got time *The Munsters* as well. They turned up and I decided to have a bit of fun since they were a lively trio. The drummer was the vocalist but his singing on *Stingray* was too perfect and I wanted something a bit more deadpan and got the bass player to do it who didn't normally sing. I also worked out a blinding drum pattern. The track came out brilliantly so to further experiment I got them all to swap instruments when they did *Joe 90* and mixed this take with a normal take which gives the track a unique feel. They had only learned the bare bones of *The Munsters*., so I got them to just jam the version and this came out really well too.I was spoilt for choice but decided *Stingray* would go on the first themes album and the other 2 tracks would go on volume 2 of the 60's. I didn't want to drop *The Adams Family* so it became a 13-track album. I got the buzz again for doing these themes and with two tracks in the can already I wanted more and quite naturally wanted Box Office Poison to do some (we slightly cheated on Vol.1 as the tracks under B.O.P were ones I had done under the prototype name of Ministry of Defiance and I was the only B.O.P member on them.I had always loved the film *The Ipcress File* and its theme written by John Barry, one of my heroes was also brilliant. The koto sound has always been a key ingredient of B.O.P's 'Pop Noir' sound and dominates this track. However, unable to get hold of the original track to learn, the Jazz/Punk attitude needed to come into play here. Effectively we just jammed and improvised with me doing a basic percussion track then koto with some dub type effect and cello, Ron then added some whistling after doing his sax track. Although the tune is recognisable the second half of the track is effectively a new piece of music made up on the spot and not in the original. Two years later 'Portishead' were doing a similar thing and got successful with it. A group called 'Mono' did something similar 5 years later and also seemed influenced by our track *Checkmate*.
.Although I was a big Kinks fan I did like The Beatles and Yellow Submarine was considered a bit of a cult film and I had always liked the track *All Too Much* in it. There was no way I would have done the title track, as it is very commercial pop and very distinctive to The Beatles but *All Too Much* had possibilities. Before I could record that another band hit my radar. I went to a Gerry Anderson convention and the band playing there was called Adventures of Parsley. They specialised in playing concerts of themes and did a decent version of *Captain Scarlet*. So I signed them up to do it for the next cult themes album and quickly recorded it with them. However, there was a problem. There is both an instrumental & vocal version in the show and it was the instrumental I really wanted but Parsley's brother was in the band and he didn't play anything, only sung, so Parsley wanted to do a vocal version to keep his brother happy. In the end, I came up with a solution. I worked out an arrangement that incorporated both and although he wasn't so happy that's what came out (Although decades later when released on 'The Andersons Are Go' download compilation album I made them into two separate tracks) Overall I was impressed with the band, so much so I proposed a 2nd theme, the original *Casino Royale* theme (originally done by Herb Alpert) It was from the 1967 James Bond spoof comedy cult film. I was impressed with Parsley's organ playing on this track and since I thought the track *All Too Much* needed a better organ player than me I enlisted his services. We had a band meeting to try out the track and I felt it needed another drummer and Joanna said she knew just the right person, a guy called Big Al Meany (It seemed a sign as the baddies in Yellow Submarine were called the Blue Meanies).

I always had ambitions for B.O.P to become an 8-10 piece outfit playing gigs etc and me playing less in the studio (Just concentrating on producing & punk cello) and this seemed like a good start with us now being a six-piece for at least this track. But then came the main problem I always had with musicians, unreliability, we were not even doing gigs and only needed to rehearse one song yet it took 3 rehearsals for everyone to finally turn up. Rehearsal done we hit the studio and a very psychedelic version of this song was done featuring Al on drums, Parsley on organ, Ron on sax, me on punk cello & normal cello & extra percussion and Louise on lead vocals and some backing vocals by Joanna. There is some brass in there but I suspect that was done on a keyboard, as we definitely didn't have a brass section as much as I would have loved one.
Whilst in the studio I took the opportunity to do an alternative version of 1995 & Checkmate with this line up. After this recording, I did broach the subject of doing some gigs but Al informed me he was about to emigrate to New Zealand & of course, Parley was on loan from his own band who gigged a lot so the live idea got shelved quite quickly but the two did make one more impression. But this short-lived line up is often forgotten about but at least they made it to record unlike the very early version of the band.

CALL MY NUMBER ONE

Although you can press up some product and sell it at gigs that is a means to an end and very low level. Growing up I was mad about record labels, music and trivia and so when I got my first label Waterloo Sunset it was a dream come true and like all labels you dream of getting a number one hit. Growing up it was exciting watching your favourite group or record going up the charts and sometimes getting to number one. So any record labels ambition was to have a hit and preferably and number one hit and if you were the artist you had the same ambition (sadly these days a number one hit is not very exciting at all and most people don't even know what is number one)

I kind of managed to have a number hit with Eleanor's notorious debut single *I Want to Sleep With You*. As many will know it went into the midweek official chart around number 36 but then it was thrown out because of the free condom. However, in Northern Ireland, it was number one. The distributor E.M.I told me many shops over there were ordering many hundreds of copies every single day. So I phoned up the biggest shop in Belfast (I think it was called Caroline Records) and spoke with the manager to see why it was doing so well. I thought it would be the condom. They told me it was initially the sleeve as many Mods came in and got it because she was on a scooter. Then word got around that it was, in fact, a very catchy pop song and then the condom and media furore about it just kept things crazy. Paul Hardcastle's 19 was the official number one in the UK and the shop confirmed it was the best selling single except all of a sudden for 10 days Eleanor single had outsold this 5-1. I phoned a few other shops in Northern Ireland and it was a similar story so if there had been such a thing as a Northern Ireland only chart *I Want To Sleep With You* would have definitely been number one but sadly there wasn't a Northern Ireland chart. I also heard it was shifting a similar quantity south if the border. Eleanor ended up having a massive following on both sides of the border and several tours were booked but got cancelled due to the troubles out there. (She still has lots of fans on both sides today. She is pictured on previous page)
Anyway, this book is about Box Office Poison and we were no less ambitious and a number one was our goal but would we achieve it? Well before you can achieve that you need to get your record labels releases in all the record shops and if you were not signed to a big label you had to be distributed by one and so this was my next port of call.
After visiting all the major companies about distributing Future Legend Records only 2 definite offers came in, one from Polydor and the other from Sony. Most of the majors have what is called 'bolt on' companies, who deal with the sales and day-to-day liaison with Indie record labels whilst Sony and Polydor get on with the actual deliveries and payment side of the things. Polydor's was called 'Grapevine' and Sony's called 'I.L.C'. Former associates of mine ran both. The music business can often be a small world. George K was my label manager at Pinnacle and Bill K had been one of those directors at Big Wave records who wanted to sign Ministry of Ska.

George obviously knew a lot about my back catalogue since they previously went through Pinnacle and he rated me as a producer and marketing person. Although he offered me a definite deal he was quite negative about expectations of any big success for the label but thought it could pay its way and be viable.
On the other hand, Bill was very enthusiastic and offered me a better deal, which was a P&D deal similar to the one I had at Pinnacle where they pay for the pressings as well as distribute the label and he maintained with Sony's clout they could get a cheaper deal on pressings than I could. I thought since he was more positive and with them paying for the pressings this would free up more money for promotion. So, I signed with Sony and although Box Office Poison was my priority we agreed the first release would be 'Themes from the 60's Vol.1' (I was already thinking about Vol.2 of course). Volume One would be released at the beginning of January 1993.

CHAPTER ELEVEN

READY STEADY GO!

With a distributor in place and a release date for the labels first release we could now focus on the main business of both B.O.P. This meant designing record sleeves and most importantly making those all-important pop videos.In many ways, your first single is the most important as it might be your only chance to get a release. (Pre Itunes) it's no good making a great record that sits in your garage collecting dust. To have any chance of a hit you need to let as many people in the world know that your single exists. With over 1,000 singles coming out every week that is very much an uphill task, especially when you are competing with the major record companies who have big marketing spends. Although a big chart hit was not acquired by Eleanor Rigby's debut single *I Want to Sleep With You* it sold a respectable 10,000 copies for an independent. (today that would get you a top 10 hit) Also, I'm still meeting people 30 years later who remember the free condom campaign with the release as it made such an impact. This time around I thought I'd steer clear of the controversial angle and try a new idea out. I thought the key to our success would be our promo videos. Although we couldn't compete with £50,000 major record companies videos we could get a very decent video done for a tenth of that, which would stand a chance of getting played. As ever I was looking to break new ground and came up with a master plan. We would be the first pop group to put out a 3D pop video. 3D film had made a minor comeback so we searched around and finally found a company that said they could do the 3D video for the budget we wanted and they were so eager to get our business they threw in doing a video to what would become Eleanor Rigby's next single as well. Of course that wouldn't be easy with no Eleanor but we managed it.

1995

I wrote a special script for *1995* that would make good use of 3D effects including cello bows going into the camera, tambourines and crystal balls being thrown in the direction of the camera, also, zooming down into a Wizards pointed hat and entering into a crystal ball to take you on an adventure in a miniature Nostradamus type world and much more. With the 3D test shots done I set about guaranteeing us T.V exposure.
Apart from Top of the Pops, The Chart Show on Channel 4 featuring only pop videos was the most important show to be seen on to break a record. I approached them and informed them about the 3D pop video and offered them the world premiere, which they were very keen about. The only query they had were about the 3D glasses. Both Smash Hits and a T.V specialist magazine were keen to get in on the act and give away 3.D glasses with their magazines. Because I had more than one magazine interested I even asked them to cover the costs of the glasses. One agreed to share the costs and the other asked to see the pop video before they would commit to paying for the glasses. So, with exposure of this size, we were destined to get mass exposure and publicity for the single's release, which was the key to making it a success. This would also guarantee that the shops would stock the single as well. However, in life and especially in the arts an obstacle or downer is never far away. After 2 hours of filming, the 3.D camera broke down. Most of the film crew were used to working on the likes of The Rolling Stones videos but were helping out their director friend on the cheap as a favour. So, it was decided there was no time to fix the 3D camera and a 16-mm film camera was borrowed to complete the shoot.

Because the filming had to be done at night and a lot of time had been lost because of the problems, much of the original script had to be scrapped, turning the video into more of a performance-related one. (Which is something I wanted to get away from). The initial story was based on Nostradamus and his predictions in a whole new weird world via the crystal ball. Although it has to said, many people liked the video that did come out, overall I was very disappointed, as I know how good it could have been.The video was shot in a bombed-out church in the middle of Stoke Newington cemetery in North London. It took half a day to clear the rubble out. A few months later The Manic Street Preachers said 'Thank you very much' and used it to shoot their video for 'La Tristesse Durera'

We constantly felt like Vampires on this shoot trying to complete the filming before the sun came up .(And looked like them: Good job there were no apprentice Van Helsing's walking by). The shoot was done in the middle of winter and poor Louise nearly got pneumonia in her Victorian underwear. She was in bed for weeks afterwards recovering. (We artists do suffer for our art) Our videos then started to take on an unusual anomaly. Ron and Jo both appear in the video but are not actually on the record. Also featured were drummer 'Big Al Meaney' and 'Parsley" playing the harpsichord. Both as stated in an earlier chapter came in to play on All Too Much. So that is the only time you see this six-piece version of Box Office Poison. However only Louise and I were were actually on the 1995 record.

Rare stills from 1995 Jo, Russ,Ron with louise in background Below Ron.Parsley,Jo, Lou,Russ & Al

CHECKMATE

To maximise exposure and sales it made sense to make a video for *Checkmate* since the single was a double A-side. Although a few problems cropped up, making this video was easily the most enjoyable experience by far for all the band members, especially Louise who counts it amongst her most memorable experiences ever. (Much better than freezing to death on the previous one)

During the height of Eleanor mania, she headlined a gig at a Mod rally in Wales. Not far away was Port Meirion the home of the iconic Prisoner Village. For those of you who don't know what this is. In the 60's there was a famous but weird T.V. show called 'The Prisoner' starring Patrick McGoohan, who had made his name in the equally cult T.V show 'Danger Man'. It was about a spy who resigned but wouldn't give a reason and he was kidnapped and transported to this weird village where everybody was referred to by a number and not a name. Patrick M was known as number 6. His famous quote was 'I'm not a number I'm a free man'. In the show, he was always trying to find out who was number one since he only ever got to meet number 2, who was always trying various tricks on him to find out why he resigned. Also, it was impossible to escape since a big white balloon that could suffocated you, hunted you down. Anyway, that's the gist of the show and it has a mass worldwide following still. I was always into the show because I had the same philosophy, that I am an individual and not a number or a sheep. So, when Eleanor and I were nearby for her concert it was a golden opportunity to visit The Village and get some good photos of her there. The architecture at The Village is unique. Designed in the twenties by Sir Clough Williams-Ellis, it features a mixture of Mediterranean buildings but in general, is like no other place in the UK or anywhere else and definitely worth a visit. Another famous feature was a giant chessboard with human pieces. Since the B.O.P track was called *Checkmate* there was only one destination to shoot the video. Also, an actual episode of the show happened to be called *Checkmate*. The question was, could we afford to make the video there? Luck was on our side for once. The likes of the BBC would often be charged £10,000 per day to film at the village. I sent a copy of the single to the owner of The Village pointing out we were an Indie label on a tight budget but would do The Village justice and generate even more awareness for it. Luckily he was already aware of who I was as he'd liked the version I did of *The Prisoner theme* on The Waterloo Sunset version of Themes from the Sixties. He also liked the B.O.P single I sent him. So we got a great deal of having The Village for the whole weekend. We would get to stay in the special chalets including Number 6's room and other interesting rooms, we could have one meal free and this would be for 8 people all for just £500. They would also put the giant chessboard out for us, which wasn't normally out. Luckily we had timed it for the off-peak season, as I doubt we'd have got such a deal any other time. It was the bargain of the century.

After being let down by the previous video crew via the 3D episode, I looked elsewhere for someone to make this video. With my overall budget being severely eaten into I also needed to keep the cost down. A local band called 'Earthling Scum' had sent me a demo of their music and mentioned they were also video makers. So I went to see them and negotiated a deal. I could see they were fairly competent and that camera work & editing was their strong point. I wasn't 100% convinced about their previous ideas though but thought them worth a chance and because they wanted a record deal I enticed them to stick to a strict budget and I'd put them on the next Cult Themes album.

After giving the video makers, who were known as Yetti and Mister Bunny many weeks to come up with a script, come the day to go to Port Meirion they had come up with zero, claiming they preferred to improvise. I'm all for that but you do need some structure to hang things on. So on the way to Wales, I wrote the basic script, which was to feature us as disappearing chess pieces on the giant chessboard plus a spoof of The Thomas Crown Affair. Then cover every inch of the village and end up on the stone boat performing.

Filming a pop video at Port Meirion was not a new idea and a couple of bands had filmed videos there before but to my amazement, they had just stood in one place in the village and not shown the village off to its fullest. XTC and Magnum had just stood by the arches, which could have been anywhere. Even one of my favourite acts, Siouxsie and The Banshees just stood by the stone boat. Many people since like Supergrass and others have made better videos but ours is considered one of the best because it truly shows off the Village.

The shoot in general went very well, the only slight problem as usual was when dope reared its ugly head once more. It turned out the 2 video directors were dope heads, so I banned them from smoking anywhere near us. This made them always anxious to get the filming done quickly so they could go back to their room and have a joint but I wouldn't let them go until I was happy with a scene, since I had now taken on the mantle of director.

But all in all, it was a job well done and the video would prove to be our most popular over the years and one that would even pay for itself. Normally pop videos are a write off for promotion and most make a loss. Mass T.V plays can net some revenue, as can a 'Best of' compilation but so many Prisoner fans heard about it and wanted to buy it we obliged and sold it and made a profit.

Louise was a lovely girl but as I pointed out before she wasn't the brightest person on the planet. It was not surprising to learn that she left school at 15 to give birth to her daughter. Anyway, we were all in the minibus feeling hungry on the way home from Wales and got stuck in a traffic jam outside a chip shop. So I turned to Louise and said 'We are going over the border back to England very soon did you change up all your Welsh money?' She said, 'no, I didn't realise it was different money to ours what does it look like?' The fivers have Red Dragons on and there are Leeks on the pound coins says I. Louise looked in her purse and replied 'I don't have any Welsh fiver's but It looks like I've got quite a few Leeks on the one pound coins. They were in fact Thistles.

But I said yes that's them, you can't spend them in England they are worthless, you might as well buy us all fish and chips with them to get rid of the money. She said O.K and everyone piled into the fish and chip shop. It was only as people were eating their meal that we started laughing and I finally let Louise in on the joke and the few whose meal she had paid for reimbursed her the money. But I'll say one thing for her; she takes a good joke and found it as funny as everyone else.

The same can't be said for 'Yetti' who made Louise seem positively bright with his behaviour. Not only was he a dope head but as the video company person, he was responsible for working out a budget and sticking to it. As we approached the M25 towards London he said we needed some petrol and so we pulled off the motorway to find a garage. Once we found one we assumed he filled up the tank and we were on our way. No sooner had we got back to the motorway than the minibus broke down. At first, Yetti said he didn't know what the problem was and we had to call the A.A., but then Ron checked things out, as he knew a bit about cars, only to find that it had run out of petrol. How could this be as we had just filled up at a petrol station? Yetti then came clean. He only had 50p left of the overall budget so had only put 50p worth of petrol into the bus. How stupid can you get? He planned to get the A.A to tow us home to save paying any money out of his own pocket for more petrol, which at most would have been £5. I kid you not. He wasn't finished there as the next day we got a call from the van hire company since Anne had paid for it via credit card. The van was due back at 9 am but by midday, there was no sign of the van. The hire company called Yetti and just got a sleepy voice saying he was just leaving. An hour later still no van and the company contacted us again. We got onto Yetti and he said he was just leaving at 2 pm. Anne got charged an extra days hire on her card which we managed to deduct from Yetti's final payment as a video editor. We also heard that Yetti and Mister Bunny had actually pushed the bus into the hire place without petrol in it. This wouldn't be the last encounter with Yetti as I had to produce his bands recording for Themes from the 60's Vol.2 and this was the next thing on my agenda.

Rare stills from Checkmate video

CHAPTER TWELVE

THE REAL DEAL BEGINS

1993 arrived and Future Legend Records launched. I knew by the market research I'd done that Themes from The Sixties Vol.1 would do well and 3,000 copies were pressed up. But as the old saying goes if you want something doing right do it yourself. When I told Sony about the Themes album they said it would be lucky to sell 300 copies, as they didn't get the concept. It then became like a self-fulfilling prophecy and surprise, surprise, they were struggling to sell the album, selling less than 300. It soon became clear why this was the case as I listened to their sales patter. I'd written out a sales sheet and this had not been used at all, instead of pushing the track-listing they were trying to sell the themes album on the artists featured, most of which retailers hadn't heard of. The retailers that had taken it were buying it for the Eleanor Rigby tracks or the fact that they remembered the album from the Pinnacle days. I complained to Bill K and he just turned around and said that's the best they could do and if I wanted to show them how it should be done I was welcomed to try. I then blew his mind.asked for a phone and a list of shops. I stayed there for the rest of the week. The result was more than 3,000 albums sold with more required and it continued to sell eventually reaching a 5-figure sum. Needless to say, they were embarrassed and they offered me a job as head of sales on the spot. In addition to this, I went into a petrol station one day and saw many cassettes on sale and thought this was the ideal place to stock the themes. The company that supplied the garages were 'Pick a Tape'. I made an appointment with them and they wanted to order 30,000 tapes of the Themes album. I thought what a great result and told Bill at Sony but he said he couldn't authorise pressing up that quantity and I couldn't afford to press up that amount myself. Pick a Tape were also asking for sale or return so I could at least understand why Sony wouldn't go for it with my label, even though they did such deals for their own label. I'm certain we could have shifted the majority of those tapes, as I remember an acquaintance saying to me that the themes albums were perfect driving music and he always had the tape on in his car.. But that's how it goes. The reason all this is relevant to the Box Office Poison story was, apart from me producing all the tracks and running the label this would be the first introduction of B.O.P to the public via the Cult Themes album. The whole concept of the album was to help break new acts through these new versions and if people liked the sound of those tracks it might get them into the bands original material. B.O.P's two tracks did prove popular and I even got a number one hit off the album as the producer of Eleanor Rigby's *You Only Live Twice* track when it was released as a single but it was a bit of a dilemma as the tracks didn't really represent what B.O.P were now doing and it was a new line up. The 2nd themes album would be more representative of us but before that, there was the small matter or releasing out debut original single *1995/Checkmate* (Cassette below)

With such a new genre of music and no following, I felt college students would probably be a good target audience for us to start with and I was lucky enough to be invited by the head of the UK Students Union to an exclusive concert at Oxford University because I had an Indie label. It seemed like a good opportunity to start both the buzz on B.O.P and FLR. The headline act was a great band called 'Blink'. The support act that day was a little- known act called 'Oasis'. Who were yet to release their first single. I met the entire band but confess I wasn't that keen on these loud mouth Mancunians and when they asked my Japanese date for the day, Naomi and me to go for a drink I decided to be polite and oblige them. I found Noel Ok and had a brief chat with him about songwriting, which proved interesting as he confessed he had been influenced by Eleanor's Censorship album and had all her singles as well but added The Jam, T-Rex and Slade were his biggest influences. However, I wasn't keen on his loud mouth brother Liam, especially as he was chatting up Naomi, so I took off instead to do some interviews with many college radio and magazines since it was their once a year ENTS outing from all over the UK. This proved to be the right move on a business level, as I was to discover in the coming months for both the label and especially B.O.P

With the Box Office Poison single about to be sold in by Sony, I was in a sweat going on the sales team's previous track record with the Themes album and wasn't surprised to learn they had only 50 sales in the first week. I knew I'd have to get involved in the selling yet again. I had a go at Bill about the poor sales staff and how they were once again selling the record incorrectly. He then said it was my close ties with the theme's product that made it easier for me to sell it but doubted I could repeat the trick with B.O.P. I then said I could go out into the street and pull the first person I saw in and teach them how to sell the same quantity as me within a few hours. The reply from him once again was, prove it. Luckily for me, I had a work experience girl, Andre at my label coming to meet me for lunch and she was waiting outside. So after a quick bite to eat I dragged her in pretending I didn't know her and set about teaching her to sell the release. That afternoon she sold 500 units by following my instructions and I.L.C./Sony were flabbergasted and offered her a job on the spot. She decided to take it. Luckily she had already done her workload for me and I still had 2 other staff. I could also see the benefits of having someone inside the I.L.C. camp to look after my interests. Because the B.O.P release was so crucial I also once more got on the phones myself. The result was a staggering 4,000 singles sold in (on 4 different formats). Once again I was offered a permanent job and turned it down. The most this lot had sold of any new acts single was a few hundred copies. I.L.C./Sony then started advertising for new staff and had a big rethink about the sales patter finally.

Of course, getting records in the shops is one thing. Getting exposure for them is another and this part of the proceedings was well underway. Unfortunately, pluggers are the parasites of the music business. The top ones are quite good and the few bits of help I have had from them over the years has proved beneficial. But as an Independent, you can't afford these very top people and are looking at more shark-infested waters. We were introduced to one plugger called Nick B who had got airplay for some well-known acts and he was very positive about getting airplay for us. As he concentrated on radio and T.V I then hired dance pluggers 'Full Blast' and this proved to be not too bad, gaining quite a bit of dance club play for *Checkmates* 12" single. Many DJ's said it was refreshing, original, hypnotic and exciting and with decent airplay could go all the way. We even made the DJ's top 10 dance charts.

With the big opportunity of the 3D pop video lost I put out a press release to try and get some mileage out of it by saying that the master tape for this groundbreaking video had been stolen out of the director's car and I was offering a reward for its return. So at least when we chased T.V people they knew who we were. However, Nick B struggled to get any T.V on the release but I managed to get both videos one spin each on MTV and a fortnight's play-list at Peter Robinson's massive video screens at Oxford Circus in London. I also did interviews and the videos got played on various Cable T.V shows. All other T.V shows wanted to hold off until they saw if we got a chart placing. Nick was also struggling with radio plays so I used a few of my contacts. First off, there was Gary Crowley who was a top cred DJ and a fellow Mod who I'd met once before and was a good friend of Paul Weller's. He loved *1995* and started to play it a lot. Then it started to get requested a fair bit. Also, DJ's on XFM radio started playing it as well. Finally, I contacted my college contacts and it went out to the college radio stations. Within a month it was one of the most played records on many college radio stations. Typical comments from DJ's were 'This new style of music is like a hurricane of fresh air'. It wasn't surprising that it did well on college campuses since college kids are usually the first to pick up on new things. These people were also massive fans of our Cult Themes as well. So, with it doing well with both college kids and dance clubbers, some mainstream airplay was all we needed for a big result from Nick to storm the top 40. But even with what I had done we were sure the single would chart because 4,000 sales would equate to about the top 60 and a definite top 3 in the Indie charts. Finally, Nick came through for us. Sadly it wasn't play-listed on the all-important 'Radio One', which guarantees a top 40 place. But he had got BBC's GLR radio station to start playing the single. This was a big radio station in London so not too bad. This also resulted in us being offered a live session on the Lucy Longhurst show.

AN UNUSUAL LIVE DEBUT

As I had mentioned previously I had thought about B.O.P playing live but had problems getting people to rehearsals so scrapped the idea. So we had never actually played live together as a group. Here we were about to make our live debut, not at some small gig but going out to millions of people on the radio. Because of the Punk-Jazz attitude, I revelled in it. With a week to go to the show the rest of the band however were wearing their brown knickers. Things then got worse when we were told there was an electrician strike at the station. This meant we couldn't use electric keyboards that used some of the harpsichord and other sounds. Parsley who had been enlisted to play keyboards then decided to play the accordion, which he'd only played once before. Ron was the most nervous since he had to improvise on *1995*, since Dave had been the one who played on the record originally and not him. Luckily, we only had to do 2 tracks and I chose *Magic* as the second track. We did a few rehearsals and I noticed the girls could carry the melody regardless of what we played. So I thought it would be all right on the night as they say.

I liked the edgy feeling in the green room before the show but everybody else was rushing backwards and forwards to the toilet. The moment of truth arrived and we went onto the show. Lucy introduced us and then asked me to do a small interview with her, as I was the songwriter before we played. My interview went so well that instead of it being 3 minutes it was extended to 20 minutes because of the controversial things I was saying. The phones switchboard had lit up like a Christmas tree because a lot of people listening felt the same way I did about the way the music business was going. The first thing was obviously about the need for a new genre of music. Secondly, I was championing vinyl, which Sony in particular was trying to kill at the time.

They had claimed a few weeks before in the press that they didn't have an anti-vinyl policy. I knew this to be untrue as Sony had told me personally that they wouldn't press up 12" or 7" vinyl for Eleanor's *You Only Live Twice* release and wouldn't press up any vinyl at all for B.O.P's release, so I paid for B.O.P's vinyl pressings myself. I said it was all about money, as Sony just wanted everything to come out on CD. But they were shooting themselves in the foot. One example was, as a DJ I could buy three or four 7" singles for the price of one CD single. Therefore giving exposure to 4 acts with vinyl. But if everything changed to CD my budget would mean I only played 1 in 4 new releases. Also, young kids with not much pocket money couldn't afford more than one CD but could get into 4 acts if they bought vinyl. But then there was a theory that Indies benefited most from vinyl because it was cooler to buy, whereas the masses that bought Celine Dion for instance didn't care about being cool and would happily fork out for a CD single. They also wanted to get more and more people into buying CD's so they would buy their whole music collection again as well. (Sony invented the CD Player) Anyway, I said a lot about the Indie versus the majors in this interview. I also learned about one final music business scam before I went on air and exposed that as well and once again it was my distributor Sony who were in the frame. Our single could have easily been number one in the Indie charts and definitely top 3 because we shifted quite a few thousand. But when the Indie charts were published we were nowhere to be seen even though we knew we'd sold more records than the number 3 single. This was because the Indie chart rules state you are not eligible for that chart if a major label distributes you, and Sony was a major so we were disqualified. The number one Indie single summed up the hypocrisy of the whole thing that week as it was 'Oasis' debut single and that was on Creation Records and distributed by Indie distributor Pinnacle, however, Creation was half owned by Sony. So in the true sense of the word Creation were not 100% Indie yet Future Legend Records was 100% Indie and disqualified, It was crazy.

With the controversial interview now over we began to play our single *1995* Live for the first time. It sounded unusual but lived up to the Jazz-Punk billing and I liked the edginess of it. The band were a lot more nervous about doing the second track *Magic* as they had rehearsed it a lot less. So, as a ruse to cover any mistakes, I said to the DJ on air that we were now switching vocalist from Debbie Detroit to Jo Sharp, however, Jo needs to get a certain timbre sound in her voice and in order to get this sound so she needs to sing naked. But because she is a bit shy we had to wear blindfolds, therefore, you may hear the odd mistake. Lucy played along with the ruse and we did the number, which wasn't too bad, although it did have a few mistakes. The next day all people were asking about was, did that girl sing nude on the radio. It caused a real buzz with the media and helped sales of the record. (belowDJ Lucy Longhurst)

With the Indie charts a no go area we waited to see if we managed to get into the main chart and didn't. I can't say it surprised me, quite apart from no plays on Radio One I found record shops less than helpful, especially the chart return shops who are very blasé and rude because they mostly get free product. We had decided not to give all our singles away for free but did do buy 2 get 2 free deals to persuade chart shops to stock it. I wasn't trying to hype the record into the charts but I did go into 3 shops in Croydon and the first 2 summed up our problem. The first shop claimed they didn't have the single and had never heard of it. I knew this to be a lie, as I had been the person who had sold it into them via Sony. Suddenly, I looked around and saw a copy of the cassette single along the counter. I picked it up and said 'what's this?' I thought you said you never had it? He looked at it like it was a piece of shit and said give me a quid and it's yours. I paid him but he didn't even ring it up on the till or log it as a chart sale. The next shop was no better. They claimed also not to know anything about the single and I asked if I could order it and the guy just said, 'I can't be bothered. Finally, I hit HMV who did know about the record. They had one copy left. I'd sold them 4 via Sony so three had sold, so that was better news. Ron's mum also went into a big shop in Crawley who claimed not to have the record and she asked to order 4 copies for her family. The assistant then said we don't do customer orders go somewhere else. Record shops and attitudes seemed to have changed a great deal for the worst since my day managing them, so when they finally went out of business I didn't shed any tears for them. But with only 1 in 4 shops clued up to the record, a chart place was a distant dream. At the end of the day the single, although not charting did make an impact, from college students to clubbers and we had also got a decent amount of press cumulating in one magazine saying the single was the best single of the decade and college radio voting it one of the best singles of the year. So we had at least made an impact and many acts more famous than I had failed to get a chart hit the first time around.

After all the cockups that went on with our releases via ILC/Sony, I wanted out of our contract especially when I saw my statement. Because we had achieved very decent sales of all releases I was at least expecting to make a reasonable profit to plough back into future releases despite it being a P&D deal but the statement had a minus figure on it. I was to learn a valuable lesson that day, never trust a verbal agreement, get it all in writing. You may remember they told me when they agreed to distribute my label that they could get manufacturing done cheaper than me. Instead, as I looked at the statement it had cost 4 times what I would have paid. I pulled out the mastering costs and argued about that straight away and they eventually made this the normal price but then added some biking costs for delivering tapes instead, something I also never asked for but was common practice with major companies. Next, they had agreed to take 1,000 of the 4,000 B.O.P singles back from shops, which was outrageous. There was no sale or return agreement; it was all on firm sale so there was no way this record should have come back. It turned out they had sold in a Roy Castle charity single to shops that had flopped big time and shops were up in arms about being misled about something to do with this single. As part of an apology the I.L.C. team had agreed to take back a percentage of other stock they sold in over the past few months and mine was part of that batch. Next up they had managed to lose quite a few copies of Themes from the 60's Vol.1 in the system which they thought had been sold but were now presumed lost. The contract stated that they were allowed to lose up to 10% of the stock via damages so they wouldn't pay for this missing stock either.

After a lot of backwards and forwards arguing I claimed they owed us about £5,000 and they claimed I owed them the same amount. Several other labels distributed by Sony who wanted to take them to court and sue them for various rip-offs then approached me. But Sony had been clever in that they had a clause making the I.LC team responsible for any problems. So, then people wanted to sue I.L.C. whose staff were always quitting because of their poor sales. As the horror stories were reeled out at the meeting, I found that some labels had been ripped off to the tune of half a million pounds. As well as the scams they had perpetrated on me they had also recommended various contacts of theirs to do the plugging and make videos etc for these other labels (all of which got zero results) I thought about joining in with these people to sue ILC but remembering Bill's previous track record with 'Big Wave' I thought it unlikely we'd end up getting anything except more in debt with lawyers costs. With Sony not being liable I thought the best policy was to walk away from it and get my contract cancelled, which is what I did. Since we were both claiming £5,000 off each other we met in the middle 'Zero' and I walked away from the deal.

First release on label. Sleeve designed by schoolgirl as a pat of a competition.

CHAPTER THIRTEEN

THE MASTERPIECE

Learning from my mistakes with Sony/I.L.C. I did 2 distribution deals this time around. One for the new Box Office Poison single *Mysteries* with an Indie distribution company called SRD in order to get in the Indie charts and another deal with BMG /Intoto to release our other releases starting with 'Themes from the 60's volume 2'.
1994 started quite well as I did a big interview for Songwriting' magazine where I amazed them with how I did some of my songwriting. I had managed to write many songs without chords. The interviewer thought this to be impossible and asked me to show him how it was done. You see, ask most musicians how they write songs and they'll usually say they start with chords. With Box Office Poison songs I never wrote this way at all. I composed most songs on the cello and since the cello is a note instrument there are no chords. I'd start with a cello riff and then lay down an alternative riff. I'd then do intricate percussion sounds followed by singing a vocal melody over the top of this. The sax would usually play lots of notes that would waft atmospherically around in the track. I then added multiple breathing takes to build up the sound to make backing vocals and finally, I may add a few notes from other instruments like a harpsichord or on one occasion a toy piano. I liked arpeggios and would put those in sometimes on the harpsichord but am not sure if that constitutes any sort of a chord. Many songs would be complete like this. But with some others, I would then add a few chords to fill things out more if I felt they needed it. My track Alien is the best example of this way of writing and when I played it to the interviewer, he agreed there didn't appear to be any chords except on the outro where I had played and orchestra riff. The interviewer was astonished and wondered why no one had ever composed this way before. I think it may have had something to do with cello players mostly being classically trained and only reading music. So, whoever writes the music thinks in terms of writing out the music the standard way whereas I just improvise and have no restrictions on the way I think. This also led me to play new types of cello riffs that hadn't been done before as well. This was because when I got a keyboard I just messed about till I got something I liked on the cello sound on the keyboard. But it turned out that a cello player couldn't physically play what I was playing on the keys because the notes were too far apart to reach. But you can play them on the keyboard. I also tried out every conceivable song structure going. Many people just stick to traditional ways of songwriting. I once started a song with a middle 8 and many times with a chorus. Other songs had no chorus at all and some had 2 different choruses. I'm not saying I'm the only one to use many different structures. I know other people probably have done so as well like Bowie and Nile Rodgers always starts with a chorus on nearly all his songs. Also the Jazz songwriters who were often responsible for writing many of the Cult Themes tunes do things differently. This is why I found re-arranging their work a nice challenge and here is how I went about it. .

THEMES FROM THE SIXTIES VOLUME TWO

Although I had already tried out some innovative things in production, such as using crisp packets for percussion and a paper album inner sleeve for a snare drum and many other things on 'Nightmares'. It was with Volume 2 of the Sixties that I came of age as truly, the successor to Joe Meek in my opinion and that of others. The track that sums this up is *DR WHO*. I had this idea to record the track like a Chinese whisper. I got every person who did work experience for me play a bit of the track without knowing what the other person had played. After having listened twice to the original *DR Who* theme. I started it off and then other people did keyboards and percussion etc. An Opera singer did the final session and I got her to wail along to the track, which was unmixed. Then she asked for a glass of water and started to gargle, so I made her gargle through the whole track. I then picked up 2 teacups and rattled along to the track adding lots of echoes creating a new rhythm track. I took what I liked from other peoples playing and the end result was a hot track, which lots of people liked and were amazed to learn what was actually going on in the track. Years later I learned that Delia Derbyshire was the brain behind the sounds on the original DR. Who theme but because she worked for the BBC Radiophonic workshop and was female she never got credited but she is a real cult figure now and I sing her praises at every opportunity. She was like a female Joe Meek back in 1963. (Sadly she died before her cult status got as big as it has now) I hope she liked what I did with the track if she heard it from the other side. I have already mentioned many previous recordings done for volume two. Much of the album was about repaying favours although having said that I'd have put most of the acts on anyway. I'd done Earthling Scum's *Babarella* track and band member Yetti had made hard work it as usual. I only put up with him because Mister Bunny, his partner had some talent. I, of course, owed them a favour as they'd done our promo video for *Checkmate* cheaply.

As I said I believed in Joanne but was unable to get her a solo deal for her material and invited her to join B.O.P but as she was late to the party and Louise was the main lead singer I thought I'd let her do the final track on Themes from the Sixties Vol. 2 as a solo artist. I gave her the James Bond theme *Thunderball.* This version is equally as good as the Tom Jones version with Jo's voice in excellent form. (In truth it was a B.O.P track featuring Jo). Little did I know how important this album would be in the scheme of things and it put both Future Legend Records and me on the map. With volume one I had paved the way for this new idea of breaking new acts via new versions of Cult Themes, so by volume two people were aware of them and according to many, most were better than the originals. This was borne out by great press reviews plus the recognition we had started a new trend. Come the time to sell the album to the shops I instilled in the BMG sales team to follow my patter and not use theirs because of what had happened at Sony. But this time around I was not interested in selling it myself. They listened and it achieved good pre-sales but not a patch on the previous volume but reorders were starting to come in fast due to 2 major bits of airplay. The all-important BBC Radio One was playing the album on The Mark Radcliffe Show and this generated a lot of interest. Secondly, Mark Lamar was not only playing all the tracks on his GLR radio show but also using *Casino Royale* as the new theme for his show (which he kept for 2 years) because of the latter, lots of offers came in for Parsley to do live shows but Parley wasn't speaking to me and stamping his feet in the corner like a little kid because I had put out the combined version of Captain Scarlet on the album when he only wanted the vocal version, so his band missed a good few opportunities. Eventually, Mark Lamar got hold of him via another source and Adventures of Parsley did a tour with Mark and comedienne Jo Brand. I understand Parsley got other offers from this and his career took off purely because he was on 'Themes from The Sixties Vol.2'. (His band had been going for quite a while before this but never had this sort of action before). I never got any thanks or acknowledgement from him. (That's the music biz for you) Next, some D. J's called the Karminsky Brothers contacted me and asked me to meet them, which I did. It turned out that lately, they had been playing both volumes of my Cult Themes albums along with some assorted other themes at this club and the world-famous Madame Jo Jo's club in Soho. This Cult Themes night had become their most popular night with people coming along dressed up like James Bond, The Man from Uncle and Lady Penelope etc.

At least half the music played or requested was from our themes albums. I then heard the same reports from DJ's up in Manchester and other places in the UK, it had now become some sort of fashion trend or scene and F.L.R. were at the musical forefront of it. Soon the press were writing about the trend and more was to follow. (Both Mysteries & Themes from the 60s Vol.2 covers were designed by Dieter Marsoner our graphic artist extraordinaire early on in the labels history).

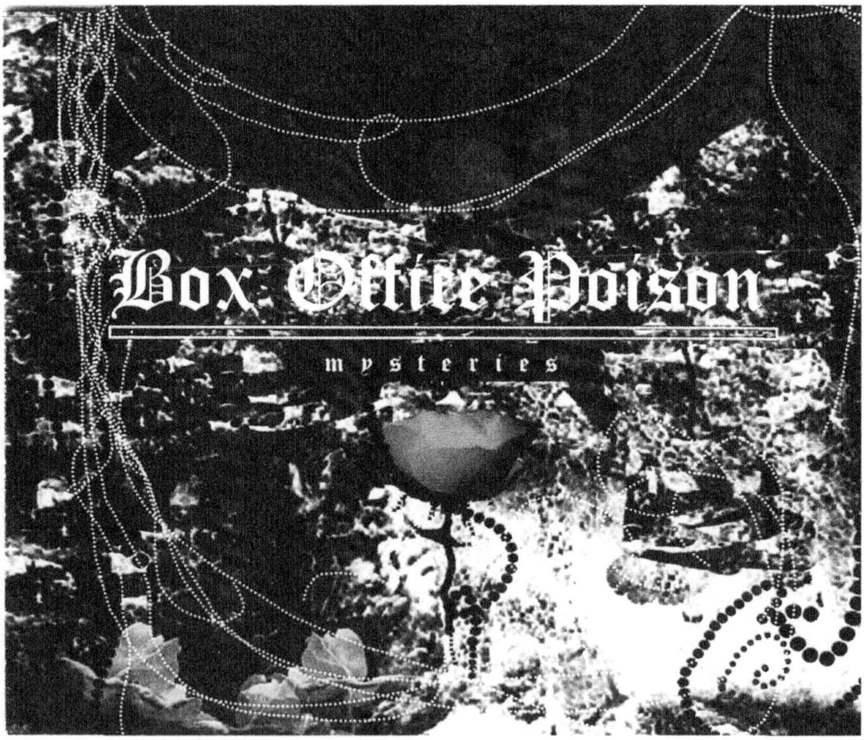

MYSTERIES

Higher................higher and higher......Let me take you higher

Dream, dream of me, I'm in your head. I'm in your head
No, you're not dead. You're not dead. I'm in your head

Mysteries of the world unite; Now and forever let's take flight
Hanging heavy on your eyelids, Floating thru' the pyramids

Open up your mind and you will find. A different kind
Hello mystery, hello dream. Now you can see me, but do not scream

NO! Do not scream, I'm in your dream. I'm in your dream
I am in your head; I'm in your bed. Yes I'm in your bed

Mystery, oh mystery, Mystery, you're my history

Time hangs so heavy on your eyelids. On your eyelids
Now, you're floating thru', floating thru' the Pyramids

Open up your mind and you will find that you're not blind
Oh mystery, mystery, don't you agree, we make a good team

Now your time has come. Don't be scared. Do not run
Now your time has come. Don't be scared. Do not run

CHAPTER FOURTEEN

MYSTERIES

Anyone hearing the track *Mysteries* always says it's a masterpiece and our *Bohemian Rhapsody.* It has many twists and turns and is an epic 6-minute long single. So, the priority for 1994 was to make a pop video for this track. With us not making the sort of money we should have from our Sony deal, pressure was on to keep costs down, so I came up with the idea to have a video makers competition amongst college students to make our next video. The idea was to take the top 3 ideas and make them into videos using college equipment and the best video director won £500. Sadly 2 out of the 3 video directors short-listed dropped out and a guy called Michael D ended up winning by default and co-directed the video with me.

My idea was to film in the woods with a beauty and beast vibe, plus another theme of a female mannequin coming to life and becoming the singer in the band. Another idea was to make instruments out of things in the woods like branches of trees and so on. The other director, David wanted to experiment with colours and shadows indoors. There is quite a lot of innovative stuff going on in this particular video. You may also notice there is an extra band member in some shots of the video. This was Chris Eddington who joined as bass player and after playing bass on Teenage Sex (which would be released at a later date) he then left, deciding it wasn't for him. He doesn't play on *Mysteries* but as I said previously we have a habit of featuring band members featuring in videos they are not playing on.

SRD only managed to sell about 500 copies of the single into shops and so we were not expecting to make the main charts but hoped now we had Indie distribution we would make at least the Indie charts. But with this being a 6-minute groundbreaking single it was never going to be easy to get airplay.

I also did some dance mixes of the single on 12" vinyl and these got the best results with one DJ saying he had a queue of people at the end of the night asking what the single was and felt like bootlegging it as there was so much demand for it. It made the DJs top 10 charts once more and college kids also loved it and many of the colleges put it at number one in their yearly chart. So on an artistic level, we had done well and the single also got good reviews but mainstream success was not forthcoming and our radio and T.V plugger struggled. I managed to get the usual one-off plays on MTV and Cable TV for the video but this time we lacked support from ace DJ Gary Crowley. I went to see him for a drink and thanked him for his previous support and we talked a bit about the Mod years but as a Mod he said, *Mysteries* was far too innovative and not at all Mod and not his taste, whereas *1995,* despite its innovative sound still had a bit of a Mod feel and song structure about it (Not surprising since Eleanor had done it first). Our plugger finally came up with a few plays on Jazz FM but then said he hit the jackpot by getting us a live spot on a mainstream I.T.V program called the James Whale show. He was known as being an obnoxious controversial DJ but he did like to showcase new talent on his show. So this meant putting a live line-up together as this track needed more than the 4 of us. We drafted in some new band members from another band called Elysium and started rehearsing. We were then informed we had to join the Musicians Union. Everyone was reluctant but our plugger said the show would pay £200 per band member so this would more than cover the M.U fee. But I thought the law had changed and you didn't have to be a union member anymore. But the M.U said it was advisable we joined and mislead us a fair bit. We were pencilled in to do the show but week after week we kept getting shifted to another date which pissed everybody right off as most people were working and had to keep booking time off work. The plugger was too timid to have a go at the show, so I went down to see the show's producer, Mike Mansfield, a right old Queen and well-known in music business circles. A production assistant initially tried to help and told me our video had been lost and this was the reason for us being switched. (I couldn't understand the reasoning behind that since we were playing live). So I started looking for it in their office. As I was bent over a desk Mike Mansfield came over and started chatting me up. (I think it was my tight white trousers that got his attention). I told him the problem and he said it would be sorted out immediately and gave me a definite show date and then handed me a contract to sign. But as I read the contract I saw it said the fee was £200 for the whole band and not per person. He also told me that we didn't have to be M.U members. As we had all joined the M.U we would in effect be out of pocket, not good news. Mike blamed the plugger saying he had misunderstood the fee but the plugger was adamant that he had got other acts on the show and they had got £200 each. I told the rest of the band and as you can imagine they were not a happy bunch and were having second thoughts about doing the show as they felt cheated and I agreed with them. When you added all the date changing to the equation we took a collective decision, that should the date be moved one more time we would not do the show. The date was moved yet again and we said we no longer wanted to do the show. The plugger then refused to do anything more for our record. However, the record would start to get recognition in some unexpected quarters. My brother and I were barely on speaking terms for many years because of a fall out in our teens but he had broken his leg skiing and it worked out a lot cheaper for him to come back to London to get it fixed. He called his so-called mates to pick him up at the airport but all let him down. When he had lots of money and was spending it on these shallow friends they were always hanging out with him but he had recently lost money on

the stock market and wasn't so well off hence why he had to come back to the UK for treatment on the NHS.
Anyway, to cut a long story short my mum called me and asked if I could pick him up from the airport and despite rarely speaking I picked him up because I held no grudge on my part. He was deeply touched by this and we ended up having a heart to heart talk about things. He couldn't understand how I was popular and respected and rarely had much money yet he had been rich, treated friends all the time and then been let down by them. He thought life was all about possessions, status and how much money you had. To some extent, this is true with a certain type of person but real friends will like you if you are penniless. He doubted that he could give up his materialistic lifestyle but felt he had learnt a lot from our conversation. So, after this, we got on much better and he used to phone me a fair bit from America.He was a top hairdresser who had worked for Vidal Sassoon and at this point in his career, he was doing lots of famous peoples hair in Hollywood. He was always dropping names and I remember my mum coming back from seeing him and she had a picture of her dancing with Brad Pitt and she asked if I knew who he was since she hadn't heard of him. Also, she said my brother was cutting Sharon Stones hair while she was there and Michelle Pfeiffer was offering to make everyone a cup of coffee while she was waiting to have her hair done.
So, why am I talking about my brother all of a sudden? Well, because we were getting on, I sent him a couple of copies of the *Mysteries* single and he was playing it in his salon one day and the sexy actress Roseanne Arquette came in to get her hair done and upon hearing the single whilst there she said, 'That's a brilliant track who is it?' My brother told her it was my band. She then said I'm just off to have lunch with Madonna any chance I can have a copy to give to her since she has just started her own record company Maverick and would probably like it. So my brother called me saying is it all right to give a copy of your single to Madonna. I thought he was winding me up at first but then he explained what had happened and naturally I agreed.
A few weeks later I'd forgotten about this and my phone rang and the voice on the other end said, can I speak to Russell and I asked who it was and she said, Madonna. I don't know why but I think because I told a few people Madonna would be getting my single, I thought it was one of my friends winding me up. So I said, 'Who is it really'? She just said call me back on this number and gave me her number, which was a California number. I called back and a maid answered saying, Madonna's residence then passed me on to the material girl once. I apologised for this misunderstanding. Then she said I've heard *Mysteries*, which I think is fantastic. It's a great production and arrangement in particular and very original. I've just got my own record company now and may be interested in signing your band. Have you got an album we can listen to? I said yes and she gave the address to send it to at Maverick Records. Naturally, I sent it off next day.

Around this time I was also looking for new management, as I wasn't keen to get stuck with it. I then read an article about a manager called Wayne Forte, a New York manager who managed David Bowie and Nine Inch Nails. In the article, it said how he got off on managing creative and innovative acts. So, I tracked him down and gave him a call and we got on very well and he asked me to send him some stuff over. He liked it and offered to manage B.O.P for a trial period and asked me to come over to New York at the earliest opportunity.

America and Americans was very much the flavour in my life at that time because within a few days I got a call from an American journalist called Dawn who wrote for many top U.S publications including Rolling Stone magazine. She said she was coming to London to do a series of interviews with pop stars and said I was beginning to get a reputation as some sort of music business legend on the underground scene. She had been a big Eleanor Rigby fan and had followed my career with interest ever since and got my book and the recent B.O.P releases. Since I like doing interviews I readily agreed and the following week there she was in my abode pen and notepad in hand or was it a Dictaphone? Dawn (pictured at foot of the page) was from New Jersey. She had a nice sixties image and looked like she stepped out of a sixties girl group. She was very cute but also quite short. The interview took place and soon after we found ourselves in bed together. I'd only known her a few hours but sometimes you find that sexual chemistry just compels you to each other like a magnet. I hadn't thought beyond that moment or that there might even be a hidden agenda to any of it. I saw her once more for another sex session before she left and she invited me to come and stay with her in New Jersey and that she would get me a lot of publicity and exposure in New York for B.O.P. Since Wayne wanted to see me as well I figured it wouldn't be long before I found myself across the other side of the Atlantic.

Meanwhile, Ministry of Ska was back on the agenda. PWL records run by Pete Waterman and known for selling millions of records of Kylie Minogue he had heard and liked Ministry of Ska tracks he had heard on the latest *Cult Themes* album and asked to see us.Dick and saw his head of A&R but felt he was taking the Mickey by expecting us to do several dance remixes of the recordings at our own expense. (They knew Dick had a proper recording studio).But they were not offering any money upfront plus PWL had their own studios. Dick refused to do anything until PWL parted with some cash. My attitude was let's do the remixes at his studio it wouldn't cost us anything and I'm sure we'd then get anoffer. Dick was adamant he wouldn't do it. I think part of the reason was we had just recorded a new version of the classic *The First Time Ever I Saw Your Face'*, written by Kirsty McColl's father Ewan. Dick used to go out with Kirsty and they were still friends so played her our version of the song and there was talk of us doing a duet. With it being written by Kirsty's dad this would naturally get quite a bit of publicity and possibly get a release via Virgin who I think Kirsty was signed to at the time. So Dick felt we had other options. Since M.O.S was more of a sideline project to me I left everything up to him and besides, I had arranged to go to New York where I felt success for B.O.P was just around the corner. At the end of the day, both the PWL deal and the collaboration with Kirsty fell through. With only a few tracks left to finish an M.O.S album, which ended up being called 'Rarin To Go', we decided to release it on Future Legend Records the following year then pursue licensing deals abroad

CHAPTER FIFTEEN

THE NEW YORK AFFAIR

It was 100 degrees in the shade when I hit New York in the summer of 94. A friend of Dawn's met me at the airport as Dawn was out of town on an assignment. She was interviewing Harry Nilsson (who died not long after this.). Dawn lived in New Jersey not New York but that's only across the river, so it was close enough. I then passed the time away chatting with her friend. Dawn arrived home later that night and within half an hour we were making passionate love once again. The next day I learned that she was going to do a kiss and tell book about all the rock stars she slept with. Strangely, I'd left a few erotic messages via her answerphone when she was out one day in anticipation of my forthcoming trip to America because I'm prone to do such things. She wanted to know how I felt about featuring in such a book. I wasn't too bothered about it as long as the information was accurate. She then confirmed she'd kept all the sexy answerphone messages as proof. I just said, good luck and don't forget to send me a copy. That night we met up with some local celebs in the shape of a band called 'The Waitresses' who had just had a big hit with 'Christmas Wrapping'. It turned out that they were also fans of Eleanor's music and there was some talk of a songwriting collaboration between us and me producing the band in the future. The next day Dawn and I hit Greenwich Village, which was definitely my cup of Cappuccino. We then visited some local record companies like 'Bar-None', who had a few worldwide Indie hits with the band They Might Be Giants. I followed this with some promotion for Box Office Poison singles, which I had managed to get my exporter' Caroline Exports' to send over to all the shops in New York to tie in with my visit. Wayne had sorted out some interviews for me to do and I thought it could translate this exposure into some sales, as my interviews often did that. The music was also played of course. So, I did interviews with T.V. radio and press and our videos got quite a few airings leading the editor of Billboard Magazine to say that those videos and the music were the best things he'd come across in many years, especially from the UK. He then started touting B.O.P in Billboard Magazine as the next big thing. This was definitely a good start. On another earlier trip to America, I was supposed to meet up with my godfather in New York but didn't because he was ill. Well, this time around I finally got to see Edward. He had always been generous to me as a kid and his offer to pay my airfare if I came over was a typical gesture by him. He took Dawn and me out to dinner where he told me he had eagerly followed my career via my Mother. I gave him copies of some of my releases and a few days later he wanted me to meet up with him for lunch again to meet an influential person he knew who he said had been trying to track me down (all very intriguing). His name was Charles Craig, an agent who represented John Barry. It turned out that he was very impressed with all my productions and arrangements, especially the way I had interpreted some of John's work including the Bond Themes. It transpired that John Barry was ill (I think it was throat cancer) and Charles had a lot of work lined up for him but felt his illness may involve John taking a lot of time off. John, confirmed to him I was on his radar and he had loved my productions and arrangements (which he would confirm in person to me a few years later). So, the question was, would I be interested in taking Johns place if he had to take a lot of time off. I was buzzing of course. Naturally, I jumped at the chance and agreed although it's not the ideal way to get such a job. Me doing the next James Bond theme, how brilliant would that be? That was one ambition that was on my bucket list for sure. Just producing and arranging the Bond theme covers I'd already done including the number one hit 'You Only Live Twice' was somewhat of a high but to actually write a Bond theme that would be the ultimate dream.

I told Dawn about the news and she wanted to meet Charles and asked for his details. It turned out she was a bit of a hustler in some ways and she was keen to blag any useful contacts I had, she also wanted to meet Wayne who I had only had a quick meeting with so far. I wanted to go on my own to my next meeting with Wayne as I thought it gave a bad impression if it looked like I had some sort of girlfriend tagging along. Dawn got the hump about this since she said that she had gone out of her way to introduce me to her contacts and I should do the same and a small row developed at which point I saw a side of her I didn't like. Also, since I'd been with her this time around the spark that had been there in the UK had dimmed slightly and because of this my eye had started to wander but where it ended up was a bit of a shock to all concerned.

I had my meeting with Wayne and we drew up a battle plan. He was pleased the initial interviews had gone well and that the B.O.P tracks had got radio and T.V. play but he was especially happy that Billboard had really liked what I was doing. He thought the next step was to chase up Madonna and wanted to know what the latest was. After Madonna had initially called me about my track *Mysteries* and I had sent our album 'Beyond the Twilight Zone', I had chased up the people at Maverick Records regarding this but the manager there had not made any decision on it and were waiting for Madonna to get back off tour. Wayne said he'd chase this up for me. He then went on to say that labels like Maverick might not be the best label for me adding, that artist labels are often a vanity thing and something the mother company (In this case Warner's) give to their artists as part of a new record deal to make them stay with them. Artists often lose interest in after the novelty wears off and I may find myself stuck on a duff label going nowhere. He added that with the innovative music I was doing the major labels wouldn't give it the time of day and at best would just put out one single and drop us if that single didn't do anything. On the other side of the coin were the independents, who could make you very popular and sell lots of records in New York or California but sell zero in the rest of America. So, he identified the best way forward was what he called at satellite label. This is a smaller subsidiary label funded by the major labels that gave acts time to grow. He said there weren't that many but these would be a perfect fit for Box Office Poison and this is where he would concentrate his efforts after he'd chased up Maverick. As far as the management went, he thought we should have a trial period of 6 months and if happy with each other sign a proper long-term deal once he felt there was something worthwhile on the table. This made sense and so we both agreed on this as the best course of action.

I had always been a big Bowie fan and always loved the track *Lady Grinning Soul* from the Aladdin Sane album. I felt it a perfect cover version for B.O.P to do. So, a few months before my American trip I'd done a demo of it with Joanna on lead vocals. I mentioned this to Wayne and asked if he could pass it on to David for his opinion. He then said David would be coming in later that day and he'd play it to him and let me know what he thought. I went back later to see Wayne about photo sessions and a few other things and who should I bump into coming out of an adjoining office but David. Yes, mister Bowie himself. I told him who I was, then asked him straight out did he like the new version of *Lady Grinning Soul.* At first, he wound me up. I hadn't realised he had such a wicked sense of humour. He said, so you're the person who ruined my song.

Then he laughed and added don't look so devastated I loved it really. He then went a bit more serious and asked about the sax lines in particular. Apparently, he had done something similar on the demo with him being a sax player but then didn't use them in the end. He said it was uncanny how both the lines and where they went were so similar. I retorted 'It must be the Brixton Air'. So he asked, did I know Brixton? I said I grew up there.

A light went on and we were thick as thieves after that for an hour or so talking about old Brixton haunts like the Ram Jam Club and the all-night Ska parties. Rather than hang around the office we then decamped to some secluded bar not too far away to continue our conversation over refreshments. We then spoke about music and he said he'd like to hear a few more tracks, especially our original material. Luckily I had a CD Walkman and a few CD's with me, so he listened to a few tracks. Like most people, he loved *Mysteries*. We then spoke about being multi-platform artists. He told me, never let people try and pigeon-hole you. That's why he was always one step ahead of everybody. Obviously, he also acted but certain people thought that he shouldn't and just stick to being a singer/songwriter. He also dabbled with fashion and was a painter, which I didn't know. I then told him that I was a decent photographer and some of my images had been considered iconic and added I was also a scriptwriter, author and had been a top DJ. He then joked that we both must have been Geisha's in a previous life. He then mentioned the English translation of Geisha meant 'Total Artist' and we both seem to fit that category. So I asked him, why are there no male Geisha's only female ones. He wasn't sure. He added he saw no reason why a male couldn't be a Geisha; he thought it might have something to do with the Courtesan element of being a Geisha. He added that the uninitiated often think a Geisha is a hooker but that is a common misconception. This was due to the Second World War when many hookers used to dress like Geisha's because the G.I's were attracted to that look but none of those girls were real Geisha's although it's possible some may have been down on their luck. He then returned to the Courtesan element saying, Geisha's were total artists but also highly sought after companions. However, it was never about sex, having a Geisha on your arm was like having a rare work of art. You were the curator and got to enjoy it whenever you wanted but it was also there for the world to enjoy as well. He continued, it's unlikely a male Japanese man would want such a life but in Europe, there was an equivalent. He said Casanova was a Courtesan but probably had no artistic talent but there were some artists like Leonardo Da Vinci and others who did need to marry up being a Courtesan with being an artist in order to get the bills paid and many musicians such as Mozart and Tchaikovsky all had patrons of the arts and some may have had to thank these patrons with extra favours. I knew Tchaikovsky definitely had to. He spoke a lot more about the subject but in conclusion said, we were probably destined to be secret male Geisha's. However, I do remember around the time of Aladdin Sane he did wear Japanese clothes and face make-up that was almost Geisha-like so he had already done it to some degree. He then went on to advise me about getting publicity for my band before revealing he was thinking of getting into directing pop videos and films. So feeling a bit cheeky I put a proposition to him. Would he direct the pop video for *Lady Grinning Soul* when we released it? I thought it would prove interesting since it was his song. I was curious to see how he would approach it. He agreed it would be an interesting project and he would love to do it providing he wasn't in the middle of anything major when it needed to be done. He said it was always good to keep challenging oneself and the very nature of being a Total Artist keeps things fresh, as each day you may be doing a different art to the day before, it keeps you on your toes, keeps you focussed and you rarely get bored.

The final bit of our conversation was about Aliens and his 70's music. I said almost jokingly that all his biggest successes were to do with space or Aliens and was there a reason for that? He replied, it never hurts to have a bit of help from your Alien brothers and sisters. So, did he believe in Aliens then? He then laughed and replied 'what makes you think I'm not one? I said, are you? I think he loves a bit of intrigue but I also have an open mind. He said, firstly two-thirds of the planet is underwater and cannot be seen, that could be a pretty good hiding place if another species wanted to live on this planet without being detected. Just as I was digesting that morsel of mind-blowing info he asked me did I know about the theory that all humans had dormant Alien DNA in them and sometimes it gets switched on somehow and that person suddenly excels far beyond even the best this planet has to offer. (Usain Bolt may be a good example but Bowie himself is probably a good example): Also the X-Files covered this subject a few years later saying it was based on real evidence. He added the people who are switched on can usually recognise each other and it may not be a coincidence that we both have Geisha attributes. So, a bit shocked I asked him if I was Alien? He corrected me saying, no human is Alien but some humans have part Alien DNA switched on. Take a look in the mirror it's usually in the eyes. Of course, Bowie has very unusual eyes but I remember Eleanor talking about this same subject and mentioning our eyes previously. All I will say is my eyes do change colour a lot from Blue to Green to Grey. People often comment that my eyes are a different colour each time they see me and that is very unusual. Eleanor had the same. I also tend to be 10 years ahead with new art or music ideas I come up with. I think maybe I have said too much already. Bowie may have been winding me up of course but I somehow thought he was just opening my mind to further possibilities and my mind has always been open and expanding ever since. I would have liked to have talked more with this fascinating genius but he had to get off to some engagement or other, so I asked about seeing him before I went back to London. He said he was going to be in and out of town over the next few weeks and to check with Wayne and if he was here we could grab an espresso or something somewhere. Just as he was about to leave I remembered something important I had wanted to ask him but was so thrown by meeting him I nearly forgot. As a kid one of the first scripts I wrote was 'Cosmic Hero' (I still have it) It was based on many of Bowie's songs and Alien based, I sent it to him via a guy called Michael Lipman, who was managing him at the time. So I quickly asked David did he ever get the script? He said no, but that's typical Michael not to pass something on. If we grab a drink you can tell me more about it but I really have to go right now. I felt I had drained every last drop out of this chance encounter and was hoping there would be more.

Sadly, Jo who sung on 'Lady Grinning Soul' for B.O.P left the band not long after this and the track was shelved for a few years until we got another singer (Who would be B.O.P's ultimate pin-up and talent but more of her later). The upshot was when the release was scheduled for release I contacted Wayne and David about him directing the video but he David was on a world tour at the time and so couldn't do it. Shame. I tried keeping in contact with David over the years. He gave me an e-mail address at Bowie Net that was one of his new projects at the time and sometimes he would answer and sometimes he wouldn't. (Such is the life of a superstar).

The last time I heard from David was when I produced 3 songs of his for 'Cult Themes from the 80's' early in the millennium. He loved all 3. Cat People, This is not America and Absolute Beginners. I will elaborate more when that part of my story turns up.
(Below: 2 of Bowies Geisha looks and right me as teenager with mine. I must have had a premonition, as I am now a full male Geisha)

I was still buzzing from my meeting with David when I returned to Dawn's place. They say never meet your idols but he far exceeded my expectations and he is still probably the most interesting person I ever met. Dawn had left me a note saying she'd gone on an overnight assignment to L.A and would be back the following day. She added a PS that her Mother was coming to town for lunch and may arrive before she returned and I should entertain her if she didn't get back in time. The next morning her mother did indeed turn up. She was slim, sexy and gorgeous and I have to confess my heart almost missed a beat. Not to mention, causing a twitch in another part of my body as I opened the door in my underwear since she had woken me up. She looked me up and down and said 'You must be Russell. I've heard a lot about you.' She came in and I offered her a cup of coffee and we sat at the kitchen table and talked for a while. She was one of those people that although you only just met you feel you'd known for years. I felt my stomach all aflutter the more I stared into her eyes and I could see it wasn't a one-way thing. I got up to make another cup of coffee and to my embarrassment; I had a massive erection, which she duly noted. As I slowly made the coffee I was thinking only one thought I'm dying to shag this vision of loveliness, what shall I do about it. Before I could come to a conclusion, Dawn came back and it felt like my life was put on hold. We all went to lunch and then discussed going for a night out to see a sixties girl group The Ronettes or the Crystals (I don't remember which). I spent most of the lunch just staring at Dawn's mum. The strange thing now is I can't even remember her name. Anyway, that night we hit the concert, which was at a dinner club and I sat next to her mum. I could feel the electricity all night long going back and forth between us and the mere touch of her knee brushing against mine nearly sent me over the edge. Dawn then went to the ladies room and her mother and I had a quick snog and this just confirmed things. We then agreed to meet up the next day. Dawn picked up on the fact I fancied her mother but couldn't believe her mother would fancy me. She also thought her mother too old for me. I don't know how old her mother was but she looked like she hadn't escaped her thirties yet. I then spent some time with her mother, which naturally caused a big rift between mother and daughter. I felt I could have really fallen for her mother but her mother felt guilty about the whole thing and wanted to end it. She seemed to think that Dawn had long-term designs on me,

which was the last thing I wanted as I had more or less gone off Dawn anyway. When I returned to New Jersey later I was most definitely in the doghouse. Dawn threw a sleeping bag at me and I had to sleep on the floor in the living room. She then informed me that in her book of Rockstars she slept with she was giving marks out of 10, she was going to put my marks near the top but now I would be sure to get bottom marks. With such an uncomfortable atmosphere in her place, I moved out to a hotel in New York for my last few days in America.
On the last day, I had another meeting with Wayne. He said he'd spoken with Maverick and the situation was as follows. Madonna loved B.O.P's music but the rest of the people at the company either didn't like it or didn't get it at all. Since they are the ones who have to push the product and not Madonna they were not keen to sign me.

He advised me that even if Madonna herself wanted to sign me because the key promotion people were not on board or enthusiastic, the product would bomb and I wouldn't be able to get another deal after that. He said we should pass on this deal and see if he could get something elsewhere for me. I agreed and that's how things were left. Some month's later Wayne reported back to me that he had managed to get a company called 'Echo'. Interested in us. They were just the right label. However, they were having problems with their funding and we had to hold off a while to see what happened. The company then went out of business a few months later and that was the end of any potential American releases. (*Many years later Dawn sent me a complimentary song she'd written about me. I guess I was forgiven*) b

THE MUSIC GODFATHER

Not long after my return from America, I was to meet a music business legend, Don Arden. Initially, it was his son David that contacted me. Don had just sold his record label 'Jet Records' to Sony. Jet records had many hit acts including E.L.O and Ozzy Osborne to name but a few. In fact, his daughter Sharon would follow in her father's footsteps by managing Ozzy and marrying him into the bargain and become a major T.V celebrity years later under her married name of Sharon Osborne. In fact, her going off with Ozzy caused a major family rift and they weren't speaking at the time I had dealings with the Arden's. Anyway, the Arden's had made 70 million on their deal and were looking to invest it in new Indie labels and since I lived not far from them I was worth pursuing. I had a few meetings with David, himself no stranger to controversy, as he had not long been out of prison for kidnapping and torturing an accountant who had ripped him off. I got on well with him and he loved most of the music on my record label. He said they would be interested in becoming partners and pay one million pounds to come on board. The final decision was down to Don and myself. So, I finally got to meet the legendary Don Arden, a well-set bearded man now in his sixties. Don had become famous in the sixties as a manager of groups like The Move and The Small Faces. But his most notorious stunt was hanging another manager out of 10th-floor window by his ankles when the said manager tried to steal The Small Faces off him. He was also known for terrorising record executives with his hard man image. As we chatted Don told me his version of events about this famous story. He said he wasn't a gangster and had hired actors not heavies when he took retribution on Robert Stigwood (manager of the Bee Gees) who tried to steal The Small Faces from him. He went on to say you have to realise he was trying to steal the food out of my babies mouths and he had to be taught a lesson. He added that after that incident nobody else in the music business messed with him. I'd heard also about him having ties with the Mafia and confronted him about it, to which he replied the music business if rife with Mafia people at one level or another so there is no way of not dealing with them at some point but it wasn't anything to be concerned about. Reservations out of the way we started to discuss the business in hand. He was very keen on Eleanor's look and material and said she could easily be one of the most successful singers in the world. He wanted to know if there was any way of tracking her down and persuading her to resume her career. I said I knew there was no chance. He thought Ministry of Ska to be a bread and butter act that could build up a big following. He then turned his attentions to Box Office Poison with me saying they should be the priority act. He said it was fine to push B.O.P in Europe via these groundbreaking records and they might do well but he didn't see B.O.P happening in America unless we changed the style of music so he asked about doing special mixes for the U.S.A and adding guitars because he thought the songs were extremely good but needed dumbing down a bit for America. It began to sound like we would sound like E.L.O part 2. He even went as far as to say I wrote very catchy pop songs and then set about making them less catchy with the experimental elements (I did do that sometimes). He concluded by saying we won't see eye to eye on everything and although we will be equal partners he'll have 51% of the company and the final say on most matters regarding the business and I can have the final say in the recordings & production. He added, he had other labels to see but there was an offer on the table for me of one million. I had a lot to think about and had a week to think it over. Next up I saw my lawyer Judy. She said, you know Don Arden's reputation. I nodded. She added, If you purely want to earn lots of money and don't care about control of your life or career then go for the deal. If you care about your music and don't want to be owned for the rest of your life then turn it down. After hearing that. I decided to turn the deal down.

(Above The Don)

CHAPTER SIXTEEN

TRULY INDEPENDENT

Come 95 my distribution contract was up for renewal once more. I wasn't too devastated to part company from BMG & SRD, as they weren't brilliant but we had managed to keep afloat as both the Themes 2 album and especially the Best of Eleanor Rigby Vol.1 had sold well. We were approached by a new company called 'Else' but after a day watching their sales team I rejected that deal. When you are aiming for the charts or a high profile you do need a major distributor. But I had a rethink and thought in 95 we won't play that game anymore and would just seek out a credible Indie distributor that could relate to our music and put us in shops that were likely to generate sales for our type of releases. We found 2 such distributors in 'Greyhound' and 'One Stop'. The latter specialised in Ska and Mod releases and the former did well with vinyl, cult stuff and cutting edge music. So firstly we got our normal stock into the shops to help pay the rent. However, the timing was very bad for Box Office Poison. Ironically the label was set up to push us and now we had run short on funds just when our album Beyond the Twilight Zone was due for release. So we ended up doing a low-key release for it. But my other band looked like it had a much better chance as One-Stop did very well with Ska music, so I had to go back in the studio to finish off the debut Ministry of Ska album Rarin to Go. As well as innovation the album has a lot of humour to it. One humorous song was about an accountant called *Norman* and once again I did my trademark of getting a few drunken girls out of the local pub to do backing vocals and this worked a treat on this track in particular. Another popular humorous track, *Condom* found me on lead vocals, which I covered in an earlier chapter. If you like Judge Dread, you'll love it. After the popularity of *Skankin with the Toreadors*, I decided another classical piece should be plundered and we did a very good version of *The William Tell Overture,* which suited Ska. The most innovative track on the album is called *Ras.*, which is a Jamaican word. It starts with one of my special intros, me singing a bit of the song in a drunken manner then kicking over a lot of bottles. I then decided to create a new genre of Ska with this track called Ska Surf, featuring Surf guitar. Ska music often features a lot of vocal noises that make rhythm sounds and some almost sound like the words 'Check it out' and 'Cha'. Overemphasising this was another of our trademarks. We also decided to call ourselves the Cha Brothers as producers of this album because we always argued over who the producer was and whose name would go first. I produced most but 30% was co-produced.I also started work on Vol.3 of the Cult Themes album of the 60's'. So the last track recorded for the M.O.S album and the first for the new themes album was a Ska Surf version of *Rawhide.* We never did much promotion for Ministry of Ska but the album got rave reviews. Many called it, 'Groundbreaking Ska'. and 'Taking Ska one step beyond all the sound-alike Ska bands'. The album sold out and became collectable fetching £70 on the collectors market not long afterward (no doubt it's hit £100 by now). If it hadn't always been a side project for both of us who knows where it could have gone. (But I will revive it at some point).

TURMOIL

One reason I decided to concentrate on Ministry of Ska at this point was that, despite B.O.P's album finally getting a release there was a lot of turmoil within the ranks of the band. Louise (Debbie Detroit) had announced that she was going to leave the band. To be honest Louise had never been 100% into the music, she was more of a mainstream person into people like Barbara Streisand and Madonna, and so cutting edge never sat too well on her shoulders. Although, she loved certain songs she saw B.O.P very much as a stepping-stone for her career. She was obviously excited when Madonna was interested but with that not happening her interest in the band began to wane. She also liked dance music and had been approached to front a dance band. I had talked her out of leaving the band a few times before but this time I knew it was time for her to go, especially with nothing much happening for us at that point after the big push in America hadn't quite paid off. Although, we still had Jo on lead vocals we were suffering from music business prejudice. I had never stopped trying to secure a major deal for the band but I often got the comments from A&R people saying 'Lose the fat bird for starters'. Of course, everyone liked Jo's voice but said she was holding us back visually. The reaction to Louise was mixed. Some people liked the look of her but didn't like her voice and others like her voice but thought she was ugly. Because I wasn't prejudiced I had stuck by the girls. Jo was also never 100% into the music and was still keen to have a solo career and just saw B.O.P as 15 minutes of fame in case it never happened for her. So, I started discussing the situation with Anne. To my surprise she informed me she had always secretly fancied being a singer and since she was into the music 100%, could she give it a go. I was shocked, to say the least. Anne looked good and had a lot of style, so I said why not. After a few singing lessons, I thought we'd break her in gently with a Cult Theme and got her to do the Bond theme *From Russia with Love.* But first, she would need a name. Most pop stars have made-up names that make them more memorable so I came up with the name 'Mouse'. This came about as a result of 2 things. She once had noisy neighbours and was scared to complain yet she was scared to make a lot of noise herself and I accused her of living like a Mouse and had started calling her this as a nickname. Around this time she was into computers and graphic art and could forever be seen playing with her Mouse.

THEMES FROM THE SIXTIES VOL.3

Although we were leaders of this new Cult Themes scene, success was by no means assured with 'Themes from 60's Vol.3'. This was because the most well known themes were on the first 2 albums. There were just enough Cult Themes to fill the third album and our reputation for the first 2 would guarantee exposure. Running short of funds I managing to blag a deal with a studio called Skyline run by a talented engineer called Jez after Dick and I reached strained relations whilst finishing off the Ministry of Ska album at his studio. Because the album is heavily B.O.P influenced and we often seemed like the house band here are the details about this album.

Department. S (Box Office Poison) : It's often said that Box Office Poison have a loose feel on some tracks. This is because of our Jazz/Punk attitude. It was also a rebellious attitude against the numerous bands saying they want to be as tight as a ducks arse. However, B.O.P were capable of being like this but choose not to be. This track shows that the arse of this particular duck was squeezed to perfection. So much so, it's hard to tell this version from the original. The only real give away sign is the punchier feel, the sound effects and Ron's new sax line & my cello tipping it towards Pop Noir. Although there is some cello, I decided to concentrate on production, as I tend to do with Themes in particular. It was a very harpsichord dominated song and needed a good player to help knock it into shape, so former B.O.P keyboard player Paul Polden was persuaded to come back for one last performance and he truly excelled himself.

From Russia with Love (Mouse) : This is a very powerful version of this Bond theme with Mouse making her solo debut on it. Surprisingly John Barry didn't write this but Lionel Bart (famous for the musical Oliver) did. However, John Barry did an instrumental version of *Russia* on one of his own albums. The original was a bit laid back to suit Matt Munroe's easy listening singing style. So I decided I'd make the backing track more like the John Barry version but with vocals. Mouse then decided to sing it in a syncopated style. Many familiar Box Office Poison sounds came on board with the cello and tympani to the fore making it more 'Pop Noir', but also very Bond and I'd say a lot more so than the film original. It was well suited to B.O.P's style. The final bit of originality added to the track was Mouse speaking the end in Russian.

The Pink Panther (Ron Rage) : When it comes to carbon copies of the originals, it doesn't get better than this. Some might say this album is almost like a Box Office Poison album and with the first 3 tracks all effectively done by B.O.P or its members with a few others to follow I can understand this. But since at the time of recording Ron and I were the main players in B.O.P I gave him a solo track as a reward. But all the credit for this track must go to Ron (Real name Ron Howe). He did all the work here. I only pushed him to do the sax again if I didn't like it and mixed the track.

The Happening (Chelsea Monday) : On this track, I was taking the girl from the pub or street to its natural conclusion. In my book Music Business Bastards (How to do well in the music business without getting ripped off) I said it was possible to take someone off the street and turn them into a pop star. I was about to prove my point. I wasn't saying anything new, since my idol Joe Meek had done it on many occasions and more recently many actors and actresses have been turned into pop stars. But it has now reached silly proportions with Karaoke singers now being made into pop stars via those dire Simon Cowell reality shows. *The Happening* was a cover of an obscure Supremes track used for a psychedelic film from the '60s. It's not an obvious choice to do but since I love Motown and The Supremes in particular I couldn't resist it. The track was pencilled in for B.O.P singer Jo Sharp but she was having backing band problems. So I asked studio engineer 'Jez Larder' to knock out a basic backing track for her and I'd then embellish it. But when the session arrived Jo didn't. Life then became stranger than fiction. An actress friend of Jez's called Anna turned up at the studio to say hello. Since Jez had been ribbing me about the comments in my book about creating pop stars he thought it was time I practice what I preached. So, I asked Anna if she fancied being a pop singer. She was reluctant at first but having done a bit of acting she decided it might be a good exercise for her. The finished product turned out great and I did some photos of her and re-christened her Chelsea Monday.(Guess which day we recorded it?) When the album came out we were inundated with fan mail and one or 2 offers for her. In the end, she decided to follow a career in acting, but doing this track didn't do her career any harm.

For A Few Dollars More (Box Office Poison): Ennio Morricone was one of the main influences on me and my 'Pop Noir' genre, so it was a natural to cover my favourite tune of his but at the same time, it was a bit intimidating as well. How could I better my idol? The answer is I couldn't. This version is done like a cross between the film original, the Hugo Montenegro cover but we added a bit of an Elizabethan feel to it. I wrote a whole new string section in the second half of the track, so at least you always got something extra for your money .It ends with some Clint Eastwood humour.

Georgy Girl (Megiddo) : This album certainly covered a spectrum of musical talent in more ways than one. From novices like Chelsea Monday, we come to award-winning folk act Megiddo. What better song for a folk act to do than *Georgy Girl* (Originally done by legendary folk hit act The Seekers). But as usual, I decided to turn things on their head and suggested that instead of copying the bouncy original to turn it into a haunting ballad and it worked a treat. To add atmosphere to it, not only did I put long repeat backing vocal drifting through the whole track but the sound of the sea washing against the shore. It could be considered folk Noir since it has my distinctive Pop Noir feel on this track and shows how my production is recognisable when not doing B.O.P tracks.

Thunderbirds (Surfin Dead): I have always placed a lot of importance on intros, as this is something that initially grabs a listener's attention. I wanted something that would sum up one of my favourite shows as a kid and the main part of the show was someone calling for 'International Rescue' when in trouble. So I added some radio tuning, then went to the nearest pub as usual, chatted up the first girl I fancied and got her to do the voice back in the studio. But this one was particularly easy since all she had to do was say 'Calling International Rescue'. But it certainly added a new dimension to the track. The band decided to do it in an Eastern European meets Pets Shop Boys style, which also worked well.

Star Trek (The Federation): To reward the studio engineer Jez, I let him put a band together to do a track and this was it. Sometimes a producer's job is not to interfere if things are going well and I let Jez get on with it. This is done in a seventies-style disco version featuring original Moogs. I basically put the icing on the cake by getting Chelsea Monday to do some B.O.P style backing vocals on it, and then mixed it bringing out the catchier parts of the track.

Windmills of Your Mind (The Thomas Crown Affair) (Jo Sharp) : .Jo had let me down by not turning up to do *The Happening.* She was giving her solo career a push of her own at the time so I decided to part company with her as a B.O.P vocalist but to soften the blow I let her submit a track of her choice and she decided to supply this track which I had no input in. It was smooth but bland, but it's worthwhile as she is a great singer and it was a Cult Theme.

Randal and Hopkirk (Future Legend All-stars): Effectively another B.O.P track this features, Ron , engineer Jez and myself improvising to this track. Apparently, the track was never released by anyone else, so all we had to go on was a 30-second clip from the T.V show and made the rest up. It has a weird but cool feel to it. The weird feel comes from the fact that the 3 of us involved were all pulling in different directions. Ron certainly lived up to his name 'Ron Rage' on this occasion. I gave him this name after the 2nd session I ever did with him where he flew into a rage for some small reason shocking me. Fortunately he was good most of the time but that's how I came up with this name for him.

The Beverly Hillbillies (Surfin Dead): At the time of recording this, a record called *Cotton Eye Joe* was at the top of the charts. It was Hillbilly dance music. So the band adapted this style for this track. (Which I thought was an excellent idea considering the tracks title) But to add to it I put in a few Ministry of Ska trademarks (like hups). The band also put their trademark Eastern European feel in the middle, which was brilliant I thought.

Rawhide (Ministry of Ska)**:** This was where I perfected the Ska Surf sound for Ministry of Ska. Although I did some Co-vocals & percussion, Dick was a good guitarist and I wanted to concentrate on perfecting this new genre as producer pushing for that twangy guitar mixed in with the Ska beat and I nailed it. Many M.O.S tracks are popular but recently many have caught on to the Ska Surf sound and this is the track that has done it.

The Self Preservation Society (The Italian Job) (Earthling Scum): There had been a big demand for this track for some time. Due to union problems regarding actors compensation for singing this in the film it couldn't be released. So, when Earthling Scum suggested it. I was pleased. However, Earthling Scum are probably the worst musician's to appear on any themes albums. Having said that, they were more creative than most good musicians. (A contradiction I know) A live concert of theirs I saw is still one of the best I'd seen. The Scum Boys were always a handful to deal with, but because I can be known to be a little eccentric at times myself I thought I could usually control them and relate mostly to what the band were looking to achieve. Engineer Jez however, was often mister straight and had a nightmare time with them. The Scum were always liberty takers of the first order but this time they went overboard. A few of the band members, Mr Bongo and Mr Sax hadn't turned up to the recording session I was producing and although the studio was fully booked the band bribed Jez to come in late one night to accommodate their 2 missing musicians. I couldn't make this session as I had a previous engagement, but Jez agreed to do it thinking it would be a few hours recording at most and a nice little cash bonus. But he should have known better with the Scum boys. They turned up with 6 additional people, tied Jez up to the chair and took over the studio until the break of dawn and to add insult to injury left Jez with a cheque that bounced. Jez was not amused. I managed to smooth things over and salvaged the track and it has become quite a classic. The album came out on vinyl and CD and it did quite well but went into overdrive as a download/streaming track. (it is often used as a football anthem as well)

The album cover was the first designed by Annie Mouse, although the basic Idea came from me and it is Anne/Mouse who is the mystery silhouette.

(The cover + B.O.P line up on Themes from the 60s Vol.3 below

CHAPTER SEVENTEEN

AUSTRALIA

If you had told me that Box Office Poison would be the 3rd most popular British group in Australia after Blur & Oasis, I doubt I'd have believed you but we were and it all began with a call from a girl called Moira who ran an Australian record company called 'Girl Zone'. She'd got some Eleanor Rigby releases on export and done well with them and wanted to know if I'd be interested in doing a licensing deal since as the name suggested they specialised in girl acts. I mentioned B.O.P of course since we were a female singer fronted band and she said she'd check us out. Part of the deal was that I distributed her main release also called 'Girl Zone' in the UK. I got some coverage but a compilation of unknown acts & unknown songs would never sell much. Our releases were doing considerably better in Australia. 1,000 Eleanor CD's sold out quickly and they were also getting a lot of interest in B.O.P. so, Moira asked if I could come out and do some promotion. I said that if she covered the cost I would. Anne who was now lead singer was very happy with this news as her parents and brother had immigrated to Australia and she hadn't seen them for ages so she would come with me. So we committed to 6 weeks in Australia from the beginning of December 95 to the middle of January 96.

I was looking forward to going to Australia and the first stop was Perth where we stayed with Anne's brother's family. This included 3 daughters who'd heard and liked B.O.P's music whilst living in the UK. I met Anne's parents for the first time and we got the obligatory when were we going to get married since we'd been together for about 5 years. I'd always had a policy of going somewhere hot when it was cold in the UK, so it was especially good being in Australia at this time of the year because Britain was snowbound. As I watched this white Xmas UK landscape on the T.V someone called me into the garden and it was 100 degrees and it was a case of 'Throw another Shrimp on the Barbi'. I didn't mind the heat but there was one annoying thing and those were the flies. You were constantly waving them away non-stop. I can now understand why Aussies were those hats with the corks on. We took in a nice few bits of scenery and we did a promo tour of all the college and mainstream radio and one T.V Show where they played some B.O.P videos. To keep costs down only I went off to Melbourne where Moira and Girl Zone Records were based and I stayed with her, her husband and daughter. After doing a few press interviews on day one I was told our pop videos were getting a lot of plays on the mainstream pop shows. They then asked me where I wanted to eat. It turned out that a brand new Hard Rock Café had opened in town and it was the hot place to go. I said let's go there and I can sign some records and get more publicity. A phone call was made but the manager wasn't there so a message was just left and we made our way down there. It was a funny situation. Their daughter was a big Kurt Cobain fan and she heard his guitar was amongst the memorabilia that would be on show, so she was looking forward to going. Moira's husband had been in a moderately successful band called The Wallabys', so you can imagine his shock when the bouncers stopped him at the door and wouldn't let him in. It was mostly bookings only and there was a dress code and his attire of t-shirt and scruffy jeans didn't cut it. He mentioned the group he used to be in but it just turned into a row. I as ever was dressed the part and stepped forward pulling several records out of my bag saying, I've come all the way from England for a signing and the manager and journalist are waiting for me inside. The people with me were my record label and to avoid some bad publicity they should let us in. We got in and

saw the manager and explained I was only in town for the day. Fortunately he had seen our videos on TV & liked them and so asked me to do a signing.I also knew the owner of the chain (who happened to be a friend of my brothers in Hollywood so I knew his name). Once I mentioned his name to the manger and gave a secret password my brother had given me, we were shown to the best table in the house and given a free meal. I duly did a signing and had some photos taken and did a quick interview with the DJ inside and he played our records. Moira's husband was embarrassed by the incident but I found it all a bit of a laugh. The next day Moira had me doing interviews right left and centre. Then I went shopping and she bought me a nice top and called me a natural star. I was careful to behave myself as I noticed Moira had taken a big shine to me. I then met up with Anne in Sydney to do more promotion. I was pleasantly surprised to learn as I attended an interview at the top radio station in town that B.O.P were considered currently the most popular British act after Oasis and Blur. They told me that other British bands didn't treat Australia with respect. They'd spend 2 or 3 days on promotion if they were nearby in Japan, then go home. I'd done nearly a months worth of promotion by then and was featured in all the media frequently. Moira was very pleased as our video for *1995 (which was timely)* was voted video of the month on one influential T.V show and all the publicity had started to generate sales of our singles and album on Girl Zone.
Sadly, Australia does not generate huge record sales as people are so spread out and the record-buying population not that huge. I was told 10,000 units was considered a brilliant result but we never reached that, we did make a profit though to plough back into the record company and for me to live on. Plus the trip was covered. We continued to do business with Girl Zone for a few years but they eventually went out of business and our deal ended.
I really loved Sydney & Melbourne but then we returned to the relatives for Xmas. The highlight for me was going out fishing for crabs since this was a new experience and I managed to catch quite a few which were served up as part of an Xmas family banquet. We then flew to Alice Springs and hired a car. Alice Springs seemed to be the capital for the Aborigines since they seemed to outnumber the white population. They were a strange but intriguing bunch and one night we were walking across woodland in near-total darkness and stumbled on a camp of Aborigines where we were invited to have a drink. We didn't stay long but heard about some of the injustices done to them. There seemed to be a lot of prejudice around from both sides. After a few days looking around Alice Springs, we drove towards Ayres Rock, one of Australia's most famous landmarks. On the way, we encountered a twister coming down the road. Instead of thinking about where is the next turn-off I was thinking 'Photo Opportunity'. So Anne and I got out of the car and started snapping away as the twister came ever nearer. Finally, when it was getting too close for comfort we started to leave but the car stalled a few times creating a heart in the mouth moment. Because so much sand was being blown around we thought it might have somehow got into the engine. Finally, the car started. Luckily for us, the twister diverted as we drove down the road although we still encountered strong winds, pouring rain and thunderbolts were crashing all around us and deafening thunder that shook the road. I found it all quite exhilarating. The next day we did the Ayres Rock climb. But to get yet another perspective on things I went up in a hot air balloon and travelled over it as well. Anne didn't fancy the hot air balloon so went on a Bush Tucker tour and ate some grubs. I know which I thought was the best deal. We returned to Perth for a few days for Anne to spend time with her relatives and then returned to the UK via Singapore.

CHAPTER EIGHTEEN

THE CANNES EXPERIENCE

No sooner had I arrived back home from Australia than I was off to the South of France. One of the biggest music industry events of the year takes place at Midem in Cannes, France. It resides in the same place as the Cannes film festival. However, Midem is not an award dominated event but a rights fair. Records companies from all over the world exhibit their wares, do deals and showcase their artists at live gigs. The major companies are always there but the Independent record companies have to think twice about attending because of the cost but it's a chance to do deals with the big boys, some succeed but the majority fail and as I said it's not cheap to attend. I met several Indie record company people I knew who had saved up all year to go, spending an average of £3,000 on just 5 days. Yours truly however with a nickname of 'Ace Blagger' saw this as a challenge and managed to do the whole trip for less than £100. Just as well really, since funds were tight. But I thought it's worth doing Midem at least once in my life. At worst it would be an experience and at best I may do a few deals, preferably for B.O.P but for other releases on the label as well. So, how did I blag it for such a low price when most people spent a fortune on flights, hotels, meals and drinks (A coffee was £7 and this is the mid-90s), not to mention the entrance fee which was about £500? The answer is talent. I was still keeping my hand in as a journalist and writing for a magazine called 'Tab' at the time. Although payments were minimal, there were the benefits of going to gigs for free, as well as getting complimentary CD's and so on. So I contacted the organisers of Midem to say I wanted to cover the event for an article about the music business. They duly awarded me a dated free pass for 2 days. Once the 2 days ran out I wasn't supposed to use it and pay for more days if I wanted them. But I just turned the pass around and walked in confidently & quickly for the other three days. All the lamented passes were on a piece of string with a sponsor's name on one side, so as long as the doorman saw this they never asked to look closely at it especially if they had seen your face a few times already. Secondly, a journalist called 'Ron Cooper' who wrote a European magazine called 'Zabadak' had called the debut Box Office Poison single the best in the last 10 years. So, I naturally sent him all the record labels future releases and did an interview as well. He also asked me to contribute articles & reviews from time to time. We built up a very good rapport but we hadn't actually met. I felt it was about time we did. It just so happened that he lived in Cannes and so he offered to put me up for the duration of Midem. So, with my entrance and accommodation sorted out all I needed was a flight. I managed to get a cheap return flight for £64-00 so things were looking good. To get things off on the right note I took Ron and his nice wife Aicha out for a Chinese meal and we all hit it off tremendously well. Although I'm naturally shy I can sometimes be the life and soul of the party and when I left they both said I left a big hole in their life even though they'd only known me a few short days. I was very touched by that.

The next day it was down to business and exploring Midem. As a journalist, I got lots of CDs, T-shirts, memorabilia and so on for free. Many stalls had free refreshments from coffee to something a lot stronger and some had food. So, there <u>was</u> such a thing as a free lunch! Working in the music business for over 10 years also meant that I bumped into quite a few people I knew. One such person was Larry Page who asked me what had become of Eleanor. He was back managing The Kinks & The Troggs. (Who were hot again because of the song *Love is All Around* written by lead singer Reg Presley and used in the successful film 'Four Weddings and a Funeral.) He told me not managing Eleanor was his biggest regret in management. He added she could have easily hit the top and was shocked she had disappeared.

The PRS (Performing Rights Society) had a stand and I knew most of the staff and got myself free refreshments whenever needed because I was a music publisher and they let me use one of their rooms to play my F.L.R. CD's for clients as well when needed (result!).

Next up, I spied a damsel in distress. She was blonde and America and looked like she may have been the blueprint for a blow-up doll. Bright she wasn't but distressed she was. I asked her what was wrong and she explained that she'd lost her manager and didn't know anyone else at Midem and had just found herself in a compromising position and was very distressed by what she found herself doing. I thought this bore further investigation. So I blagged some wine and a few seats from a nearby stand and her story began to unfold. Her name was Trish and she was a singer in a cocktail lounge in Las Vegas where a manager had spotted her and said he'd make her a star. They had recorded an album in Nashville at her cost, which even included a famous brass section The Musical Shoals. Her manager had said Midem was the place to come to get a deal but she had to pay her own flight but he would cover the hotel cost. When they arrived the previous night she found just a double bed in the room and now knew why he had agreed to cover the hotel cost and was told if she wanted a deal she had to get intimate with her manager, so she slept with him. Today they had started to see his contacts. He had already lined up a dinner date for her with one of his contacts without him being there since he said he had other business to attend to. Then half an hour ago they visited another contact at a record label stand (which was near where we were sitting). They had gone into a room and it was made clear by her manager that in order to get a deal with this label she'd have to give this guy a blowjob and that's how business was done here. The manager left her in the room with this other guy and she reluctantly gave him a blowjob. But she'd come out feeling dirty and ashamed and the manager was nowhere to be seen. I asked if I could have a copy of her CD to which she replied she didn't have any. She then went on to say they hadn't been manufactured in time but would be there the following day. Now, I have heard the expression dumb blonde but now I have met the definition of such a person. With Midem being once a year you'd think any manager would have everything ready months in advance and to turn up to with no CD's smacked of a scam. I wanted to help the girl but wasn't sure what I could do. I tried to convince her that maybe she was being taken advantage of, then finally her manager arrived. He was a sleazy character who would have looked more at home in the porn industry. He wanted to know who I was. I told him I ran a record label and quizzed him about what he knew about the industry and was quite rude to him. I said straight out what kind of a moron turns up to Midem without a CD. He got the picture and saw I'd sussed him out and so he made a hasty retreat with Trish in tow. I saw Trish again the following day and things had gone from bad to worse. She had ended up sleeping with another client that night and her manager had made it plain that this was the only way a female singer got on in the business and if she didn't like it she could go home to her 2 bit piano lounge job and forget about stardom. I gave her Ron's phone number and said she could leave a message for me if she found the whole thing unbearable and I'd find a way to help her.

She thanked me and went on her way but to my shock and surprise on the very last day I bumped into her and she had her CD's and gave me a copy. So, although I'm sure she was being used maybe the whole thing wasn't a con after all. I listened to the CD when I got home and she was actually quite a good singer but the material was a bit run of the mill. That night I'd find it was not only girls who were expected to sleep with someone to get a record deal. As I was leaving the Midem complex one day I bumped into another Indie label guy I knew called Herbie, who offered to buy me dinner. He wanted to pump me for contacts so I was only too pleased to give him something in return for a meal. But it turned out I learnt more from him. It transpired that far from all the deals being done at the main venue most were done at hotels and in particular at the Martinez bar. So armed with that information I donned my best popstar outfit and went to the Martinez hotel bar. I ordered a cocktail and nearly fell over when they gave me the bill (It nearly wiped out my whole budget right there. .....Ok I'm just joking but I was seriously worried about buying a round of drinks) I needn't have worried as some contacts came to the rescue. However, before they did I learned something valuable. On a table near me were half a dozen loud-mouthed Yanks and they were boasting about their shopping expeditions at Midem. Each one was trying to impress the other by saying how many copyrights they had bought. Then the one who had bought the most was asked what he was going to do about promoting the acts or what sort of compilation albums he was going to put out. He turned and said, I don't give a shit about the artists and I have no intention of releasing any material. His only intention was to sit on the copyrights and sell them on for more the following year.

Since leaving Sony I'd found myself a very good manufacturer and the owner of the company Steve had just walked through the door with his staff and members of the hit band The Shamen. I stood up and said hello and from that moment onwards I wasn't allowed to buy a drink. He also offered to buy me dinner the next day, which I naturally accepted. Although he did a lot of business with me he said my records were particular favourites of his. He liked *Mysteries* in particular and said it was especially brilliant to listen to through headphones after you had taken drugs. He then asked what drugs I took when writing songs to which I said, none. He said he couldn't believe it since the music takes you to another level both with and without drugs. I had a few laughs with the lads then figured, as this was the place to do deals I should circulate. As I surveyed the scene trying to get a handle on who might be important someone approached me. He was a swarthy looking overweight Italian who could have passed for Opera singer Pavarotti. But far from being an Opera singer, he was M.D of R.C.A Records in Italy. He handed me his card with a smile saying, 'Which pop group are you in? You must be in a pop group looking the way you do'. I had a nice embroidered black jacket on that stood out with a high collar white shirt that had lots of buttons close together and a cello earring. I said I was in the British group Box Office Poison. He confessed he had not heard of us but could he buy me a drink? He got the drinks in and I began to talk about B.O.P and showed him an F.L.R. catalogue featuring the band. He said he was desperate to hear something and he pulled out a CD Walkman. So I gave him CD's Of *Mysteries* and *Checkmate* . He duly played the tracks and then said 'These are brilliant. I want to sign you. How much money do you want?' I thought to myself 'Surely it can't be this easy.' I wasn't sure what to ask for, so asked him to make me an offer. He said £50,000 advance and 10% royalty for a 5-year deal. He then raved about what a good front person I was and how I stood out from the crowd. I kept telling him I only did vocals on a few tracks and the girls were the main singers. But he said I had to be the front person as part of the deal. I replied I didn't think I could do it. He said of course you can, you have natural star quality and the band will not get big without you fronting it. I said I needed time to think about it so he asked me to have lunch with him at his hotel the next day and I agreed. It was a real dilemma since there was a decent deal on offer but I didn't want to be the lead singer of the band. Firstly, I felt I was too old as I was no longer a teenager and secondly I wasn't really a singer. What I had done on *Mysteries* was stylised whispers come speaking type vocal that suited the song and when I fronted Ministry of Ska I sang with a Jamaican tinged vocal. What to do that was the question? I decided that a compromise would be needed and that I would do 50 % of the vocals instead of just the odd one or 2 as long as Anne could do the rest and as the previous singers had now left that made it easier.

I met Mr R.C.A, Mario for lunch the next day. Mario piled on the pressure and the drink and said he could get me a T.V interview with Ria T.V straight away to announce the deal for publicity value if I agreed to the deal. Obviously, a paper contract would still have to be sorted out and signed. As I showed more interest the climate changed somewhat as talk turned to his personal life. He said he had big Chateaux on Lake Como in Italy and wanted me to spend the weekend with him the following week, as he likes to get to know all his artists personally. Then he kissed me on the cheek winked and said 'I'm going to make you a big star'. For the first time, it dawned on me that maybe there was more than music at stake here. So, I asked him if he had any CDs or a catalogue of artists he'd signed. Sure enough, he pulled out a few CDs and a catalogue. All were nice young men with cheesy grins and suntans, jet-black hair and blue eyes. I had visions of being chased around his Chateaux until he got what he wanted. Still not being comfortable about being the lead singer I decided reluctantly to turn the deal down. My suspicions were confirmed when I met someone else who knew him who said he was known to be a bit of a bum bandit.

That night I went to one of many functions and spied the most beautiful black girl or any sort of girl I'd seen in my life. She was a DJ called Elaine and I made a beeline for her. We hit it off instantly as we were both South London people. We had a quick snog and I felt this had strong potential to go somewhere serious. The love bug was clearing its throat and about to sing. She then said let's go back to her room, which was at the same hotel where the party was. I don't mind saying that I couldn't quite believe that such a Foxy chic was interested in me but there was chemistry and I could feel it. But just as we were about to step into the lift her manager came running over and grabbed her saying some important people wanted to meet her. I wasn't sure whether or not to go with her but followed along despite a look of disdain from her manager. Then suddenly, I was blagged myself by an old music business pal and Elaine seeing this said 'I'll catch up with you later'. She came over to me later with a big America posse of Hip Hop artists and said she was going to a club with them but it may not be my scene. I was keen to get intimate with Elaine but knew I'd feel like a spare part in such company. So we agreed to meet the next day at Midem for lunch. We met up and she informed me she was going back to the UK early and we exchanged numbers and she asked me to promise I'd call her when I got back. I did just that and we agreed to meet for dinner but at the last minute, she cancelled.

A few days later she invited me to a launch party for a T.V show she was going to be hosting for Sky or MTV. She was already a popular DJ on a radio station. I'll never forget this party experience, normally I stand out from the crowd, but I had a lot of competition this time around but stood out for a different reason. Limousines were rolling up to a venue near Tower Bridge as I arrived. I went into this packed-out party to find I was the only white face there. Initially, I got a lot of suspicious looks and one person even called me mister Policeman. Others were more complimentary commenting on my stylish dress sense. I also got on well with people I spoke with because of my Brixton upbringing. However, there were also a few shady gangster types. I finally caught up with Elaine and she did an interviewed with me for her TV show talking about Ministry of Ska as well as B.O.P followed by another secret snog. But she was so in demand it was impossible to get much sense out of her that night, so I said I'd call her. I called her and she told me she had a lot on with the new show but did want to see me when things were less hectic.

I thought someone as hot as her was likely to be on a roller coaster ride to the top and I could see myself being messed about but because I fancied her so much I decided to give her one last call a few weeks later. We finally met at her place in Streatham and a magical night occurred and I was very smitten with her. We were supposed to have dinner the following week and asked me to call to let her know I was on my way just in case any last-minute thing came up. However, when I called some guy came on the phone and said he was her new boyfriend and that I shouldn't call again. However, I didn't want to give up that easy as she was a bit of a femme fatale for me. So I went around her place to encounter a few gangster types who threatened to kill me if I didn't disappear sharpishjo. Elaine came out of another room and insisted they leave me alone and offered to walk me to the car. As we made our way to my car she said her life was a bit crazy at the moment with huge deals going on to make her big but some of it was gangster money and they thought they owned her. On one hand, she was very excited to realise her dream but on the other hand, she was very scared of the company she was keeping but it was her crazy ride and she didn't want anyone else getting hurt. She said she liked me a lot and in another life, she'd definitely want me as a boyfriend but the timing and circumstances were not right and for my own safety, I should stay away. We kissed and both almost said together see you in another life.

I never saw her again and although she initially made a big splash including presenting Top Of The Pops a few times, she then appeared to disappear from the mainstream. One assumes the gangsters swallowed her up in some way. It was such a shame. Although recently I heard she was on the comeback trail and so I may grab a word with her, maybe more!

Anyway back to Midem. After lunch, with Elaine, I did the final rounds of Midem then went to the PRS stand to get some refreshments whereupon I bumped into one Steve Buckle. After Wayne hadn't managed to get me a record deal in the U.S in 94 I hadn't stopped looking for management and 95 had brought Simon Davies to the fore. He took me for a few drinks where we met several music business people and after hearing B.O.P he offered to manage us. His priority band at the time was 'Peepshow' and he was trying to get them a deal but he promised once that deal was secure we were next. However, he also managed a girl called Shelly who used to be in Bucks Fizz (She was drop-dead gorgeous and the girl who replace Jay Aston when she departed).

But she had major turmoil in her life as she had a serious stalker problem and Simon had to keep disappearing to deal with it. I gave Simon 6 months to get something going for us but all that turned up was getting a film company interested in doing my homeless song *Backstreet Boulevard* (Which subsequently fell through). We also had a meeting with Simon Williams of Fierce Panda Records, which also didn't lead anywhere. So, I found myself manager-less once more. Then as I said, at Midem along came Steve Buckle and we got talking on the PRS stand.

Looks-wise he was reminiscent of Dudley Moore minus the charisma. Anyway, talk soon got around to B.O.P and I played him some music at the stand. He thought both B.O.P and the themes were exceptional. He also said I was the best record producer of my generation and he could make me a millionaire in 3 years if I just wanted to be a record producer and nothing else but I might have to produce a few acts I didn't like. I told him if he wanted to become my manager B.O.P had to be the priority. He then agreed to become our new manager. He told me he managed one of the 2 ex Bros Brothers and soul singer Linda Lewis. He was also well in with Australian Impresario Reg Grundy.

So all in all Midem was not a waste of time. Although a few record companies who said they would be into licensing our releases fizzled out I had made some good contacts and got a new manager. I thanked Ron for putting me up and he was very pleased when I gave him 3 carrier bags full of CD's and T-Shirts as a thank you. I kept the most famous acts CD's and then sold them at the record and tape exchange back in London and guess what. The money I received ended up covering the cost of my airfare. So in effect, my Midem visit had cost me nothing at all. Sometimes good business can be as much about how much you save as how much you make.

(Below Russ with Ron from Zabadack magazine in Cannes D.J Elaine)

CHAPTER NINETEEN

A STAR IS BORN

Whilst Steve put some packages together to take around record companies I concentrated on my first release of 1996. After the success of 'The Best of Eleanor Rigby' I decided volume 2 was in order since I had enough material to fill another album, with album tracks, B-sides and rarities. For good measure and to keep the flag flying for vinyl I released Vol.2 on CD and picture disc vinyl featuring Eleanor on a Scooter.

We had clearly milked all the good Cult Themes from the 60's and apart from 'Bullet' (which I had overlooked). I could have left the Cult Themes idea there but I had a feeling that a seventies revival wasn't far away and we should tie the 2 ideas together with 'Cult Themes from the 70's Vol.1'. . It was another way to keep the buzz going on B.O.P as well. So, I began keeping my eyes open for the right acts whilst compiling the right track listing. I also thought I should add a new twist to the Cult Themes by including a previous hit act and get one out of retirement to do a theme. I thought to get things underway I would record the already signed talent. So first up was Mouse to do her second solo theme. She chose another Bond theme *Nobody Does it Better* (From The Spy Who Loved Me). This was an interesting challenge as I never really liked the original. It may be a good pop song but the Carly Simon track sounds nothing like a Bond theme. So I did a whole new arrangement of the song making it sound very much 'BOND' including Bond-style guitar riffs as an undercurrent. I also used an echoed cave sound for the percussion on the tracks, which added oodles of atmosphere. I was very pleased as it now sounded like it came straight out of a James Bond film. Bond fans were also quick to comment on this upon release of the album.

Steve then saw me and said he wanted a catchier sounding B.O.P song to grab the record labels attention. This wasn't a problem since as well as doing cutting edge stuff I still liked catchy pop songs and decided that B.O.P's next album would feature more instant pop songs whilst keeping the 'Pop Noir' feel and sound. I already had lots of songs written and just needed a few more to finish a new album off, which I managed to complete. I started playing them to Anne to learn and she said she wasn't sure if they would all suit her voice and not sure if she could carry the band on her own and thought I should stick with the 2 lead singer idea and find another singer. This came along a lot quicker than expected.

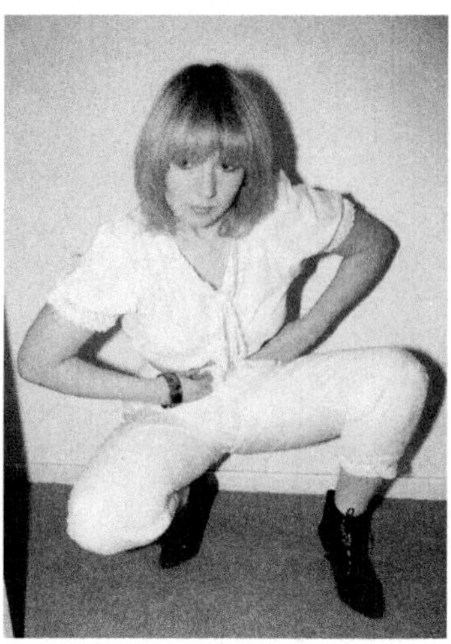

1st promo photos of Mouse above .keeping the Victorian underwear look but adding to it)

FATE

On Mother's day, Anne & I took my Mother to a restaurant boat at Camden Lock. If I said my heart missed a beat I think you know what is coming next.. 5.5", medium length dark hair, sexy and very beautiful. Her name was Lizzie and she reminded me more than a little bit of Eleanor and this caught my attention as she served up some soup. Yes folks, she was the waitress on the boat.

Of course, I've been drawn to certain people like a magnet before but the appeal of this girl was so compelling. I couldn't make out whether it was a case of me fancying her or seeing some sort of star quality in her. Remember, I was also on the lookout for a new B.O.P singer but this girl was a waitress, what were the odds of her being a singer. Throughout the lunch, I couldn't keep my eyes off her. As we got up to leave I approached her with my business card and said 'Do you by any chance sing'. She was stunned at the unusual question but replied I do sing actually and play a few instruments. I said I was looking for a new singer and if she was serious about becoming a singer she should give me a call.

Within a few days, Lizzie called me and we agreed to meet up in Camden. We hit it off immediately. She asked me about my track record and as I mentioned Eleanor she got all excited and very animated saying, she was a fan of Eleanor's music. There was brief talk about her fronting a tribute band to Eleanor as she loved her so much, then I pointed out my main thing was Box Office Poison and went on to describe the music. I then handed her some CD's. She said she'd been in various bands since she was 13 but a year or 2 ago she had become very disillusioned by the unoriginality of the music most had done and decided to give up singing. She was thinking about going to college to study and was working as a waitress just to get extra money to survive. We concluded that if she liked the music she would become the new singer with B.OP along with Anne.

The following day she asked to meet up again and said, 'Box Office Poisons music is the sort of music I've searched all my life, I can't believe I've found it at last. The music is brilliant I definitely have to be involved'. So as with all band members I thought up a new name for her and gave her a choice of two, Cinnamon or Misty. She chose Misty.
Our manager Steve Buckle and Anne both met Misty. Anne and Misty hit it off but Steve Buckle said he didn't trust Misty and thought she was trouble. Steve carried on for a while representing me and also got interested in doing something for Jo Sharp but it gradually fizzled out because when it came to choosing him or Misty I chose Misty.
I have to admit my head was in a spin over Misty as we started doing a few recordings for the new B.O.P album. Despite having her period on the day and feeling uncomfortable she did some great vocal tracks. It also quickly became apparent that she was very artistic like me and we thought in very similar ways. It was refreshing to find someone so in tune as an artist because I nearly always felt like an artistic outlaw even amongst other so-called artistic people I worked with. As well as artistically, there seemed to be some personal chemistry and so it seemed inevitable that some sort of intimate relationship would develop. Initially, opportunities were not plentiful because she had a young son even though she in her early twenties.
Because she thought I was a bit sceptical about her being a fan of Eleanor's she asked me to visit her one day to show me her E.R collection. Her mother, who she lived with, had taken her son to visit her sister and it wasn't long before the drink started flowing. Lots of flirting was going on as well as intense musical discussions then at one point she left the room and returned stark naked. She had a very nice body to go with her pretty face as she walked over sat down and put her arm around me and started kissing me. I was always in 2 minds after we met about whether or not to keep things on a business level or to mix business and pleasure. But I couldn't resist her any longer. My hand soon found its way between her legs. It wasn't long before she started getting excited and she then led me to her bedroom. After more foreplay, we were finally having intercourse. After 15 minutes her bedroom door flew opened and in came her mother. She literally pulled me out of her daughter and demanded I leave immediately. I quickly put my clothes on and left.
My head was in a spin for a few days not quite knowing what was happening especially as I was getting confusing signals from Misty. At first, she said she idolised me but it might have been a bad idea to shag each other. But her behaviour to me on the night was very much one-way traffic until I couldn't resist her charms anymore. I felt it was probably her mother talking more than her and so we had a clear the air meeting. Misty was very frank about herself, saying she was very much a heartbreaker and although lots of guys were always coming onto her, she would usually go out with someone and then treat them badly and hurt them and was shit at relationships. She, therefore, felt that since we had a special relationship in many other ways maybe it was better not to get involved in a love affair. I felt if I had in turn said let's go for it, an intense love affair would have started because I was already getting strong feelings towards her.
Misty was the only girl I'd met besides Eleanor that I could see me marrying but this also scared me. I was still very much scarred from my marriage and despite it being 5 years on I still didn't feel totally recovered and the last thing I needed was another Eleanor and then to have it end in tatters. That would have finished me off. By Misty's own admission she was likely to destroy the relationship. I also felt in her that I had found my musical soul mate and the ultimate B.O.P singer and didn't want to jeopardise this.

So we agreed to forgo any sort of big love affair in favour of working together and friendship. As for sex, I felt there was unfinished business in that department because of the way I was rudely interrupted but it would be a while later before was resolved. That's not to say no sort of sexual business went on at all, it did but in a weird way, more about that later. To add to the whole equation was Anne who as well as being my girlfriend was also the other singer in the band. I think she picked up on the fact that I fancied Misty but she also sung Misty's praises saying, she was the ultimate B.O.P singer. Because Anne & I had an open relationship, it wasn't a problem but others said they did get a jealous vibe from Anne. (Anne may have been another marriage contender had she not met me at totally the wrong time just after I split up with Eleanor and so although we had a very good relationship the open one we agreed on seem to work best).

Whether it was the wrong or the right thing to do I pitted both girls against each other when doing tracks for what would become the 'Heavy Breathing Decade' album. I had done this with Jo and Louise before and it had worked well to get the best out of the singers. For me, it was more a case of seeing whose voice would suit which track best. Anne did a good job and despite what she thought herself it brought the best out of her in many ways. So in the end Anne ended up on one-third of the tracks and Misty doing nearly two-thirds of what would be our next B.O.P album. The album also included *Is It Sex You Seek* (one track Jo had recorded during the Twilight Zone sessions but not put on the album as I was considering it as a single. This was a song you have read about with Arabic music).

(Below: rare mostly unused & unseen photos from my first photo session as Misty)

CHAPTER TWENTY

SONGWRITING

When it comes to songwriting I am not that prolific. Maybe it's because I believe more in quality than quantity. I have probably written about 100 songs in 30 years, which works out less than 3-4 songs a year. But I don't sit down and say I must write 4 songs per year either. I have gone many years without writing one song. Then in one year, I might write 10. I often get songwriters sending me tapes saying they have written over 100 songs per month. Then you listen to their songs and each one is wafer-thin. They think they will impress me by saying they write so many songs. But 100 crap songs are 100 crap songs. They would have been better off spending time making 5 songs brilliant and they wonder why they don't get anywhere. Another common error in the music business is to put out a song just because you wrote it regardless of whether it is any good or not. This is what leads to many one-hit wonders. They say everybody has one great novel in them. I think most songwriters or bands have one great song in them and the rest are ordinary.
There are probably 1,000 great songwriters on the planet over the last 100 years who have written classic song after classic song, maybe less. But there have been hundreds of thousands of acts and songwriters who have contributed one great song and no more and many who have not even come up with one great song.
As a record company M.D and music publisher I get sent at least 500 tapes or CD's a year. Sadly today people send some online links (But I never listen to online stuff but do listen to physical copies of things) Out of those 500 I usually find one person who can write more than one really good song. Then there are about 10 who can write one really good song and the rest, well the less said the better. So to me, the smart thing to do is when you are putting out an album you should make it the strongest album possible. How many albums have you bought in your life after hearing a single only to find the rest of the album a real let down and waste of money, too many I bet? So, my policy with B.O.P was to have each track good enough to be a hit single. With Eleanor Rigby it is considered I wrote 4 classic songs *Over and Over, 1995, Think for Yourself and Love on the Phone*, plus 3 reasonably good songs with good lyrics in *Getting Through The Day, More Than the Truth and Censorship. Mod Girls* had an interesting arrangement and very good lyrics from a Mod perspective but the music was very much second hand Motown. Since feedback from fans and reviewers alike were positive I can say that I was an above-average songwriter who had written more than one great song. But had I written a classic? On the Mod scene, some would say I wrote at least 3. In the wider scheme of things perhaps *1995* which I redid with B.O.P could be considered a classic since it was called single of the decade by one mag and made the record of the year by many colleges. Gary Crowley, no stranger to playing classic records rated it highly as well. *Think For Yourself* would also go on to be a classic of some kind as well. I also went on to write some equally as good if not even better songs later on for my latest band 'Psykick Holiday'.

With material on Box Office Poison's Twilight Zone album, I think I came of age as a songwriter. Although I redid a few of the stronger Eleanor Rigby tracks like *1995 and Love on the Phone*, probably the pain of divorce was responsible for some other great songs, *Cry Out the Pain* being a great example. This is often the case with songwriters. It is in their darkest hours they can come up with their best work. Being happy with your perfect life usually results in banal love songs. I think the reason songs and any form of artistic work are so good is because art is part passion and part emotion. Forget the teachers or reviewers who often judge things on technical merit at the end of the day, great art hits your emotions and makes you feel something, that's what counts.

If you look at a painting and it moves or affects you in some way that's great art, not someone who drew a line the correct way or used a slightly different colour to someone else. The same applies to music. These days there are scores of songwriters who are churning out by numbers pap songs that are recorded by manufactured acts and bought by 7-year-olds. They are played on the radio as background wallpaper music so as not to offend the lowest common denominator and within a few months, these records are quickly forgotten about. I'm not looking to blow my own trumpet because at the end of the day if you get my music you will be the judge and jury of it and I'll be happy to hear your feedback via my publisher. But I know many people who have most of my releases and play them still. Most songs also still sell or get played daily or at least weekly and people putting their hand in their pocket, parting with hard-earned wages is the only review you need. I have even had people writing to me saying they'd rather go without a meal to buy my record instead if they only had limited funds. I also noted early on how my songs affected people since a few people said they joined C N.D (CND) after hearing *1995*. Although, I wasn't preaching in this song I just painted a picture with words and sounds to portray what it could be like if nuclear weapons got out of hand. Likewise, I'd get people writing in saying I had a bereavement or and illness and it was only your songs that got me through it. You then realise two things. Sometimes being a songwriter can be a heavy responsibility and 2, just how powerful songs can be to change things or get a message across. So, all my songs have many depths to them. On the surface some may seem like catchy sing-along tracks, others more moody and evocative. But scratch the surface and somewhere in the song, there is a serious message that someone could learn from or relate to. Also, it has been noted that the truly great songwriters put their heart on their sleeves and bare their soul to the world, which is not an easy thing to do. My song *Cry Out The Pain* most certainly does this lyrically but what makes this an extra special song is the music and arrangement also conjures up that pain.

CRY OUT THE PAIN

A wedding ring in a bottom draw, two cold hearts that beat no more

Passion reels at the thought of pain, it's back in town again

You shook my confidence and made me feel lo., Life has no meaning with nowhere to go

A breathless body lies on the floor. One poor soul who couldn't take anymore

I wish I could cry out the pain. Because I never want to feel it again

I wish I could cry out the pain, No, I never want to see you again

I'll eat my heart out if there's a shadow of doubt and sell my soul to the devils tout

To put my heart on the line and stop this, this decline

I wish I could cry out the pain because I never want to feel it again

I wish I could cry out the pain. No, I never want to see you again

Crying Crying, Crying Out the Pain... The Pain..... Crying

It has often been said that even listening to the instrumental versions without the lyrics can conjure up the feel or vibe of the songs subject matter, which is no mean feat. But this is part of what 'Pop Noir' is all about. It's like a three-minute Film-Noir epic in song form. The most common one that affects people is *Backstreet Boulevard*. People say they feel like they have been in a doorway or experienced what it's like to be homeless just by listening to that song. I know it can't possibly let you experience homelessness in reality but the way I did the music including using discords makes you shudder and the lyrics conjunction up the experience. Likewise the track *Alien,* one of my favourites (I wonder why) conjures up an Alien feel, it also puts across a stark message but is also tinged with optimism with the odd thought-provoking line. *Think For Yourself* was redone very differently from the Eleanor Rigby guitar version and was dominated by cello riffs, which afterwards influenced many pop songs. You get lots of classic guitar riffs but this features a classic cello riff. Lyrically this is one of my favourite songs and I would fine-tune the music, even more, when it later became a single. The lyrics are anthemic like, and the song is also Matrix-like, as I'm trying to get people to wake up and smell the coffee and take off their blinkers to life. It also combines the 'Prisoner' philosophy of I'm an individual, not just a number. This song also marked my foray into pro women's rights stance. People are often shocked to find out I wrote this and other songs because it seems to come from a female perspective. But bearing in mind I was writing for a female artist in Eleanor and then Misty and other B.O.P singers, for the song to come across well the singers had to believe in what they were singing. I remember quite a few of Eleanor's female fans saying I love that song *Think For Yourself,* It really says what I feel. When Eleanor informed them that I wrote it you should have seen the confused look on their faces. Girls especially related to the line 'Say no you people ruling your life. From when you're a daughter to when you're a wife', so, how is it I can write such lyrics? Well certainly I'm in touch with my female side, there is no doubt about that. But it's mainly because all my friends over the years have always been girls and I have hardly ever had any male friends since I left school. I'm sure there will be quite a few girls reading this that have experienced an overprotective father or a possessive boyfriend since my friends tell me this is the norm.

Likewise on the 'Heavy Breathing Decade' album the song *Come with Me* captures the essence of a female orgasm. One girl bought 15 copies of this album because she said that the track summed it up so perfectly and wanted all her friends to have a copy but more about this album in a while. I'll just finish off with some 'Twilight Zone' track info first. *Checkmate* was more of a thrown away track lyrically but musically, especially the 12" version is a musical orgasm and a track my cello teacher said could have been written by one of the great classical composers. I don't know if I'd go that far but musically it is an interesting track, with its thrusting cello riff, fingering arpeggio harpsichord and screaming sax and hypnotic percussion grooves.

When I'm asked if I have written any classic songs or if you ask any fans of my music this question one track comes up more than the rest, *Mysteries*. This is considered a bit of a masterpiece and one person even said it was our *Bohemian Rhapsody* and if we had been a famous band putting it out it would have been number one. Maybe this relates to it being 6 minutes long, having many different moods and textures to it. It also builds up from start to finish with a few surprises in it and just when you think the song can't go up another level it does. It also has another unusual feature which is every time you listen to the song you discover something new in it. You almost think that someone broke into your

home and replaced your copy of the song with a new version. That's because of the unique production and arrangement I did on it with that in mind. Also, the dance and French and Spanish versions have another different feel to them again. The arrangement is very intricate with over 16 different percussion tracks interwoven into each other. The choice of musical instruments and sounds used are unique on this record. It's highly doubtful that anybody else will have used the same combination of instruments on another record. Every instrument has an important part to play in the track. But the bits I'm most often asked about are the intro on the 12" version and outro on all versions. There is a sound at the start that people are not sure what it is. It's actually me sitting on a squeaky chair moving around on it about to play the cello intro that is in itself a bit unusual as I start playing one cello sound and another suddenly joins it halfway through. The koto also plays an introductory riff. The outro is unusual because it's a harpsichord playing a fast percussion riff. Basically, I used to experiment on a computer when trying out songwriting ideas and I'd play a percussion riff on say a high hat. Then switch my keyboard sound to harpsichord to see what it sounded like playing this riff. It sounded unusual so I used it. DJ's in particular seem to like this outro. Anyway, I could write pages more about the instruments used and so on. But it would become boring so I would just say listen to the track you won't be disappointed.
I've already covered *Magic* elsewhere but lyrically it is considered a classic and I won a 'International Poem of the Year' award for it long after it came out as a song. It's also one of my favourite lyrics.

Love on the Phone was an E.R song that many DJ's said was the catchiest song on her album 'Censorship'. I have added new twists to this version by adding a String Quartet middle eight and 50's Andrews Sisters type backing vocals. Overall it has more of a classical music feel to it.

Sad World was the instrumental track that was going to be used for the BBC's Olympics theme. As previously mentioned it has many moods and textures to it and many world instruments are used in it such as Pan Pipes, Chinese Xylophone, Red Indian drums, Spanish Castanets. The key phrase lyrically in this song is 'Does anyone learn from the things that they do?' Too many people in life are too quick to blame others for their own shortcomings or mistakes, and as long as they do that and do not take responsibility for their own actions they will not move forward in life.
Probably the weakest song on the album is *16 year old***.** Although as a pop song it has 2 choruses that are both very catchy and reflects the difficulty of being 16 and all that entails, musically I couldn't quite get the sounds I wanted on this track especially Spanish style trumpets, which I couldn't afford to hire. It also had a Wham/Motown type beat that has been done better. As I wrote it for Eleanor it would have been more Motown and possibly much better musically & vocally. But it's still a very good song.
We're all insane is a Bowie-esque affair, reminiscent in part of *Sound and Vision.* It has clever lyrics and is an anti-love song. It has an unusual arrangement but is still quite catchy. It was inspired once again by Eleanor and the incident where she tore up my Valentines card; only in this song she throws flowers down a wishing well. (Artistic license)The final track on ' Beyond the Twilight Zone', *We Are the Future* gives a few clues to time travel whilst sign-posting a few warnings. It's another unusual but catchy song that also features a few discords with overtones of the classic single *In the Year 25-25.*

For every very good song, I write there are probably two I discard as rubbish.

The point I started off making a while ago was about the quality of songs and not putting out songs just because you wrote it. My problem used to be the opposite. Even though I'd written good songs and had the power to choose them as singles I tended to make other peoples songs the A-side and started off putting mine on the B-sides when in fact the reaction was it should have been an A-side. I then had the confidence to see that I was writing really good songs. My Eleanor repertoire was written over 5 years. Taking a long while to get somewhere in the music business can be soul-destroying but it does have an upside, it can give you time to build up a catalogue of good work. You often find it is acts that have been around for quite a while before getting a record deal who put out classic debut albums. My Twilight Zone songs had been built up over 7 years, so I knew I had the strongest possible material by then. Ego can be the major downfall of many. My policy is I only want the strongest songs on my album because that's good news for people buying the album but also it can be good news for your longevity because the better your album is the more chances you'll get to make more albums, whereas to rush out a duff album means probably no more albums will come out. Sometimes it pays to play the long game. It will be up to others to judge whether 'Beyond the Twilight Zone' is a great album or not. In hindsight, I would say it's a good album but not a great album. It does have many songs that are highly rated by others and I still think the less well-known songs will eventually find new legs and if done right could also become highly rated. So in that sense, there are no duff songs on the album but I would go up a level in the future with Psykick Holiday in my opinion.

But if you are not great at writing lots of very good songs in one go what do you do? Well, smart people like David Bowie and Madonna knew just what to do. Bowie may have started off writing great songs on his own but by the Diamond Dogs album, he was co-writing quite a few tracks. It also helps to do a great cover version of a well-known song (if you can better it) or discover another song written by someone else that hasn't fulfilled its potential. Bowie has done all this when he found himself baron of a great collection of songs. It only really failed him once on the 'Tonight' album but this too had 2 great singles on it *Loving the Alien*' and *Blue Jean*. Incidentally, these were the only two written solely by him on that album. The problem with that album was he was under pressure to follow up the hugely successful 'Lets Dance' album. But 2 singles on Let's Dance were co-written, *China Girl* with Iggy Pop and *Cat People* with Giorgio Moroder and despite the *Lets Dance* track being solely credited to Bowie, producer Nile Rodgers input to the track was massive as anyone who knows his Chic production will know. Nile Rodgers cropped up again on what would be Madonna's turning point *Like A Virgin* and produced that album. But the importance of record producers is another story and maybe I'll tell it in this book and maybe I'll tell it in another book. Madonna co-writes nearly all of her songs and is good at picking the right songwriters and producers to work with. To write as many hit songs as she had on her own would have been impossible since she was no John Lennon.

Although, I didn't set out to copy Bowie or Madonna's master plan I did realise that I was not prolific enough to write albums full of strong material year in year out. I knew that co-writing was one way forward and covering other people songs was another to create the strongest possible album each time. That's why most album releases I've been involved with are considered classic albums. Eleanor's Censorship is a classic Mod or Brit-Pop album that still stands up today. It has even had a documentary made about it and cited by many big music stars like Shirley Manson of Garbage who says it's one of her favourite albums ever and a big influence.

Ministry of Ska's 'Rarin To Go' album, although not in Bob Marley's league is a classic in its own way. Beyond the Twilight Zone is very relevant as it was the first 'Pop Noir' style music album and certain tracks went on to influence people like Goldfrapp and others.

All the Cult Themes albums are also considered classics in their own right despite these not being original material. But they are an exercise in how it is possible to better original tracks rather than just do lazy karaoke covers. I'll cover the Heavy Breathing Decade album in more depth in another chapter but what I will say is, that particular album was a classic combination of all of what I have just mentioned. Strategic co-writes, cover versions of unknown classics and at least 3 of the strongest songs I have ever written on my own.

WE'RE ALL INSANE

If love is the answer, the question is a dancer

That tangos with your mind and grabs you from behind

We're all insane.........we're all insane

You scare me with your problems; destroy me with your lies

You scar me with your cheating; You're the lover I despise

You're all insane........you're all insane We're all insane.........we're all insane

Win me today, lose me tomorrow. You're the creator of your own sorrow

We're all insane.........We're all insane So insane......................so insane

You threw my flowers down the wishing well. You gave me love but you gave me hell

You threw my flowers down the wishing well

CHAPTER TWENTY-ONE

CULT THEMES FROM THE SEVENTIES VOLUME ONE

With Mouse's track recorded and Misty being a new member of B.O.P it made sense to record B.O.P's and a solo Misty's track for 'Cult Themes from the 70's Vol.1'. First. I had decided the 2 B.O.P tracks would be *The Persuaders* (from my favourite composers John Barry) and *The Chase* from Midnight Express by Giorgio Moroder. Around this time I had acquired a small 4 track recording device and bearing in mind what I had gotten away with on 'Themes from the 60's Vol.1'. I thought I'd be cheeky and record some of the tracks for this album on it as well as in a proper studio and see if people noticed the difference when released. With *The Persuaders* being an instrumental we'd did it on my home set up. Although I'd invented 'Pop Noir' I still felt I hadn't quite perfected it and *The Persuaders* was the track where I thought I finally nailed it. I don't know if it was Misty's presence or that I just got more confident in my punk cello playing but it all came together on this track although not at first. I knew Misty could play keyboards so got her to do them on this track whilst I did percussion and strings. We finished it quickly but it sounded exactly like the original. We sat there looking at each other and said what's innovative or 'Pop Noir' about that, next to nothing. So we scrapped the track and started again with Ron involved this time. The new version of the track starts with him doing some raw sax and this is close to his best work. The ultimate 'Pop Noir' sax is what I call a seedy improvised Jazz sounding sax wafting out of a Jazz clubs at 4 am in the morning and echoing along the street. Although it's an instrumental track I wanted Misty to do a haunting backing vocal sound on it and suggested a few things. This type of atmospheric and haunting backing vocal is very much a typical 'Pop Noir' vocal. Misty as usual exceeded all expectations as she breezed through some improvised vocals. The other key element was my punk cello improvisation that adds eerie sounds, raw sounds and Dolphin, Wolf and Whales sounds with lots of slides and trills put through an echo unit'. Then the producer in me takes over to add menace and atmosphere to the proceedings starting with either low timpani rolls or low tom drum beats. Then comes the harpsichord riff. The first part of the track is a slight variation on the original riff and it builds up a nice stairway to the main part of the song where another atmospheric sound comes in. It's a sixties organ sound with different effects on it to give it both a dreamlike and nightmare type quality. (The band 'The Psychedelic Furs' probably uses the nearest thing I have heard to it before). Another key element of 'Pop Noir' and me as a producer is the way I use reverb and echo in recordings. Joe Meek was the first to use these to good effect in the 50s & 60s, often gaining criticism from companies he worked for and that's one reason he launched his own Independent record label in 1960. So he made his critics including other studios eat their words as *Telstar* and in particular, *Johnny Remember Me* (swamped in echo) both hit number 1 and both sold over one million copies. Joe also invented his own echo units. Others were quick to latch on to this but Joe's stuff was always more distinctive. By the time I came along the engineer type producers were in full force and they used echo according to some manual that said it had to be done a certain way. Although this can enhance a track it doesn't add a whole new dimension to a track. So I decided to experiment with random echo according to nobody's rules and this made the tracks a lot more interesting by putting out of time echoes and random ones. It was like having an extra instrument in the track playing something that was impossible to play & grabbed people's attention. I used in time echoes reverb & other effects as well

John Barry told me when I met him that he loved all the new bits of music and the atmosphere of this *Persuaders* version, then added with tongue in cheek, I hope you are not looking to blag royalties for it. I wasn't of course. I was more interested in being an innovative record producer. The other track, *The Chase* was perfect for us to do with an atmospheric and hypnotic groove; we could improvise other instruments in and out of the track at random making it very original. Whilst at this recording session Misty told me about a band she'd seen called 'The Incredibly Strange Film Band'. They actually specialised in film themes so ideal to go on the album. She gave me a flyer of their next gig, which I attended at The Weavers in London. I met up with Pat McGarvey, the leader of the band afterwards. I asked him what his plan was for the band. He didn't know who I was and I kid you not, he said his ultimate ambition was to be on a Future Legend Records 'Cult Themes' album. He couldn't believe it when I told him who I was and that he could now fulfil his dream. It also turned out he was inspired to put his band together because of me starting the Cult Themes trend. The I.S.F.B.s had attended a themes night at Madam Jo Jo's with the DJ's the Karminsky Brothers, who had started playing our albums. One theme they did in their set and one of the priority ones on my list of themes to do was *Get Carter.* It had always been a great theme and was as cult as they come. However for some strange reason, the original was hard to get hold of and not on release. So, I quickly went into the studio to do *Get Carter* and it came out as cool as can be and I worked well with all the band and they tried out several things I asked them to do. I also do a thing, probably not that original but not commonly done, which is to have all the instruments come in one at a time and leave the track the same way. It starts with atmospheric bongos followed by a moody stand-up bass. It was easily as good as the original version and many people would buy this album to get this track with the original not being available. I also had a surprise ending. When I saw I.S.F.B. at their gig they also did a very good version of *Shaft*, only Pat's vocal was never going to compete with Isaac Hayes. So, I came up with an idea to turn things on their head and get a female to do the vocal. That's the only way to compete with the original. There was only one choice of course. Enter one Misty Woods. Her sexy vocal suited it down to the ground and with the bands instrumental being as good as the original it was more than well received. I remember a cutting room engineer seeing the track-listing of the album as we were about to master it and saying *Shaft,* nobody can better the original, and anyone who has tried has massacred the track. Then he heard it and said I can't believe it, this is equal to the original and even dare I say a little better because of the new slant. I also changed the famous hi-hat rhythm to a bongo and added strategic echoes but it's Misty's vocal that wins the day although I'm not keen on my little vocal bit, which Misty insisted on me doing. I sometimes tended to do an Alfred Hitchcock. He used to do a bit-part in all the films he directed and I play something somewhere in many tracks I produce. Apart from the odd word in this track I played a percussion rhythm on a clay vase but halfway through I hit it too hard and smashed it. But left it on the recording. Misty was also going through her Mod phase due to me reawakened her interest in Eleanor Rigby, so she wanted to do a Mod track and chose The Who's track *5-15* from the classic Mod film 'Quadrophenia'. This needed a big band sound and so we roped in the ten-piece I.S.F.B. to do the backing since they were coming to record anyway. Misty had a few reasons for recording this track apart from the Mod angle. She said she didn't want to be known just for sexy type vocals and wanted to belt out a number and wanted to do it in an Eleanor style as a tribute..

CHAPTER TWENTY-ONE

THE DR MARTENS AFFAIR

There are many times in the Box Office Poison story where we nearly grabbed the gold medal and here was yet another incident. I got a phone call from a guy called Simon Mills, who was a director at the internationally famous boot company Dr Martens. He asked if I could come and see him about a music project. Since Dr Martens were known to sponsor gigs and had other music tie-ins, I thought it would be worth my while.

We met at Dr Martens head store in Covent Garden London. Coffee was served in the boardroom and he began to explain why I was there. Dr Martens is looking to do a tie-in with the re-release of the Mod film 'Quadrophenia'. They had drawn up 3 shortlists. One, of the top record producers in the UK, another for experts in the field of Mod music and one, for a compilation expert. I was on all 3 lists and in most cases at the top. So, he came to the conclusion I was the only person for the job. What D.M wanted to do was borrow my Cult Themes idea and do something similar on a Quadrophenia tie-in album. They liked the idea of helping new talent via new versions of well-known songs, so asked me to discover 12 new acts and produced 12 new versions of classic Mod songs associated with the film 'Quadrophenia'. He mentioned that Dr Martens had sponsored gigs before and the logical next step was to get their own record label and could I also help them set that up as well and this album would be its first release. He asked how much I wanted to do the project and I said £20,000 was the going rate for such a project. I confirmed I'd do the album project but would still have to think about the extra-label work, as I was busy running my label. He said, although they would like someone like me to run the label he understood my position and just setting the label up and starting it for someone else to run would be sufficient. He concluded by saying he'd have to get the finance sanctioned and we should meet again the following week.

Negotiations followed the following week but he was adamant that D.M would only pay £10,000 for me to do the album but they would as a bonus distribute all my records releases in their shops and through their mail-order company. This sounded like a good opportunity but I felt they were cheap skating me on the money front still. So I asked for another £5,000 to which he said no, so I mentioned it was also standard practice for the producer to also get a 4% royalty on sales (it was actually 2-3 % but I was expecting them to knock me down) I also added that my band Box Office Poison would have to be on the album. He wouldn't agree any more money but would grant the last 2 conditions, so we agreed a deal. He said he had to get the final green light from one of the owners who were the Griggs Brothers and would call me the following week. Two weeks went by and I heard nothing so I phoned back to find that Simon had gone on holiday and nobody knew anything about the deal. Finally, he contacted me when he returned from holiday and said things would move ahead once I signed a contract with them as long as I would help set up the label and sorting out the manufacture of this debut album. Although I felt they were taking liberties because of all the extra work because of the future possibilities I took a long-term view and said O.K. Simon then dropped another little bombshell. There was now a deadline. The album launch was set for late January 97 to tie in with the re-release of Quadrophenia. Effectively, I had to find 12 acts, arrange and produce all the tracks, do the artwork and sleeve, get the album mastered and manufactured and clear all the MCPS copyrights as well in just 3 months. Finally, I was told I had to assist with the legal contracts as well since D.M were not familiar with music business contracts. I said this was far too much to do in 3 months and I also had to finish off the Cult Themes album I was doing and had already booked all the bands and studios for that project. Simon just said, you must be used to people wanting things yesterday in the music business. I said it may be possible to do it if I worked 7 days a week 20 hours a day but that was allowing for no mistakes or errors so the sensible thing would be to have a plan-B. He asked what plan-B was. I said the most time-consuming part of the project would be finding the right bands and negotiating deals with them. It often took me at least 6 months to do this on a Cult Themes album. So, what I would do is give it no longer than a month to find the acts and sign them up. If there was a shortfall we should just license some classic Mod tracks that didn't get enough exposure upon their first release and give them a second wind. He agreed to this deal and came up with a helpful suggestion. He said Dr Martens had supported a band called 'Maroon Town' in the past and they should be one of the 12 acts, he said we have already agreed to B.O.P being on the album so that makes only 10 acts to find. Since I had already just recorded a new version of *5-15* (very timely) from Quadrophenia with Misty anyway for my Cult Themes album it made sense to put this on the album to save time and it was also a key track anyway. But because I owned the copyright D.M would have to license it from my company. (My time at Sony hadn't been wasted because I had learned that if you don't get your money from one avenue you could get it from another) He agreed after hearing the track and so the clock was ticking to find 9 acts.

The first band was signed up very quickly due to the Cult Themes album. I knew a Mod music journalist called Mark Sergeant who also managed bands and he put forward 3 or 4 acts to appear on the Cult Themes album. I liked 3 of them and agreed on a deal. The most suitable act for the Quadrophenia tie-in were Lynus, an all-girl band who had just left school and were around 16 and 17 years old. They could only just about play their instruments but had a lot of enthusiasm and cheek and I got on with them extremely well. Sadly, shortly before recording their drummer left and a late replacement, a 17-year-old schoolboy was drafted in. His drum kit sounded like a biscuit tin and his playing was only just competent. So in some ways, this session had a bit of a Punk ethos and was a challenge. But I do love a challenge. The girls had chosen to do a Bond theme *Diamonds are Forever* for the Cult Themes. Well, there was no way to compete with the big ballad Shirley Bassey version so I opted for a low-fi version that really suited the bands' style and talents. The studio engineer Jez was a good keyboard player so we drafted him in to play the more difficult parts of the track. I worked out a very interesting arrangement with strong catchy backing vocals and a very Bond sounding bass riffs and the swirling arpeggio harpsichord main riff glued the song together. Lead singer Grace had a distinctive voice so the track stood out as different. Everyone involved was very pleased with the result and so I sprung the surprise news on the band that they could also appear on the Dr Martens album. The band were so excited they nearly wet their knickers and I was nearly drowned in teenage perfumed kisses.

It's a good job I like a challenge because the Quadrophenia album would definitely be that.

With the Cult Themes, I found it fairly easy to better many original themes. The biggest challenges were the Bond ones as these were so familiar to people and mostly all classics in their own right. The tracks for the Quadrophenia tribute album eventually christened 'Generation to Generation' were more daunting because they were tracks that were all-time classics and been played to death. *My Generation (Who), You Really Got Me (The Kinks), Louie Louie (The Kingsman), Green Onions (Booker T & the M.G's), Whatcha Gonna do about it (The Small Faces) etc.* Normally, I would steer well clear of covering such tracks.

Lynus chose to do *My Generation.* When you are doing covers there are 2 tricks you can use to distance yourself from the original and give yourself a chance. One is to get the opposite sex of the original to sing it and 2, do a version that is an opposite style to the original. I used the latter to good effect when doing Georgy Girl and that's why a lot of people rate this version better than the original. So, with *My Generation,* it was a case of deadpan female vocals as opposed to Daltry's angry young man rebel vocals. So they did a more pedestrian laid back Lo-fi track. It had a garage band feel with a great organ sound on it and the intro and outro are particularly creative. It worked so well it became the albums opening track. Next up was a track that has had more covers than most songs in existence, *Louie Louie.* I always knew the 2 most difficult tracks to do on this album would be *Louie Louie* and *You Really Got Me.* The A-team were needed and that meant B.O.P and the already established Maroon Town. I thought Louie Louie would suit B.O.P best but it had to be something extra special and it was. I worked out a very hypnotic arrangement with rolling pianos and a swirling organ. The drums unusually played the part of the rhythm of the melody. I conjured up a steamy scene on a hot New Orleans night by putting rain effects on the track to give it a steamy feel and my cello emulating a passing steamboat which was complimented by Misty's extremely sexy vocal. Even the engineer said he nearly came in his pants listening to her singing it; she even put a cherry on top by changing one word in the song. Instead of 'I smell the roses in his hair' she sang 'I smell the sex in his hair'. Ron too had one of his finest hours on this track doing sax. Although Mysteries remains his finest hour on an improvised level the solo sax spot in Louie is brilliant. Ron also played on Green Onions. Anne did a very good version of *Louie* as well since she was co-vocalist with B.O.P but as soon as Misty did her version she shrugged her shoulders and said 'I can't compete with that it just suits the track down to the ground'. Anne was a good vocalist but as she herself said, Misty was in a different league sometimes because she oozed star quality and had a very distinctive voice and was great at improvisation, which is what B.O P were all about.

B.O.P's version of *Louie Louie* was so hot that the following year a radio show on XFM in London did a whole hour-long show playing all the different cover versions of the song and asking their audience to vote on which was the best version. Our version won with the original in second place followed by The Kinks and Motorhead.

Despite not ending up on lead vocals for *Louie,* Anne got some compensation and kudos by having her finest hour on this album. I got her to do *Whatcha Gonna Do About I.*, It knocked everybody's socks off. Although she may not agree I think the rivalry between her and Misty in the singing stakes really paid off here because the girl I had been going out with for so long would never have been capable of such a vocal 6 months before. She sang 2 different counter-melody lines in 2 different singing styles, neither, of which I had heard before. It even shocked me. Was this really the girl who only learned to sing less than 2 years ago? One vocal was strong but breathy whilst the other is whispery but very raucous which is a very difficult thing to do for any singer. The backing track is lively enough but it is the vocals that make this track a winner. (Years later her version of Louie ended up on 'Mirror Image', her solo album, also proving popular)

So there I was with a third of the album sorted out but the rest proved to be a tricky operation. I had approached another Mod label, 'Detour' and asked around about new talent and gone to a few gigs as well. But what happened via Detour was a typical example of what I was up against. It's funny how nobodies suddenly think they are big somebody's when they get a sniff of a deal. It goes right to their heads.

Three bands were put forward by Detour. The first band were just plain dumb and couldn't see the bigger picture. Dr Martens had already told me a minimum of 10,000 copies was going to be pressed up of this release. (A big opportunity for any artist). This first band said we only do original stuff we don't do covers can't we put an original track on the album. (Which part of Quadrophenia cover version tribute album did they not understand?). The second band who lived up in Scotland wanted a limo to bring them to London for the recording session and to be put up in first-class hotels before they'd even consider signing a contract and all they'd previously done was have one Indie single release that had sold a few hundred copies. The third band insisted they wanted to produce themselves. Since I was hired as the producer of the album this was a non-starter and when I told them this they dropped out. Another half dozen acts were approached and eliminated for one reason or another. But I was running out of time. I usually took 6 months to sift through hundreds of tapes and CD's and go to scores of gigs before deciding on who would be on a Cult Themes album and to condense this into a few weeks was nigh impossible.

Since I was about to record a Ministry of Ska track for the Cult Themes album I thought it made sense to do an M.O.S track for Dr Martens as well. Then with Maroon Town booked in to do' *You Really Got Me*' that would be the album half-done. It looked like the plan-B, of half new versions and half licensed Mod classic would be the best that could be done in the time allocated.

I then met up with Simon at D.M headquarters to give him an update and say plan-B had to now go ahead. He listened to the tracks recorded so far and was very excited by them and said the jewel in the crown by far was *Louie Louie* by Box Office Poison. He commented that he had just let me put B.O.P on the album as part of the deal without knowing what we sounded like. Now he wanted to hear much more of the band as he thought that we were a bit special. So, I gave him a tape of some of our tracks. Within a few days, he called me saying B.O.P had to be the first signing to the new D.M. label. We would get a decent advance and a big promotional budget. It could be up to half a million. This sounded like good news, to say the least. He seemed genuine about it but he was also geeing me up about putting the new label together. Simon also agreed that there wasn't enough time to find any more new acts and I should now concentrate on licensing some classic Mod tracks as agreed to complete the album and sort out the sleeve. This proved a lot more problematic than expected. I had a list of about 20 tracks I wanted to licence, of which I only needed 6. Polydor owned quite a few. They had The Jam, The Chords and The Purple Hearts. I thought they might be reluctant to license a Jam track but the other 2 bands only had a few minor hits, so should be easy to obtain. It seemed Polydor were thinking about doing their own Mod compilation so they wouldn't let any tracks go elsewhere and if they did, wanted a fortune. Next up I wanted a Secret Affair track but BMG wanted an astronomical fee to license it. This was ridiculous since the songs hadn't seen the light of day for over 15 years and apart from the Mod scene, few people would care about such tracks.

D.M had given me a budget of £500 license money per track. I'd also got various advances for the newer acts. What made things extra good for the acts were the contracts. They couldn't believe how artist-friendly they were. Usually, the opposite is the case. But D.M's contract department didn't have a clue about music contracts so they asked me to write them, which I did, favouring the artist. D.M then just checked a few bog standard legal things and that was the contract and it got signed off. So I was very popular with the artists.

Finally, I found a company who were not too obstructive or unrealistic. Stiff Records had 2 tracks I wanted. One, *Free Yourself*, which was a top 10 hit for The Untouchables and *Here is My Number,* a very minor Indie hit for Eleanor's former rivals Makin Time. They agreed on a deal for both tracks.

Despite the rivalry, Makin Time and Eleanor were always quite friendly and supportive of each other. They were very happy with this deal as well. After The Jam, the 2 most successful acts of the initial Mod period were Secret Affair (that I'd drawn a blank on) and The Lambretta's. whose record company were also unrealistic. But I'd met the lead singer of The Lambretta's, Jez Bird' on the odd occasion and he didn't live that far from me so I gave him a call and met up. I told him about the reluctance of Rocket/Phonogram to let his tracks go on the compilation.

Luckily there has always been a big loophole in the music industry regarding music copyrights. The label you're signed to usually pays for the recordings. So they own that particular recording. But if you are no longer signed to that record label and choose to record a new version of the track yourself, you own this new version and not the original record company and therefore you can put out a very close copy of the original without any trouble. Jez thought this the best way forward. He didn't want to redo *Poison Ivy,* his biggest hit and preferred to do *Da-a-ance,* another quite big hit but not as well remembered as the first hit. This made good business sense for him as he wrote the song and would get extra songwriting royalties via the D.M. album. I was happy to oblige. Jez had his own recording studio between Brighton & Lewis, so I went down to give him a helping hand. It was at this point I remembered my new idea to feature a previous hit band on a Cult Theme album, so asked Jez if he fancied it. He quite fancied doing the theme from *Starsky and Hutch*. So I became an honorary member of The Lambrettas for the day (as the band had recently split up but Jez retained the name as he was the main man). So just the 2 of us knocked out the theme as well as the new version of *Da.a.ance*. I ended up playing percussion and brass stabs on the track as well as producing both. It is a blinding version of *Starsky & Hutch* and easily as good as the original and even Huggy Bear (Antonio Fargas) loved it when I played it to him at London's 'Starsky and Hutch club' where the club owner Mike Tanousis was also a big Cult Themes fan and a particular fan of my production. So much so he asked me to produce an album for 'Huggy Bear' (Antonio Fargas) but that's another story.

With The Lambretta's tracks boxed off, I contacted another old Mod mate of mine Tony Meynell of Squire who had been one of my favourite Mod acts. They'd had a few minor hits, the biggest one being *Walking Down The Kings Road.* They had however been on the all-important 'Mods Mayday' album, which was amongst many sparks that ignited the

Mod revival of 79. Tony had been very supportive and a fan of Eleanor's when we came onto the Mod scene and always used to say that *I Want To Sleep With You* was one of the all-time Mod classic records that every Mod had to have in their collection. Luckily Tony was also shrewder than many other Mod acts and had always retained his copyrights so when I asked him for a track it wasn't a problem. But he did say it would make a nice change if it wasn't' *Walking Down The Kings Road*. So he asked me to pick my personal favourite out of his vast repertoire. I always loved his song *Does Stephanie Know*, (it also tied in with Quadrophenia's main female character), so I chose that one. With my deadline, fast closing in I was only 2 tracks short and the answer to complete the album was right in front of me and a good financial bonus to boot. I owned some Mod classics in the form of Eleanor Rigby's singles and The Reaction single *Make Up Your Mind*. So with these 2 acts included the album was finished in the nick of time.

Like Tony, I thought rather than include Eleanor's most famous track, which would be *I Want To Sleep With You,* I would include another track, (also considered a Mod classic) that hadn't got as much exposure, *Over and Over.* Often likened to a lost Kinks classic although an original written by me.

With the recording and licensing part over I thought I could relax but major problems were just around the corner. Next, I had to do the mastering. This is where you fine-tune all the tracks to make them the same levels and do any last-minute edits and put it through a system that makes it possible to make CDs from. I normally had a few places I liked to go where I'd get good results but at such short notice they were all booked up and I had to make do with a place in Camden that I'd never used before. During the process, I kept questioning the sound of the speakers saying the tracks didn't sound right. The guy was adamant they were industry standard. But he kept disappearing and finally took off for an hour leaving us in the lurch. Misty had come with me and she agreed with me about the sound. She also caught the engineering coming out of the toilet smoking dope, which he put out before he came back into the control room. This helped explain why he was very un-together. For a short while I felt I must be having some sort of breakdown because of overworking and hearing things wrongly but what made me realise I was right was the licensed tracks. The engineer said the studios I'd recorded in must have created the sound problem and their speakers were not as good as his. But this didn't explain why the licensed hit such as *Free Yourself* also didn't sound as good as when it was released as a single. This is when the engineer stormed out. Finally, a compromise was reached. I wasn't happy for it to go to the manufacturing stage. But the engineer knew Dr Martens were paying the bill and said they should have the final say and if they were not happy I could redo the mastering elsewhere. I don't know if it was time pressures or inexperience but Simon at D.M gave the O.K to this mastering and manufacture was due to go ahead. I'm still not 100% happy with that release and a few reviewers picked up on the same thing as I did but many other people don't have a problem with it and liked the release a lot. Maroon Town were especially happy with the production I did for them. Kinks fans also liked the interesting modern Ska production and arrangement I had done on *You Really Got Me.*

Before the CD could be manufactured the MCPS had to be paid to get clearance from the songwriters/publishers. This took a bit longer than expected and nails were being severely bitten all around. Since nothing could be done until at least a week into the New Year I decided to take a much needed holiday break.

Before I went there was a big boost that made me happy. Simon had asked me to write my own contract terms and he would see to it that B.O.P got a few hundred thousand pound advance and half a million-pound market spend for our first releases on the Dr Martens label. At last, I thought a decent push would be behind us. Misty too, was ecstatic, as was the rest of the band. So whilst away I drafted a contract for my return. However, when I returned, all was not rosy in the D.M garden. A most bizarre incident and one of those where the writing on the wall was getting blurry had happened. Anne had become very good at doing artwork and CD sleeves, so I gave her the D.M. sleeve to do. It should have been straightforward. But as she sent the proofs to D.M they started complaining about the bands' text. The reason? The bands had dared to mention other product they had out. I couldn't see anything wrong with this at all. As a record company doing Cult Themes, I was always happy to include information about bands other releases or gigs as giving exposure to the bands was a major part of them being on a Cult Themes album.

I got onto Simon and he said it wasn't him but the companies managing director who had come up with this demand. As we would soon learn, this particular guy had had his toes trodden on and he was looking to make trouble. I can't remember his name now but I think it was Frank. Anyway, Simon had done this project on the say-so of one of the owners of Dr Martens, the Griggs. This M.D character was between them and Simon, who was just a marketing director but had not consulted this M.D about this project and to add insult to injury he wasn't a music lover either. (Company Politics)

I wasn't very happy and ignored the request and instructed Anne to put everything back in the booklet. She was in an awkward position as Dr Martens were paying her to do the sleeve. So I thought I better let this M.D person know who he was dealing with and not some wet behind the ears dummy.

The launch party for the album was just over 2 weeks away and they were running out of time to get the albums manufactured. Although it was clear that this M.D would prefer the album not to come out for some reason, it would be a big embarrassment for Dr Martens if come the launch party there was no CD or it was cancelled. Lots of press and T.V had already been informed about this. So I knew they wouldn't cancel the release. Simon said he'd tried his best and wasn't happy with the situation either and the only way was for me to contact Frank and get him to agree to let the text back on the sleeve but he didn't hold out much hope since the guy was a bit of a bastard.

I tried contacting Frank and ended up speaking with his P.A and insisted the text be reinstated. She came back to me and said Dr Martens are paying for everything and they have discretion over what can and cannot go on the sleeve and I had no say in the matter even though I'd put the album together I was just another hired hand and should do what I was told. My reply was 'I think you'll find I'm more than just a hired hand. I am the person who can stop this CD from coming out altogether and leave Dr Martens with a massive egg on its face in front of the media'. She wanted to know how that could be possible. I pointed out that I happen to own the music publishing on 2 of the tracks on the album and the MCPS can't give permission for the album to be manufactured until all the publishers give their clearance. All the other publishers had given clearance but the MCPS had contacted me the day before about mine and I told them I would not give them clearance until I sorted out a problem with Dr Martens. I then added that I didn't care if the album came out now or not since I'd been paid already. I was just making a stand against this injustice they were perpetrating. I could almost hear the disbelief on the phone. They thought they had one over on me and I had turned the tables on them. She said she'd call me back.

Instead, it was Simon who called me saying 'What the hell did you say?' Frank is not at all happy. However, he will agree partially to your terms but he needs a compromise.

He said you could reinstate all the text with acts you personally have something to do with but acts you have nothing to do with the text must remain as it was, edited out. I told Simon to hold his nerve and it was all or nothing but Simon said he needed me to agree to this as a favour to him. So I said I would do as he asked but just told Anne to reinstate all the text as they didn't know who was connected with me and who was not and I would front it out with this Frank and there was nothing he could do once the album was released and I felt it was just him flexing his muscles as removing the text made no sense and he'd live with it. Then I went ahead and got the album manufactured. But the fun and games of this episode weren't finished there.

The launch came around at their flagship store in Covent Garden and it was the hot ticket in town with lots of celebrities and tons of media. I arrived early and met Simon to find a worried look on his face. He then informed me I was not allowed to say anything to the media about a Dr Martens record label. I pointed out that a press release went out months ago stating Dr Martens were launching a record label and 'Generation to Generation' would be the first of many releases and the label would sign lots of hot new talent. The feedback I got was the exciting part of the news was that D.M gets own label, not a one-off album release.

The world's media were out in force and would want answers. He said he was fed up with everything that had gone on and the treatment he'd received from the M.D and had resigned over it. Since he was no longer responsible for everything, he would appreciate it if I dealt with the media as the face of the project. He then added, obviously with no label that meant no deal for B.O.P. I wasn't happy of course but said I'd deal with media as a favour to him.

I met up with the rest of the band who were all very excited and Misty wore an Eleanor influenced white PVC dress and was loving every minute of all the attention she was getting. I was rolled out in front of all the cameras including MTV and mainstream T.V and yanked off to do lots of press interviews after that. The first question was always 'So why have Dr Martens decided to launch a record label?' I had to reply 'For top-secret reasons I can't talk about the label but can talk about this particular album release and the artist included on the release particularly Box Office Poison. I roped Misty in and we got lots of coverage for B.O.P. Dr Martens was suppose to give me all the press cuttings but I only ended up getting a few when half the staff at D.M seemed to be either sacked or decided to leave after this fiasco. Something strange was going on at Dr Marten and I was only getting half the story. Years later it was mooted they had a few financial problems. I can't say I was surprised because I discovered working for them over those few months without going into too many details (for confidential reasons) it often seemed that the right hand didn't know what the left hand was doing. It was a shock since they were such a big company.

The album 'Generation to Generation' went on to sell 10,000 copies in a few weeks but was then deleted. It got some good reviews and quite a lot of mainstream press, including The Independent who called me an Indie production God. This was a reference to all my work as opposed to just this release. (So that was a buzz). There was one final battle for me, however. I had to fight with Dr Martens one last time. Although I'd been paid for the project I was still due a 4% producer royalty on the 10,000 CD's and the new people in place at D. M's tried to get out of paying me. (No doubt instructed by my old adversary, M.D Frank). So I had to resort to blackmail one more time. I said I had kept quiet at the album launch about the behind the scenes fiasco as a favour to Simon but now he was gone I was quite happy to sell my story to the press about the shambolic way in which Dr Martens was run. I'd probably get more from the press for my story than what they owed me in royalties. Within 2 days I was paid in full.

Footnote: It never rains but it pours. Apart from doing the D.M album & the new Cult Themes album I also got approached to do many other big producing projects including a themes comp for Virgin.(This is Cult Fiction) I seemed to be forever turning down things that that year. (Still, it's good to be hot).

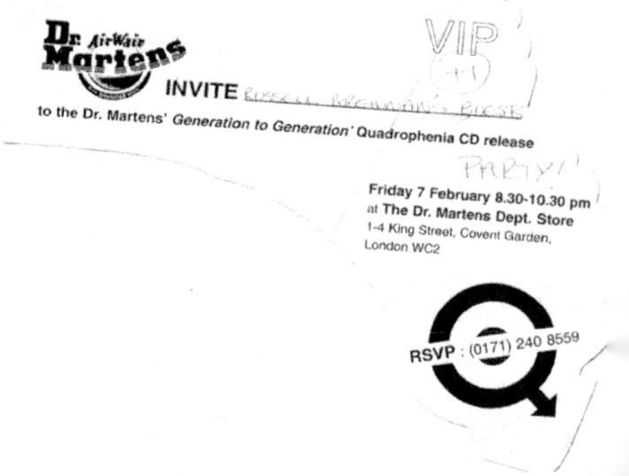

Above very rare press photos of the B.O.P line up at of the Dr Martens launch (Sadly a scan as we never got the actual photos) L-R Ron, Anne, Russ & Misty. Also album party launch invite and the album itself.

CHAPTER TWENTY-TWO

THE DEBUT

Yes sir, 96 was a pretty busy year. As if I didn't have enough to do with Dr Martens & a new Cult Themes album and other things mentioned. I had also made the error of agreeing to do Box Office Poison's first-ever live concert in front of an audience. Like everything else I do, I have unusual ideas about live concerts. Firstly, I was not interested in getting on the treadmill of playing the same old venues that all upcoming bands play. Since we effectively had a record deal we didn't need to put ourselves through that. I had always liked the idea of playing live but unreliable members at certain stages meant after a few rehearsals we never got to the gig stage. So apart from the live radio performance mentioned previously we still hadn't played a gig. I always had it in my mind to make a B.O.P gig more of an event or a happening rather than just another gig. Also, I like to get the right vibe when offered a gig. We had been offered quite a few and I'd always turned them down but after producing 'The Incredibly Strange Film Band' I went for a drink with their leader Pat and he told me that he sometimes put on gigs. He added he wanted to put on a Cult Themes Christmas special and since Box Office Poison had been the only act to appear on all the Cult Themes albums would we be the headline act. For once it felt right so I said yes but then forgot about it because of the intense period with all the albums I was producing. It was only when Pat contacted me in mid-November asking me about what I wanted on posters and flyers for the gig that I remembered it. I then informed the rest of the band who immediately panicked. We managed to have a meeting about it but I was booked in the recording studio every day until early December and couldn't do any rehearsals. Rather than get a full line-up together which would mean 9 or 10 people I decided the easiest way to do it was to run the basic tracks from a computer through my keyboard then do live cello, sax, percussion and vocals over the top. That way there would only be 5 of us needed. So with this in mind, it would be easier for Anne, Misty and Ron to rehearse on their own with tracks and then we'd find a percussion player. The gig was booked for Friday, December 13th, which was part of the appeal for me as I am not superstitious. However, Ron had a few problems with this day because he had business things that dictated he couldn't do the gig. So we managed to borrow The I.S.F.B. sax player Nick but a percussion player ended up dropping out at the last minute. So, only 2 rehearsals were done. I like it on the edge but the same can't be said for everybody else.

THE GIG

The support act were called The Six Million Dollar Band' who went down quite well then it was our turn. The gig was a sell-out and the audience were in for a night they would never forget. I remember one of the support band members saying to me afterwards, that was the most unusual gig he'd ever seen, he never knew what was going to happen next so he was glued to the spot not wanting to miss anything. It was a great start as Pat introduced me as the new Brian Wilson and Joe Meek of pop music and we opened with *The Chase* theme from Midnight Express followed by Anne doing *From Russia With Love*. I had anticipated a few problems with the computer regarding loading up songs and had worked out some dialogue for the girls to say between songs and some competitions for the audience to win some CDs. So out of the blue along would come an unexpected competition. Next up although we were short on a percussion player we had brought a lot of percussion instruments along so I asked if any member of the audience wanted to join the band as a percussion player for the next number *1995.*

A guy came up from the audience and started to play the bongos but instead of one number, he stayed for the whole set.

Misty was in fine form on *Louie Louie* but she seemed very nervous on the night and she shied away from doing too much dialogue. Anne was in the form of her life though and really carried the day and in my book was the star of the concert. This surprised me because Misty had done lots of live gigs before but this was Anne's live debut. I was really proud of her. To add to the chaos and improvisation I normally put my cello through an effects unit to get the unique sounds I use. Normally, I rest my effects unit on a table but there were no tables so I had to put it on the floor. But I only had a short pick up lead and it kept coming off the cello bridge every time I moved a bit, so in the end I just lay on the floor playing the cello, which everybody thought looked very unusual. I got up off the floor to do the vocal on *Mysteries* and this went down very well. I was also cracking lots of jokes about unusual things on the night and with it being the only time we would ever play any Cult Themes in a set it was a unique one-off experience never to be repeated.

Months after the gig I was getting letters from fans who had missed the concert asking when would we be playing again because they'd heard the concert was so unique and different to any concert previously seen and felt gutted about missing it. Because of the infrequency and uniqueness of all Box Office Poison concerts, they would take on a legendary status of their own over the years.

CHAPTER TWENTY-THREE

THE 70's

Despite all that was goings on I still managed to complete the recording of Cult Themes from the 70's Vol.1 in 1996. You've heard about some of the recordings, so to tidy things up here are the rest. The most bizarre recording session of them all featured 'Earthling Scum'. (No surprise there really I guess) I was in 2 minds about letting them do another Cult Theme after they had tied Jezz up and hijacked his recording studio the last time. But their 2 previous contributions had proved very popular and I'd seen them live and thought they were very original and eccentric so I invited them to do *The Professionals* theme and we were now back at Dicks studio and I had a different engineer making things possible as they were definitely on Jez's banned list. Still, to this day I am wondering whether this recording session was a hidden camera stunt. Yetti was his usual pain in the arse but Mr Bunny was serious about his work and managed to keep Yetti under control. The first unusual thing that happened was when a female violin player turned up and started playing along with the track. The thing was she couldn't play. It was like hearing a seven-year-old play her first lesson. I thought maybe she needed time to warm up but an hour later things hadn't improved and most people had run for cover except Yetti who kept saying how brilliant it was. I thought rather than complain I'd play along with the joke, if that's what it was. So I just said, 'excellent, ok you're done. I then just turned the track off when the next musicians came to do their bit. Similarly, the sax player was not very good either but not quite as bad as the violin player. But to top everything, the band's guitarist hadn't turned up and they wanted to rebook the studio and come back another day to do the guitar track. I told them this wasn't possible as the record company would only pay for one day's recording and one day mixing and my time was tight because of everything else that was happening with D.M etc. Mr Bunny and Yetti looked at each other and both said, 'Cougar'. They then said they would be back in an hour they had to break someone out of the mental asylum. I thought they were joking of course. So after they went I then took a coffee break and recorded some percussion. Nearly an hour later the studio door flew open and Yetti wheeled in a dazed-looking person on a hospital porter's trolley wearing a straight jacket. They then propped him up against the wall. I said who the hell is this. They replied this is Cougar he used to be the guitarist in our band but he went a bit crazy after a bad drug trip and he was now in a mental hospital, we just broke him out as he is the only one who can play the song at such short notice. I thought once again, where's the camera? The guy looked drugged up to the eyeballs, so I thought we'd be lucky to get anything out of him. But Yetti took off the straight-jacket, stuck a guitar in Cougars hand (I put the lead direct into the desk) Then they told me to run the track. He then smacked Cougars face and said Professionals theme now. The track started and Cougar played along to the track. There were a few mistakes so we did one more take after which point the guy just fell asleep. They put his straight jacket back on and said they better get him back to the hospital before he was missed. Then they wheeled him back out. Strangely enough, the track came out quite well. I even managed to use bits of the violin to good effect. Producing good musicians doing a track that is well put together is one thing but making a great track from something that is a bit of a mess is much more of an interesting challenge, so I wasn't complaining, as I love a musical challenge. Talking of good musicians, a music journalist had recommended a band called The Sweeney to do a track. No prizes for guessing which track they wanted to do. The band had already released one acclaimed album and had a great live reputation so I hoped featuring them on a Cult Themes album might help them get the final recognition they deserved to go to the next level. Doing Cult Themes the way I do them is never just a straightforward case of copying the original track. In many instances, the original tracks are impossible to get hold of (One reason the F.L.R. Cult Themes were popular because now you could finally get your favourite track). The only place you could get a copy of the music for The Sweeney was by getting a video of the T.V show. But these bits of music only ever had about 30 seconds. The Sweeney theme was a case in point. But it also had a slow bit of music at the end of the show. So I worked out an arrangement to weave the 2 together, which worked very well. This track also features an unusual percussion part. Whilst in the recording studio I came across a toy space gun that belonged to the studio owner's son. So when the slow bit of the song came along I pressed the trigger and it made a very interesting sound and once I added an extra effect to it the track was even better. Yes, folks, if it's not nailed down I'll try and use it in a recording.

The Bruce Li Foundation and Monkey, 2 of Mark Sergeant's other bands, did the final 2 recordings. Although Lynus were the stars of his stable, Bruce Li had a lot of young members looking to make their mark and I believe one, Harry was the son of a couple of members of the popular folk group 'Fairport Convention'. They were a good bunch and looking to learn from me and a great version of *U.F.O* that sounded out of this world was done complete with genuine hoax call as the into.

Sadly on every album, you always get at least one toe=rag or someone who will mess you about and Monkey won the prize this time around and so their track. *Superfly* didn't reach its potential as they were reluctant to try out any new ideas. But the track does have some redeeming features. It sounds like an urban landscape in music form, so it's very different from the Curtis Mayfield original soul version. Recording and completing 2 albums back to back as well as a large part of 'Heavy Breathing Decade' earlier in 96 was a major achievement but very exhausting. I was going into the studio at 10 am and leaving at 5 am, only getting a few hours of sleep, 7 days a week for many months. You've already heard what happened to the Dr Martens album. The next chapter will tell you what became of 'Cult Themes from the Seventies Vol.1'. *(below B.O.P promo photos for the themes and Earthling Scum (Yetti is on right)*

CHAPTER TWENTY-FOUR

ALL GUNS BLAZING

After the disappointment of Dr Martens not signing B.O.P up and the subsequent big promotional push out of the window, it was time for a new strategy. The positive side of The D.M deal was at least now I had gained some excess funds, which I could put behind B.O.P and the label. But before we could do that we needed new distribution. The likes of 'Greyhound' and 'One Stop' were Ok to put out releases and make a living but to gain major success and for serious sales, you need the right distributor. Being an Indie label meant it was important to have a distributor that understood you and this boiled down to just 2, Vital and Pinnacle. Having run into trouble with Pinnacle before via my Waterloo Sunset label because of Eleanor's disappearance I thought my chances with them would be limited and Vital my best bet. Although Vital rated my label and knew all about it they had taken on too many labels and had overstretched themselves and were in the process of dumping labels, so the timing was wrong. Life can often be about timing. A few years earlier the head of 'One Little Indian' (Bjork's label) had liked B.O.P but the timing was wrong to sign us and they were also culling rather than signing. Beggars Banquet were also interested but wanted me to fold the label at a crucial point and just concentrate on B.O.P. I'd have been happy to do this normally but the timing was all wrong. It's a shame as both of those labels would have been perfect for us.Anyway, it was looking like only one avenue was open to me now and that was Pinnacle. I saw one of the label managers there called Stuart and he was very excited about the prospect of getting Future Legend Records. He had seen me crop up a lot regarding the Dr Martens release. He was aware that I had created the Cult Themes trend and he was a fan of Eleanor Rigby's output. I then played him B.O.P's stuff, which he loved, so a deal was quickly forthcoming. Luckily most people at Pinnacle from 10 years before were long gone. All except the M.D who queried the deal at first when he heard it was me. Then he checked and found out I had paid off my previous debt and the deal went through.

The perfect release to kick it off the new deal was 'Cult Themes from the 70's Vol.1' and Stuart even knew quite a few acts on the album like The Sweeney who Pinnacle also distributed. The rest of the schedule consisted of going all out to break B.O.P. and a debut solo single for Misty, a Waterloo Sunset compilation album about my previous label and a new Eleanor Rigby single. It looked like being our biggest year ever for profile and potential sales and a make or break year. Another bonus for both Pinnacle and us was our back catalogue. Pinnacle liked selling back catalogue and made all our releases available to record shops once more. We even had to press up more Themes from the Sixties Vol.1 because every time a new themes album came out it revitalised sales of the previous ones and we had sold out of that one. The slight downside if you can call it that, is the extra expense. Pinnacle liked to see lots of advertising and posters and a top plugger on the case. A big push was put behind 'Cult Themes from the 70's' Vol.1' and it was our best selling Cult Themes album since The Sixties Vol.1 and needed repressing immediately. It was getting rave reviews and a series of concerts were done by the bands to promote the album. As usual, B.O.P were looking to do an unusual gig. The last time I'd seen the group Lynus I asked them to learn 3 or 4 of our songs as it might be worthwhile and they had. A Cult Themes launch gig was set up at The Zodiac in Oxford (A big venue owned by Radiohead and Supergrass) It would feature the 3 Oxford-based acts on the Cult Themes album.

Monkey were rubbish as expected, Misty guested with The Bruce Li Foundation doing a few of the Cult Themes and Lynus were the headline act. In the middle of their set Anne and I walked out on stage and hijacked their set it asking them to play the B.O.P songs and the new Cult Themes that I had also asked them to learn. It was very on edge, but that's the 'Pop Noir' philosophy. The venue was a sell-out and it all went very down well.Also for once, instead of being 10 years ahead, my timing was good because a 70's revival started around this time as well. I can't say I'm responsible for it but we were in the thick of it.

(Above Mouse & I with Lynus and below Misty with the Bruce Li Foundation at the zodiac in Oxford)

The next priority was to schedule some Box Office Poison singles for release and make some more pop videos and get a plugger. But first, a bit more recording was needed. With Misty and Mouse now being the singers, I wanted to re-record some of my best tracks as singles. Misty did *Think For Yourself, Alien and Lady Grinning Soul.* Her vocals took these to a new level, as her voice is the ultimate 'Pop Noir' voice. As were her P.N style backing vocal I had developed with her. To update *Think for Yourself,* I now added a new sub bass drum beat to give it a contemporary feel and developed some other drum innovation I was working towards. It added to the moodiness of the track to make it the ultimate Pop Noir drum sound. With *Alien* this was less easy to improve since I had captured the right feel with the original version. But I decided as a backing vocal, Misty and I would just stand in front of the mic breathing heavily into it. This added the perfect atmosphere and once again Misty vocal was perfect for the lead vocal.

Both Misty and Mouse tried out *Lady Grinning Soul,* Misty won out with her sensual vocal and jazzy improvised style. The original Bowie track is one of his best so it was hard to better but we certainly came up with a very dreamy and compelling version that features punk cello at its best, plus interesting percussion and sax parts that Bowie himself already liked.

Mouse/Anne did new versions of *Teenage Sex* and *16 Year,* and her vocal suited these tracks better than Misty. With *Teenage Sex*, I went for Pop Noir crossed with a Phil Spector type production. I had originally written this song for Eleanor and she had only got as far as recording a basic demo of it. You may remember I produced a guitar version for the Psychomatics as well, which everybody thought sounded like a potential hit single but since they split up it was never released. The intro to this new version is very innovative and lots of people always ask what it is. It is only clear what it is when you see the video. I am playing a drum rhythm with drumsticks on my cello strings. I also used a thing called an ebow on this track to get a different sound as well. Another appealing thing about this track is that it has a catchy lullaby feel to it. The song itself is about teenage rebellion and the flip side to the lyrics to *16-year-old* and It puts across the idea that teenagers are mostly reckless because they think at that age they are going to live forever and rebelling is the order of the day. The song came about when Avril, Eleanor's 16-year-old keyboard player heard 16-year-old and said there was another side to the coin. Because she inspired both tracks and because we didn't have a keyboard player Avril returned to B.O.P to play harpsichord on it. *(Avril below)*

CHAPTER TWENTY-FIVE

VIDEO KILLED THE RADIO STAR

With the recordings done for the singles the next step was to find a video director and do the videos. I've always been a fan of double 'A' side singles as they show that a band has strong material and it's also value for money. However, the CD format meant it would actually be a CD- EP. I decided Teenage Sex/Alien would be the first single. Early on in the label's history, I was into helping new graphic artists and an Italian/German guy called Dieter Marsoner was our main one, he did some great cover art, including *Mysteries & Beyond The Twilight Zone + Themes from the 60s Vol.2*. He was about to return to Italy but recommended a guy called Mark Aquera to do our videos. Also, Anne had become a good graphic artist & photographer as well, designing some F.L.R. sleeves. I would also have a hand in them myself. (A whole lot of creativity going on) Her sleeve for 'Cult Themes from the 70's Vol.1' proved popular and she did her most outstanding work on the *Alien/Teenage Sex* sleeve featuring the band inside a cello. Even though I'd got a new influx of funds from my Dr Martens job, with a plugger and adverts also to pay for, it was decided the videos were going to have to be made on a tight budget. This is not always a bad thing from a creative standpoint. Often big-budget pop videos suffer from a lack of original ideas and blandness although there are a few exceptions like 'Bjork's' outstanding video output. With big-budget videos, the technical side like lighting and camera work is top-notch but so what. The directors doing these types of videos often used a clichéd phrase, saying they won't get out of bed for less than £10,000. These video directors were creative once but once they made their name they seem to run out of ideas and lose their hunger. We proved with *1995* and *You Only Live Twice* that you could get a video that looks like it cost £50,000 for £5,000. So I think that's the most a video should cost. However, we were up against it this time, with only 10% of that to spend on each of these new videos. That meant ideas & originality would be key. Naturally, directors at this end of the market were still learning their trade and so it's likely some problems would crop up. So Dieter's friend Mark A, a laid back scruffy hippy type of individual was chosen. I decided to hire him for 2 videos. This was because we wanted animation in both and was told this was one of his strengths. I watched his show-reel and indeed this was his strength. I did however have my reservations about him directing people but thought I could always take over this role as I had done before if he wasn't up to it and this proved to be the case after he did a few shots with peoples heads missing. *(below the definitive B.O.P line up of this period)*

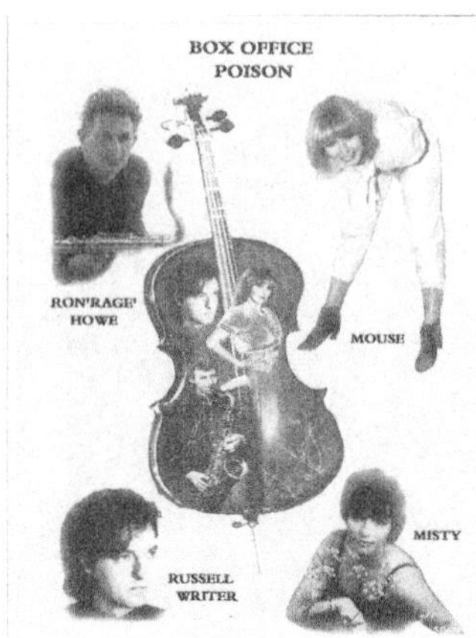

ALIEN

The main idea for the Alien Video was to do a spoof on the T.V show The X-Files about tracking down an Alien. The other idea was to have the band playing in a seedy club influenced by a scene from 'Fire Walker' the Twin Peaks movie, plus some improvisation of course. Most of the live sequences were filmed in the basement of The Embassy Club in Islington, London, as were all the Alien scenes. The remainder was shot at an under-developed part of Camden Lock that now makes up the stables shopping area and especially the 'Cyberdog' brand that coincidently I would wear a few years later. Whilst at the Camden location several problems cropped up. After filming what seemed like great footage it transpired something was wrong with the film and camera. So it had to be all done again. The second time around we were accosted by security guards who tried to seize the film. After a brief scuffle, we managed to escape with the film. However, one thing came from this, Mark Aquera used the damaged video as a backdrop for the video, which was quite innovative of him. Once again the B.O.P tradition of featuring non-band members in a video was kept. Ron decided he was now too old to appear in pop videos and declined to take part but said he still considered himself a band member for recording or live work. Misty had started dating a Mod guy called Andy and he was drafted in to mime on trumpet to the live band sequences. Andy would later play the guitar on Misty's solo release, 'Wallpaper Man & Mod Boy'.

Mouse (Anne) did appear briefly at the start of the video as 'Scully' (Blink and you'll miss her). Also featuring briefly in this video are 2 of The Spice Girls (*That woke you up didn't it*). Well, not quite the Spice Girls, but friends of Andy's who were in a Spice Girls look-alike tribute band. They feature dancing in the club. Once again don't blink. At this stage it was looking like B.O.P were just me and Misty, which was Ok for this video since we were in fact the only 2 on this particular recording anyway and there was no sax on the track. Although I didn't change my image as much as Misty I did have quite an image change for this video having different coloured hair extensions woven into my hair. It felt cool but didn't look so hot on the video so I dumped them soon afterwards. I wore a new embroidered jacket and the Matrix-style coat that I'd designed.

The cellar we used under the Embassy was a unique place and we made good use of a caged lift, which we stuck Misty in. Mark A was finding it hard to concentrate on filming half the time because Misty was not wearing knickers. (*It would have been good to have a camera on him*) Misty came up with an interesting Alien image and another image featuring a see-through PVC dress and a Bam Bam (from Flintstones) hairstyle, that looked really good.

Sadly, Mark A was not as together as we had hoped and some plasticine animations promised for this video never materialised, so the potential of the video was never fulfilled. Strobe lighting used in the video also hampered it being shown on T.V. (it causes epileptic fits). However, the video overall features some great shots of Misty in a cage (where she belongs!) Plus as already mentioned the distorted video tape effects. Many fans seeing it have rated it highly as one of the most creative videos they have seen. The same applies to many of our videos. Many say they have to watch Mysteries video 30 times to see everything in it.

RARE PHOTOS FROM ALIEN VIDEO; With the first Alien video footatage destroyed here are some rare still photos from the shoot of the main three band members. The rarest is of Mouse as she decided not to do the video 2nd time around.

TEENAGE SEX

After problems with equipment at Camden, it was problems with personnel that dogged the Teenage Sex video shoot and arguably when B.O.P became a two-piece. I was shocked to find Anne had done a disappearing act the day before the shoot and left a note to say she didn't want to be found. She had seen a program about Ritchie out of The Manic Street Preacher's disappearance and it had got to her. It seemed like the curse of the breakdown was upon me once more. I was worried sick about her not only as a band member but also as my girlfriend, which was hardly the ideal preparation the day before shooting what would be the most important video of our career. This was also her big debut as the lead singer on an original B.O.P track. In her note, she said Misty was the ideal front person and she could do the video even though it wasn't her voice. Anne added she would return once it was done.

The main idea for the video was to have some cartoon teenage characters go to a drive-in movie to have sex in the back of the car whilst playing on the cinema screen was Box Office Poison. All the footage of Anne and Misty had been destroyed in Marks dodgy camera and he had to hire another one. So maybe that was a sign that it wasn't meant to be for Anne.

Another B.O.P philosophy regarding videos is to make the location as much the star as the band so we chose the famous London landmark of 'Tower Bridge'. Other clips in the video were cobbled together from the 2nd shoot at the Camden location featuring Misty. Shooting without a permit at Tower Bridge proved a bit of a problem. We couldn't cordon off the section of the pathway we wanted to shoot on and every time we started to film a tourist would appear in the background. So it effectively took us 3 hours to get a 30-second shot. Still, that's guerrilla filming for you.

In some ways, this is our most successful video because it topped the Russian pop video charts keeping the likes of David Bowie and Diana Ross at bay. Many more people wanted to show the video but then Misty had a tantrum about it and wouldn't let it be shown because she doesn't like the fact that it's not her voice on it. The animation has some very good bits although a few bits could have been better. There should have also been more of it. The sound also needed some improvement. Still, I quite like the look of this video, it's a shame it can't be shown more. As for Anne, she recovered from her mini-breakdown and it was touch and go as to whether she wanted to continue in the band. The recording side wasn't too bad even though she was under pressure to compete with Misty. The music business is geared up to young artists and if you are over 25 you are considered over the hill, which I think is out of order. Misty was 23 but Anne was in her 30's, and this got to her after seeing photos of her and Misty side by side. The ironic thing was, at one point Anne was just as popular and just as much of a pin-up as Misty was with our fans. At the end of the day, age shouldn't come into it. Some of the most creative people are often older, such as artists, photographers and record producers. Singers like Madonna are still showing the kids a clean pair of heels although she has gone off the boil recently. Bjork and Bowie too were always ahead of the game. David was totally creative up until he died at 69. Originality and talent is not the property of youth and the opposite seems to apply with blandness and lack of ideas prevailing in music these days. How creative is it to just steal a previous hit song and stick a rap over the top of it? I think experience wins against youth every time. New things do come along but new doesn't necessarily mean better. Badly fitting trousers and street sweeping flares. Rappers rubbishing females, gun culture, limited vocabulary based around the same few words. Plastic personalities fronting T.V shows and yet another show on the general public, is that progress? Another film packed with one explosion after another, computer-generated action repeated again and again. One sequel after another and then lets milk T.V shows from our youth to make film cash in's because there are no original ideas around. Great art is now a stuffed cow or an unmade bed. Should I get excited now every time I see a spunk stain in my bed? Rap and Hip Hop is old hat it's been around since 78. Manufactured pop stars whose karaoke cover versions aren't a million miles away from 1950's crooners who got kicked into oblivion by real Rock and Rock. When was the last time youth came up with something really original? Punk was the last great youth rebellion. Rave was interesting but how different was it from hippy love in 67. New strands of music have come along but things like Drum and Bass and other so-called new music is exciting for the first few records then the same formula bores you to death. In a way, the reason The Matrix was such a great film is that it hit the nail on the head. People are living like sheep with blinkers on blindly following music, fashion and other trends so as not to feel left out. Wake up and smell the coffee people. Of course, there are exceptions and some talent is around (Lady Ga Ga.). But if you analyse things, blandness is at the core of today's society and it's filtering down to our kids who are having less and less in the way of original thoughts. Anyway, I've said my piece and hopefully, I will wake up a few people who will show me that youth can be original.

Now, it's time to get back to my story. Animation for video is a time-consuming business so this gave me time to finish off the Heavy Breathing Decade album, look for a plugger and record Misty's debut single. Let's start with Misty. You may recall there was talk of Misty doing an Eleanor tribute band, which I vetoed. I said at the time to her I'd come up with a better tribute idea. Since Misty was currently a Modette and I had a very catchy song I'd written for Eleanor called *Wallpaper Man* that Eleanor had done a demo for but never recorded properly for release, I said to Misty as a tribute she should record this song the way I'd have done it with Eleanor. Into the bargain, Misty could write a song of her own to be the B-side. As well as being a talented singer and someone with star quality I soon found out that Misty was a talented songwriter as well. I then signed her to a music publishing deal and this was one reason I agreed to push her as a solo artist as well as the main singer with B.O.P. It was a refreshing change to record one of my songs with guitars again since B.O.P never use guitars. *Wallpaper Man* was very much a guitar song and that's why I never did it with B.O.P. It had very humorous lyrics but stood no chance of airplay unless a DJ was a rebel since it was a dig a bland daytime radio. It's a little bit reminiscent a bit of The Beatles *Nowhere Man.* Misty then wrote a song called *Mod Boy* as a tribute to Eleanor's track *Mod Girls*. At first, it was a bit too close to my own song *Love on the Phone* (which Misty loved) so I had to nudge her to change it a bit. But once changed it was a lively Mod anthem. The musicians were mostly friends of Misty's. When it came to putting it out as a single I thought of a more original way to get it noticed and marketed. Since there hadn't been an Eleanor Rigby single out for 4 years I thought it would be good to keep her profile alive and generate sales in her albums with a new single. Of course, she wasn't around to record a new single. One track that had been played to death when her 'Censorship' album had come out was *Love on the Phone* and many DJ's said it would make a hit single. So I thought it high time this came out as a single. *Play with Fire* had a classy production like *You Only Live Twice & Up The Junction*, so I decided to make this the other side of the single. I then took a leaf out of Two-Tones book. When the Two-Tone label was launched featuring The Specials many singles had one band on one side like Madness and Selector or The Beat on the other side. Therefore promoting 2 acts at the same time. (This idea was in fact, nicked from old Ska records from the 60s that did something similar).

I thought it was highly likely that beyond B.O.P fans there would be very few people who knew who Misty Woods was, so to introduce her to people I thought I'd put her 2 tracks on a 4 track CD-EP with the other 2 tracks being the Eleanor ones. This way people would buy the single for Eleanor but discover Misty at the same time. Since there were similarities between the 2 she would pick up fans for future releases and B.O.P may pick up extra fans as well although quite a few of Eleanor fans had already followed me to B.O.P. There would still be a 7" vinyl single but this would just feature Eleanor's 2 tracks since she was still very collectable and especially on this format. (Below some promo shots of Misty done for the sleeve + finished CD)

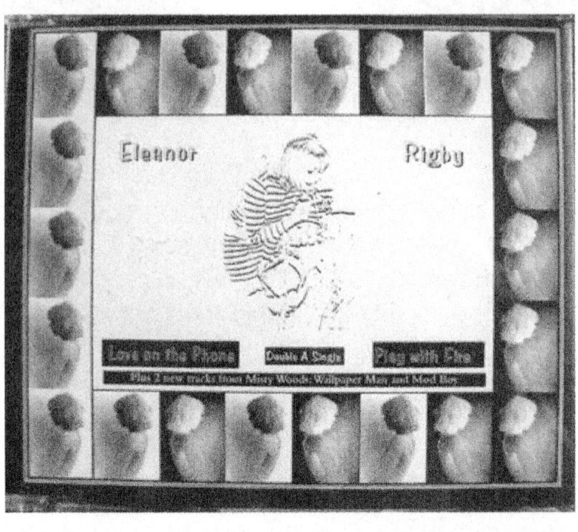

CHAPTER TWENTY-SIX

HEAVY BREATHING DECADE

After recording Misty's solo single, it was time to finish off the 'Heavy Breathing Decade' album. As I was preaching earlier, it's better to put out an album of strong songs rather than a weak album of all your own songs just because you wrote them and this was the philosophy used with this album. As a music publisher over the years, I'd come across some great songs that hadn't got anywhere but had the potential to be big hits. I decided the album would consist of some of these tracks plus songs by others that should have been hits but weren't, plus the best songs I'd written over the past 5 years that I hadn't yet recorded or released. You may recall I once managed a band called 'Europeans in Tropic'. They split up but had one song that was a real gem, *Come With Me,* so I made contact with the songwriter 'Ralph' and offered to become his publisher for that one track. However, the lyrics were very syrupy so I thought some better ones were needed and duly wrote some that would go with the concept of the H.B.D album. It was about female orgasm and it hit the nail on the head because a lot of people would buy the album for this track when released. One girl bought 15 copies saying it was the sexiest song ever written and she wanted all her friends to have a copy. The lyrics may be hot but the production also needed to be spot on to create the atmosphere of a passionate lovemaking session in a storm with body's entwined in one almighty orgasm. With sexy cello lines, storm sounds, Dolphin and Whale like vocals, punk cello sounds plus a hypnotic groove and a tingling harpsichord riff, all worked a treat. Misty was born to sing such a song and it was perfection itself. But Anne did an equally brilliant and sexy job on a spoken version of the song. The studio engineer said he got a hard-on just listening to her version. The two versions of the song bookend the H B D album.

COME WITH ME

Come, come, come with me, to an island inside of me

Oh I'm breathing heavily, Come with me

The night is young but can't you see, I just want you inside of me

Let me feel you inside of me, set me free

Whispers of love pass to and fro, Feel my body and then let go

Oh this feeling I can't control......Come with me

How I wish you could only see, how much pleasure you are giving me

Oh touch me, touch me there, set me free

Our bodies tense and our spirits flow, I wish this feeling could never go

Oh it's special with you,, Come with me

Come, Come, Come with me, to an island inside of me

Oh I'm breathing heavily. Come with me

Come come with me...To an island inside of me. Inside of me

I can't control this, I can't control this.....Come with me

Despite the 100% sexual content of this album none of my output would be complete without some sort of message. As you know Eleanor's debut single *I Want To Sleep With You,* although selling well was banned, so the only people who got to hear it were the people who bought it. I always thought this was a great shame as it's such a catchy song. However, the lyrics were always the weakest part of the song and being about the 80's lifestyle, they were now out of date. So I decided to write some new lyrics for it. I think it's crucial to keep the awareness going on crucial topics. Aids had not gone away but become low profile, so I felt it needed a shot in the arm.

One particular trend that has crept in that will cause a new explosion in Aids is the trend for anal sex. There is 10 times more chance of spreading the disease this way and also of a condom being damaged. To many, it's just a trend like tattoos and piercings. Many people may wake up 10 years from now saying what have I done and want to get rid of them. The latter two may leave a scar but can be gotten rid of, aids can't. Although you may not die now you may have to be on medication forever. I'll leave you with one final thought on this matter. You may like to buy shares in adult nappies, as they are likely to be best sellers 5 years from now. I saw an interesting interview with a Porn Queen a while ago who said she hated doing anal scenes and was glad she didn't pursue that avenue despite the pressure to do so but her friends did it for extra money and 3 years on she had to wear special types of nappies because of constant anal leakage as she put it. I guess the back passage is tight for a reason. The reason I brought this up is that I decided that *I Want To Sleep With You,* would now be an Aids awareness song. So, my new lyric tells the story of an unfaithful partner who gives his other half Aids. If the song saves one person from the nightmare of Aids it will be worth it. In fact, the life that might be saved might be mine. It's such a catchy song I can see people having a sing-along then it dawning on them what the song is actually about. Given the subject matter, the track is a pure contrast of bouncy upbeat and happy sounding music. The other thing I have added that was not on the original is a Joe Meek *Telstar* type organ solo which I really love the sound of. It was impossible to get hold of the unique organ that played this sound. So I had to mix different sounds together to re-create it.The next track is a cover originally called *Parade.* The title was one of its big mistakes and a reason for it not being a big hit. It was originally done by a duo called 'White and Torch'. It got lots of airplay and did make the lower regions of the chart. It sounded very reminiscent of some classic Walker Brothers records. I was managing Music Master record shop when it came out and many people were looking to get the record but the thing was the word *Parade* was nowhere in the song. *Don't Sleep with Him* was the main phrase. As I had the record myself, I knew which record people were talking about but knowing what other record shop staff were like I expected many sales were lost. The track itself was cello dominated and suited 'B.O.P's style. So when we recorded it, it fitted in perfectly with the other songs I'd written. I also rectified the mistake made by the original band and called it *Don't Sleep with Him (Parade).* Our original harpsichord player Avril who had also been with Eleanor Rigby had written a very good song called *Take Me Up To Heaven and Back* when in the E.R Doppelganger band, The Psychomatics and I always liked it. Since it had a strong sex angle to it I recorded it with Avril playing the harpsichord on it. Despite there being no guitars, it's very rocky and very reminiscent of the 'Doors'. Another classic song that should have been a big hit was *Strip Show,* it was by a cult band 'Doll by Doll'. I heard it playing one day in the Hard Rock Café. It's not often I seek out a DJ to ask what is playing but I was compelled to find out about this record and immediately bought it.

I did our version with lashings of atmosphere and just the right element of sleaze. One instrument I used a lot was a Russian instrument called a Balalaika that can be heard on *The Ipcress File* and I'd gradually introduced it into our sound and it came into its own on this track. I also tried out some new punk cello ideas on this track playing the cello without a bow. The sax is very 'Pop Noir' on this track as well. The final cover track to be recorded at these latest sessions had the most famous name attached to it. Elton John made an all time classic album in the 70's called 'Goodbye Yellow Brick Road'. Tucked away on the album was a controversial little track about Lesbians. *All The Young Girls Love Alice.* It had always been one of my favourite Elton songs and with our album being all about different aspect of sex it was time to record it I thought. It's a very raucous track and if further evidence was needed that B.O.P could do a hard edge track without guitars this was it. It went on to become a bit of Lesbian anthem and our version is one of the most popular versions now by Mouse (solo) & B.O.P featuring Misty.

I WANT TO SLEEP WITH YOU (part.2)

I start my day the feminine way, ooh dressed to kill

I turn on the T.V set and it says sex will make you ill

I remember a time when it was such a thrill

That was so long ago. It just goes to show but I can't say no

I can't help myself I want to sleep with you

I L.O.V.E you and you love me too

I can't help myself I want to sleep with you

I L.O.V.E you and you love me too

Open up the paper, another victim to depress

Love or joy, oh boy, my life is such a mess

You see I'm not a loose girl, I just love to love

I've seen the figures. I know the risks

But it's such a test

Seeing you, seeing me, it turns me on

I'm sexually attracted, but it's love that I want

But now you've been unfaithful and it starts to show

Now your HIV test no longer says no, It's a shattering blow

I don't want to I don't want to sleep with you. It's too late and now I am a victim too

Don't want to sleep with you. Don't want to sleep with you

CHAPTER TWENTY-SIX

HEAD YOU WIN TALES YOU LOSE

With the videos done, the first B.O.P single of 97 was going to be a double A-sided *Teenage Sex/Alien,* however, because we had to release CD's now, that meant effectively a CD-EP. The bonus tracks were a new version of 16-year-old *sung by Mouse and Psycho City.* (*Which was the first lyrics I ever wrote*) sung by me, which was almost a solo track as it's very punk cello orientated with a menacing feel which called for a male vocal. Mouse designed the sleeve below.

So it was now time for the trickiest part of the proceedings, that of getting the airplay to try and get a hit. So, a plugger was needed. We couldn't afford the top people so it was down to trawling the depths of those shark-infested waters once more. In my now considerable time in the music business, I had only heard about one honest brilliant plugger at the lower price range. His name was Scott Peiring. I had met him a few times and the first time I met him he mistook me (*wearing sunglasses at the time*) for 'Johnny Marr' of 'The Smiths' who he was the plugger for. So he was very much an Indie guitar man and B.O.P were not Indie guitar. If Eleanor had still been around he would have been the perfect plugger. Although snowed under with work he had a meeting with me anyway. He said since all his contacts were into Indie guitar he thought I would be wasting my money on him. He said my best bet was to look in trade paper Music Week for pluggers. So I looked and found one Jane Wallace. She said she had been head of promotions at Virgin and also worked freelance at all the major record companies. I had a meeting with her in a big flash West End office. Jane was in her forties with red hair and had a combination of nervous energy and confidence about her. At the meeting, she presented me with a list of clients she had worked for and one was a group I knew who had just become successful called My Life Story. She gave me details of her terms and conditions and asked me to visit her home in the Cotswolds for lunch to cement the deal a few days later. She initially wanted £3,000 but I drove a hard bargain and wanted both sides of the record pushed including videos. In the end, I got her for £1,500 upfront plus an additional £500 when the job was finished. She agreed on a 6-week campaign.

I was always sceptical about pluggers so I phoned the manager of the group 'My life Story' and he confirmed Jane had plugged an early single of theirs but was too busy to talk further.Since My Life Story used cellos and had some similarities to us and she'd apparently got results for them she seemed suitable.

Jane further convinced me, saying she had very big contacts at radio and T.V and dropped lots of names, all of which I had heard of. She even said if the worst comes to the worst she could call on personal favours of these big names to guarantee Radio 1 & 2 airplay & T.V exposure. I thought, maybe at last I had found a plugger who could genuinely get results for once. So I was optimistic and excited. Part of any pluggers job is to keep the client informed each day by phone plus written feedback once a week. She phoned me for a few days, and then it all went quiet. It then became hard to get hold of her. I finally got through and she just said she was waiting on people to get back to her. By week 2 the excuses started rolling in and Jane's confident veneer had vanished and been replaced by a highly-strung voice arguing on the phone. She's had some rejections from local radio and was still waiting on the bigger people for results. Her excuses started with her saying the title *Teenage Sex* was a problem. (Something she never mentioned when accepting the job). I couldn't believe that 12 years after *I Want to Sleep With You* I was running into censorship problems again. If people listened to the song they would hear straight away that it wasn't controversial. People like George Michael had put out tracks like *I Want Your Sex* and numerous dance tracks had much more controversial titles and were being played. So, I reminded her that the single was a double 'A' and if she had a problem with one side she should push the other side that had no controversial title. By the end of week 2, she was still struggling but said she had finally got a result. What was this big result? She had got me invited to a premiere of a Shakespeare film and there would be many contacts there to network with and I should come along. I thought that's better than nothing and duly went along. It turned out far from Jane being an A list person who could get into premiers, which is what she put across, her brother had directed the support feature and she got free tickets because of that. At the party afterwards, I was introduced to only one person of note. The person was about to produce 'The Avengers' film based on the classic 60's show and once he found out who I was he said he might like me to do the main theme. (But nothing came from it). At this premiere, I gave Jane copies of the *Alien* video to use because of the problems she said she was having with *Teenage Sex*. But more days went by without a word and when I finally got hold of her she decided to quit. She said she had now had feedback from key people and they had all refused to play the single and she was hitting her head against a brick wall. I pointed out that she wouldn't have even had time to send the *Alien* video out never mind get a reaction on that song. I then reminded her about her so-called friends she could blag favours from to guarantee airplay? I also asked her to send me proof and written feedback of what she had done so far, to which she hung up. So here I was in the middle of the most important release of my career with no plugger and everything up in the air. I tried to speak with Jane again but couldn't get any reasoning out of her and she refused to send any reports so I asked for a full refund immediately. So, as if I didn't have enough to do running a record label I had to chase her up for a refund every few days and with no plugger and major adverts coming out in N.M.E and Melody Maker I had to take on the plugging myself. With 2 videos, I felt a key area to attract attention would be T.V and so blitzed all the T.V people. I soon built up a rapport with many of them and started to get the Teenage Sex video played.

Ironically, it was the Alien one that Jane had never pushed that was a problem because of the strobe lighting effect on it. Another thing I learned whilst speaking to all the T.V people was none of them had been approached by Jane Wallace and most had never heard of her. When I hit the radio the same picture began to emerge. Also with me also getting airplay for the tracks with no massive negative response, it was clear Jane was a con artist. I wasn't even a professional plugger and I was getting results, so why couldn't someone who was supposed to be professional, not get even one result. She had also given up far too early and should have carried on for another month. I still didn't get a refund and the only thing I got was a letter of resignation from Jane. So, I said if I didn't get paid back within a month I would sue her.

Lots of people said to me pluggers are always taking advantage of people and taking money with no results to show for it and that none had ever been sued. So, I would be the first person ever to sue a plugger and people were not optimistic about my chances.

Although I managed to get about half a dozen T.V plays and lots of airplay on XFM plus selected plays on other radio stations and mass support from college radio, I didn't have the all-important mass Radio One play and so the record didn't make the UK charts. The sting in the tail was, Teenage Sex got to number one in the Russian pop video charts with Bowie and Diana Ross at number 2 & 3. Although we got a one-off payment for the video and it was the most popular pop video in Russia for one week, we couldn't capitalise with record sales because it was hard getting regular payments, so exporters wouldn't sell records to Russia. It was always a surprise to me how Russians heard of us in the first place. But we get requests from nearly every country in the world so I can only imagine interest starts at a fanzine level where we have always been popular and it trickles through from there.

Being ripped off left a nasty taste in my mouth but I was determined we would not be beaten. 97 was designated the year to go all out to break B.O.P. Because I had got involved in the promotion and plugging I had found that although initially, it was hard to get hold of the right people at T.V and radio, once you did and I got a rapport with them they would take your calls. One problem I found initially was that because of the gap between our 2nd and 3rd single of 3 years most people who had heard of the band had since forgotten about us. So I was advised that although Teenage Sex was not a runaway success the very fact that everybody in the media now knew who Box Office Poison were would help in getting interest in the next single and they were right. So the next priority was to get the video made for *Think For Yourself.* Although, this too was a double A-side with *Lady Grinning Soul*. We thought it best to get a quality video of just one side rather than stretch resources over 2 videos. You may recall I asked David Bowie to direct the video for us, as *Lady Grinning Soul* was his song. He had agreed to this, so I dropped him an e-mail but got no reply so-called Wayne and he said David was on a world tour so it wouldn't be impossible for him to do it. David had always given me that proviso that he would do it providing he wasn't busy. He even said he didn't want payment to direct it as he knew funds for an Indie would be tight but had hoped for a decent budget for the crew. So I decided with no Bowie tie in I would concentrate on my own song *Think For Yourself.* I managed to get a very good bargain from a company based at Elstree film studios, which we could use to film in as well as do a location, shoot. All for £1,000.

THINK FOR YOURSELF

Although I have ended up directing many of B.O.P's videos I never went into each production with that aim. Since I am appearing in the video I wanted to just concentrate on the performance aspect and not have to worry about directing as well. So when the video company, Ellie-J recommended a director I couldn't have been happier. His name was Teddy, an Afro-American guy who had directed videos for the likes of Tu Pac and Bon Jovi.

As seems the case with many directors I have encountered, ideas are thin on the ground and they seem more technically focussed thinking about lighting, camera techniques, and editing. Of course, all these things are important but you do need to have some interesting content rather than just a band performing or happy smiling faces dancing down the street. So once again the ideas department was down to me. My idea was to go for total improvisation at a good location that represented learning and using your mind, plus get lots of moody shots like a David Bailey photo-shoot. The only idea Teddy's contributed was to spoof an Alfred Hitchcock film 'North by Northwest' (Aeroplane sequence). This was also mainly because Ellie-J had just got a special effects unit developed by George Lucas that could put a plane doing a flyover without hiring an actual plane. Because of my idea about learning it was useful that we had a big college following around the country. The head of Keele University student union was a particularly big fan and was always asking us about playing a concert there so I called him and arranged to blag the University as our key location.

Keele was an ideal place as it had some very Gothic buildings and a very old Library amongst other things. It even had an Amphitheatre supposedly used by the famous Satanist Alistair Crowley.

Since neither Ron nor Mouse were on this track and didn't want to appear on pop videos anyway it consisted of just Misty and me. There are a lot of great locations in this video and despite the clout of the Student Union, there were some places like the 100-year-old library that we were not supposed to shoot in so we were like Spy's sneaking in to film these shots secretly. Things were going well but then the trouble started. I had planned to use the secret Amphitheatre at the college for one or two scenes to give things variety. I kept saying to Teddy let's go and do it before it gets too dark. Teddy said he wanted to do some indoor shots of Misty at a nondescript location (IE; some students quarters) first and that they had night lighting so could shoot the Amphitheatre later. I took his word but went to see the Amphitheatre to work out some shots as he did solo shots of Misty. By the time I got back the mood of the day had changed. Misty wasn't in the best of moods that day, to begin with. But she was seething by my return. Teddy had filmed some unflattering shots of her, but he wouldn't listen to her or take her seriously. When I got back she got me to look at the footage and was right, they were many unflattering shots. So I called a halt and said now let's go to the Amphitheatre to which Teddy replied I have just discovered we brought the wrong lights for outdoor night shooting and can't do those scenes. Everyone was on edge and it was getting late so a halt was called to the shoot.

A few days later we went to Elstree to film the rest of the video but there was a bad atmosphere between Misty and Teddy and Misty was saying on the way to Elstree she wanted him sacked as he was a misogynist & useless and I should take over as I was a much better director and we also had a special rapport. Rather than sack him as soon as

I walked through the door I said I wanted to look at the rough edit of our previous footage. It wasn't very good at all.

So I spoke to Jack who was head of Ellie-J and he said he would advise Teddy he was no longer needed and I could take over as director with help from their cameraman. I could also have extra days editing because of the problems. I did many interesting shots at Elstree and did a few interesting edits as well. I did it in black & white but also 2 additional versions, one in colour and a psychedelic one. It proved to be our most successful video since *Checkmate*.

(Below 2 outtake still shots from the video not used Misty followed by Russ)

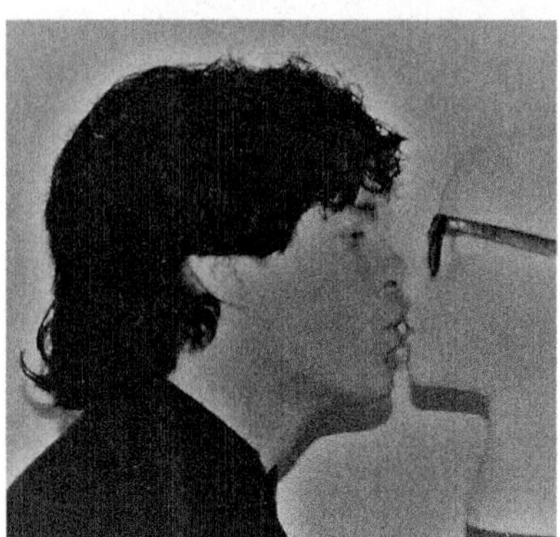

CHAPTER TWENTY-SEVEN

THE PHOTO

Whilst awaiting the manufacture of *Think For Yourself* CD (with bonus tracks; *Louie Louie and Nightmare on Elm Street*) I was asked to judge a 'Battle of the Bands' final. Misty asked if she could come with me. Since the event was being held in Brighton and it finished late she came back to my place instead of going home. We'd both had plenty to drink since free drinks were plentiful for judges. We had barely been at my place 10 minutes when Misty pointed to the famous nude poster of Eleanor for her Censorship album and said, 'So when are you going to do a great photo or poster like that for me? I want one and I want it now!'

I had done a few photo-shoots for others since that famous shoot but hadn't pushed this avenue much. But on this night it would all come together. Whilst I was thinking about some original shots and loading the film in the camera Misty had stripped off because she wanted something naked involved in the shots. I have a very distinctive cello that looks like no other because it is wrapped in black lace. I then got Misty to wrap her body around the cello but my camera flash wouldn't work. So I looked around for the best-lit part of my place, which happened to be the kitchen and took half a dozen snaps directing Misty what to try out but her sensual vibe was more than enough anyway. I knew after the second shot that it was a classic photo (as I had done when taking Eleanor's), you can just feel it and for me, photography is all about instinct and composition. This photo, now known as Misty Cello went on to be one of my most famous pictures and somewhat iconic and appeared in quite a few newspapers and magazines. It even eclipsed some of Eleanor's most famous ones. I had done many other photo sessions with Misty before and after this and there are a few classics amongst those but this photo is like that one big hit record that a band has that everybody refers to. (Which can be annoying) More recently I took my photography to a whole new level with my new muse, Maiko (aka Aurelie Freuoa) and the one or two hit wonder tag would vanish finally as I have now done scores of top photos with her.

After the photo session, Misty recorded a few music demos with me and at about 5 am we finally got to bed. I didn't have a spare bed so Misty shared mine. It was the first time we were naked in bed together since the ill-fated sexual encounter where her Mother came in and pulled me out of her. We had agreed not to get involved too heavily and as far as I was aware sex was off the menu so I tried to behave myself and sleep. Misty asked for a quick cuddle then seemed to fall asleep quickly. My arm was still around her and she suddenly took hold of my hand and shoved it between her legs and started moving it around her clitoris area. Then she let go. I got the message and carried on playing with her until she came. She just sighed and rolled over and not a word was spoken. The next day she never even mentioned it. This happened again the next time I saw her and this time I mentioned it but she claimed she didn't remember doing it. I've heard of sleepwalking but sleep foreplay must be a new one. But since Misty is an original I guess she would have an original sleep disorder.

A few days later I decided to scrap the sleeve for our new single and replace it with the new photo I took of Misty wrapped around the cello. But after a while, I messed about with the photo. It was a black and white photo so I added different colours to it and distorted it. It then looked a bit like a Andy Warhol piece but it said to me in this form *Lady Grinning Soul,* so this became the cover for the single/CD-EP. It was no surprise Bowie liked it when I sent it to him, as he liked Warhol a lot. I didn't get to speak with him but got a minimal email message from him saying 'Love this version, this vocal & photo idea, very Warhol. Good luck with it' x D. It was then when I emailed back asking about doing the video that I got no reply. Then heard from Wayne he was on tour. I then went all out to get results for this single in every area. As if getting T.V, radio and press were not enough for me to do I also decided that we should get a full line-up together to do a few gigs to promote the release in case we needed to do some live T.V shows as this possibility was mentioned.

To play the music as it appears on the record takes about 9 people so a 9-piece line-up is what I went for. Avril had recently come back to the band to record the track she had written so she agreed to do harpsichord, piano, and keyboards. Luckily she had a new flatmate 'Ness' who happened to be a cello player. As well as me doing punk cello, percussion and some vocals we needed someone to play the classical lines as well so she was in. We had Ron on sax and Mouse would do backing vocals and the occasional lead vocal. I then advertised for a drummer and bass player and duly got 2 lads who knew their stuff. Then of course there was Misty on lead vocals. We did have a percussion player as well but he dropped out so we were left an 8 piece. People wonder why I hate doing rehearsals and don't do many live gigs, well here is a perfect example of why. Although I must point out I love playing live concerts. Since I improvise the band couldn't follow me and so most of the pressure would be on Avril and Ron who knew the songs best. Ron failed to turn up which didn't create a very good impression on the rest of the new band. After chasing him up we gave him an ultimatum about tuning up as he had become a bit unreliable so he decided he would quit. So we were now short of one of the key ingredients of the sound of the band with only a few weeks to go to our gig. Because my songs are unusual and often complicated it was hard work for a brand new line-up to learn and as we spent 2 hours waiting on Ron very little was achieved at this rehearsal. Luckily the drummer knew a sax player and he agreed to join the band temporarily for the gigs and then see how things went.

With some good results starting to happen airplay wise things were looking promising but there's always a hurdle that turns up. Avril was doing quite well and Ness was starting to get the hang of things but the new trio of members were struggling at the next rehearsal. Misty had turned up late to the rehearsal and looked in a bit of a state. She had chopped her hair off with a razor and looked awful, she looked gaunt and announced that her grandfather was dying. Anne was also not herself as she had chronic backache but had made a long journey to get along to this rehearsal. An hour into the rehearsal it all kicked off big style. Misty said this isn't working (which in one sense is accurate but you don't expect 7 new people thrown together to have it spot on an hour into the first proper rehearsal). Her comment would have been best served at the end of the 4-hour session taking me to one side and saying I'm concerned that we will need loads more rehearsals before we are good enough. Anne saw the despondent look on the other musician's faces after Misty's comment and had a go at her saying she was more trouble than she was worth. Misty then stormed out and I tried to smooth things over with the rest of the band because they were ready to leave after what she said. I then ran out of the rehearsal place to talk to Misty but she had vanished. So I went back and we finished the rehearsal with Anne taking the lead vocal since she knew the songs. I had expected Misty to come back at some point but she didn't. So my first port of call after the rehearsal was to drive to her place. But when I got there she wasn't in. To compound matters, (as was the case a lot of the time with Misty) her phone was disconnected for non-payment so there was no way to contact her and get things sorted out. I thought because she knew this she would contact me but she didn't so I had to eventually resort to sending her a letter to get her to call me. (no email back then).But this gave her 3 days (because of the weekend) to fester over things and work herself into a stupor over the whole incident. She had just assumed I deserted her and took Anne's side, which was not the case. If she had not stormed off so quickly or had been on the phone or at home when I came round I'm sure this incident would have been resolved quite quickly. By the end of this ill-fated rehearsal, the band had got quite a few of the songs together. But everyone was wondering what was going to happen next. The next thing was a clear the air meeting between Misty and me where she declared she had had a mental breakdown and didn't want to be in Box Office Poison any more. I put the sequence of events to her and gradually talked her around. She finally decided that she would do one more rehearsal and do the main gig that was lined up plus any T.V shows but after that, she would have to reconsider her feelings about whether or not she would continue in B.O.P. But she insisted part of the deal was that Anne was no longer in the band and that we may need to do a shorter set because of lack of rehearsals. I'd already spoken to Anne about the incident and she had already pre-empted what Misty might say. Anne said because she thought Misty was a very talented front person she should front the band and she had herself wanted to quit since the Teenage Sex video incident anyway but was just helping out till a new singer came along. If Misty demanded she leave it wouldn't be a problem. So I agreed to Misty's terms and the gig came around.

the famous photo below + a slight variation of the single sleeve

CHAPTER TWENTY-EIGHT

A NIGHT TO REMMEMBER

The big gig we were playing to tie in with the launch of *Think for Yourself,* was at Taylor's Jazz club just off Oxford Street (London). It was a fairly intimate venue and we were the headline of 6 acts. The entire band were on edge except me, I was very relaxed. Apart from having a jug of Sangria inside me, I invented The 'Pop Noir' philosophy and I tend to live it 100%. The first part of 'Pop Noir' especially in a live context is the Punk/Jazz attitude. To me, this should be self-explanatory. Punks used to just get up and play regardless of if they were good, bad, or indifferent; it was about the experience of the moment and doing it. It was never about rehearsing for 6 months until it's so smooth it's boring. The Jazz aspect is just about the improvising aspect of Jazz and not anything else. Some people misinterpret the Jazz-Punk attitude to mean we play Punk and Jazz style music, it's not, although there is a bit of Jazz in there it says on the packet, 'Attitude'. The best music has often been about attitude, from Jim Morrison to Johnny Rotten. I'd often had arguments with the editor of N.M.E. about this. He would often bleat on about the blandness in music and say no one was doing anything new or different. I pointed out that we were. He agreed but said since we didn't play guitars he couldn't feature us. (!!!!). I then said to him the problem he had with me was attitude 'I HAD ONE'. The majority of people N.M.E. were writing about couldn't string 2 words together and hated doing interviews or if they did, had nothing of interest to say. I was too outspoken which might not only offend some readers but advertisers as well so B.O.P were a no go area for N.M.E although they were happy to take money for adverts for our latest single. I remember being championed by many fanzines, some citing our music as the best and most original in 10 years and they were puzzled that N.M.E. didn't write about us'. They thought N.M.E. were champions of new music but sadly they were wrong.

Anyway, back to the gig. When I got up on stage I didn't know what I was going to play until I got there. Even though I'd written the songs. Every time I'd play Punk cello it would be different from every other time to make it a unique experience. I hate repeating myself as an artist that's why I'm a pioneer. Despite some band members not being fully aware of 'Pop Noir' attitude, lack of rehearsals meant I got the desired effect I wanted, which was everybody was on edge and this created its own strange energy that the audience could pick up on. Because of lack of rehearsals we had to do a short set of 6 or 7 songs instead of 15. With the more complicated arrangements like *Mysteries*, I had devised a way to make it work. In this song, everybody comes in at different stages of the song so I'd go around the stage tapping people on the shoulder with my cello bow when it was their turn to come in. It was like they were being knighted or something. A lot of the audience said after the gig they loved things like that, it was so unusual. Also whilst playing the castanets on one song they flew out of my hand and under the drum kit so I jumped off stage grabbed someone's empty beer glass and a folk from a bar snack someone had just eaten and played this as a percussion instead. Misty was on form despite the previous problems and sexing it up with the microphone stand, she was also wearing a red wig as she realised how bad her hacked-off hair had looked. We got a standing ovation from the packed club and then I went to the bar to get a drink. People were patting me on the back and asking to buy me a drink saying the set was brilliant. The barman also came up to us later and said he had worked at the club for 3 years and seen bands every single night but had never seen a band to touch us for originality, atmosphere and edge, we were in his opinion the best band ever to play there. He then wanted to know if we had any release out and so I gave him details of them.

I was ecstatic about the concert myself and loved every minute of it and had the bug to go on tour and everything. But everybody else was down. All they were talking about were the mistakes they made and so on. Misty was saying the same at first but once she heard the barman's comments followed by audience members saying similar she changed her tune. I pointed out to the other band members, if one person has the right to be down it was me since they were my songs and some were played at twice the normal speed. But I was far from unhappy because the basic songs got across and it was a unique experience and the majority of people at the gigs were not familiar with the songs anyway. A few of them were a bit happier after I'd said this but everybody has their own agenda and the majority of the band said they would do any T.V shows but would see how these went down before doing any more gigs or a tour.

I went to Taylor's 2 weeks later to see another band and many people came up to me and said 'Is your band playing tonight?' Some had come on the off chance we were, others were regulars who simply said we were the most exceptional band they had seen at Taylor's. Finally, I saw the barman who then pulled out all B.O.P's CD's from under the counter and asked me to sign them. So it was clear he was not bullshitting about what he said about us. It's a shame the rest of the band weren't there. The final lesson I learned, which I knew already, was that my image worked. Since I only did lead vocal on one song and Misty is the front person you would think that most people would not remember me but it seemed everybody did. Case closed for the defence M'Lord!

(Below ; Misty & Russell: right: Avril & Ness: Next page the band with our two front people)

Meanwhile, I was getting lots of good results for *Think For Yourself* from the media. Great reviews, reasonable airplay and half a dozen T.V plays for the video. Then one mainstream I.T.V. show called 'Rock Mania' wanted to do a special on us and to play a few of our videos and do a half-hour interview.

To be honest I didn't like being a plugger but it showed just how useless or what a con artist most pluggers were. I was a non-plugger and was getting much better results than any other plugger I had worked with or heard about on the lower end of the scale. Sadly, at the crucial point in our career Misty had lost the plot slightly. When I played our videos to Rock Manias producers they were all raving about how sexy and good-looking Misty was and they were all looking forward to meeting her on the day of the interview. I turned up first and one of the producers, Cath said; I really looked the part as a pop star. But when she saw Misty with me 10 minutes later she asked if she was my secretary and asked when Misty would be arriving. I said this was Misty and you could see that she was visibly shocked by Misty's appearance. She still had her cropped hair; she also wore glasses and wore clothes that were only one step up from a tramp. Although Misty coped reasonably well with the interview she wasn't on top form and it was up to me to carry the day with amusing comments and interesting information. Apart from *Think For Yourself,* the show also wanted to play the *Teenage Sex* video but Misty wouldn't allow it to be played because it wasn't her voice on the track. She had built up such a hatred of Anne that she was being unreasonable. So we lost extra exposure on the show. Rock Mania was shown twice and with all the other promotion done *Think For Yourself* became our most successful single since our debut release. We needed one final push to get into the charts but then Misty cracked up and booked herself into a mental hospital. It was beginning to feel like De-Ja Vu. With the lead singer out of action, the best I could do was interviews with radio and press, after this, the sales wound down. So there was no hit record but we had succeeded via 2 single releases in quick succession in raising our profile substantially. At least now most media people knew who we were and 'Pop Noir' music was being talked about a lot. Many musicians started forming 'Pop Noir' music style band including Mono and Goldfrapp. We were also influencing established bands like Pulp. I had a promotion stand at a Cult T.V. & film memorabilia exhibition and my assistant told me Jarvis Cocker got copies of all our Cult Themes and Box Office Poison albums. So it wasn't a surprise when Pulps next single was the 'Pop Noir' influenced *This is Hardcore*.

Misty's timing of a breakdown was terrible because her debut single also came out. The single sold on the back of Eleanor's tracks and it got decent reviews and some airplay but with no Misty or Eleanor there to promote it the impact of the single was minimal outside of Mod circles. At best it only served to promote The Waterloo Sunset Story album release. My previous label had become collectable and with some rare unreleased tracks, rare photos and the label's story not told before it was a decent release. It was more a labour of love than a vehicle for big record sales. But I had been a fan of cult labels myself and these always made good compilations. Sales wise the album broke even but I had spent quite a bit on advertising and posters for it.

Running a record label was very much a balancing act in more ways than one. In order to get Pinnacle behind my releases, which they did, I needed to show them we were committed as a label and this meant advertising, PR people, gigs, airplay and regular releases. So by the end of 97, I had spent all the money I had earned from Dr Martens and new sales income establishing the label and its acts but we only just about broke even. The music business is a costly one to work in but I was managing to compete with the majors on about 10% of their budget per release or act. The legendary Tony Wilson of Factory record and a mate of mine said to me, staying in business was the definition of a successful Indie label

HISTORIC JUSTICE

As this tumultuous year drew to a close I was also facing a stressful court case and wondering if I was next in line for a breakdown. Jane Wallace had failed to pay back the money she had taken off the record label for plugging services that were not rendered and I took her to court. I then became the first person in the history of the music business to successfully sue a plugger.

It's a shame it wasn't filmed, as it would be an eye-opener for anyone wishing to hire a plugger. All the evidence was heavily in my favour and she had none. On a contractual basis, she had resigned after 2 weeks of a signed contract for a six-week promotion. So the judge said straight away there was a breach of contract and that if she had done any work at all it had been for only 2 weeks and that two-thirds of money paid should be refunded immediately because of that alone. In her contract, she said she would do mailouts to 200 Independent radio stations as well as all the top people elsewhere. All she provided was one proof of posting card with 6 names on it and these might not have even been for my packages. Jane said nobody was interested in the record and that's why she gave up. The judge asked her for written proof of this. She replied that nobody was prepared to put this in writing to back up her case, not even these so-called close personal contacts. I on the other hand provided proof of airplay lists and letters from media people confirming that they had played my records and videos and had not even been approached by Jane Wallace. She visibly sank when this evidence was produced because it really did sum up that she was either incompetent or just a con artist. All she introduced in her favour was her husband's testimony that she had done lots of maillots and phone calls.

The judge then said she should repay me in full plus court costs. So I got the record labels money back and she had to pay both her and my court costs. I thought that would be the last I would hear of her but I was wrong. The music business is a small world sometimes.

CHAPTER TWENTY-NINE

BREATHING

After the hectic year that was 97 by 1998 things had quietened down on the release front. We had done the singles to raise awareness now it was time to shift some albums, get some finance in and take the band to the next level. So the first priority was to finish off the Heavy Breathing Decade album. I have covered most tracks recorded already, now here's the story of the final 5 tracks. Two tracks had been knocking around for ages, both from the Eleanor Rigby period. She had done a track called *For the Video* written by David Hubbard. It was a song about making porno videos. It had always been a good song and since the subject matter was perfect for this album I decided to include it. Misty had recovered enough to do a few days recording and I had done the backing tracks for many of the songs but found this one tricky so Misty did the fairground style keyboards on it. By this stage, we had also perfected the French B-movie style backing vocals at this stage. (Also used to good effect by Goldfrapp) The other song was one that Eleanor never recorded. Her first drummer Paul had started playing a bluesy guitar riff on an acoustic guitar one day, which I quite liked so I wrote some lyrics and did a vocal melody. I had visited Denmark before I was a DJ there. It was a weekend city trip. A common thing at the time was some people put you up in their homes for a small price. (So Air B & B is nothing new). I ended staying with this gorgeous 30 something lady who wasted no time in coming into my bedroom and shagging my brains out. The reason I mention this was because when I returned to the UK I found I had NSU (a relatively small but irritating venereal infection). A trip to the V.D clinic was then on the cards. So this is what I wrote a song about, calling it *Penicillin Passion*. It's a very jaunty catchy little number with some humour to it. With other more appropriate material coming along all the time for Eleanor this song was sidelined to the demo box and forgotten about. Because of the nature of the H.B.D album, it was a perfect song to resurrect and record. It's the least 'Pop Noir' track of the album but it does have a lot of innovative touches to it. There is a thing called a guitar harmonic, which is situated at the furthest end of a guitar. It has a unique sound to it. I had this sound and a bottle sound on my keyboards, so I used these for some of the riffs in the song, then added a nice muted trumpet to the track as well as the usual cello. This track also has some great sax on it, which is a story in itself. B.O.P were back down to a two-piece of Misty & me when we started to record these tracks then out of the blue I got an e-mail from a girl called Abbey who said she was a sax player looking to join a band and could I help her. I said it just so happened we needed a new sax player. She asked when and where I wanted her to do an audition to which I replied 'We are recording at the moment and since improvisation is a key part of the sax work why don't you just come along and play on the tracks. If I like what you play you'll be on the record and in the band straight away, if not I won't use any of your contribution and look elsewhere for a new sax player.' She thought it was a bit of an unusual way to do an audition but came and did a great job, with Penicillin Passion being perhaps her best track. Most bands practice many months before recording or gigging. Here was Abbey with not even one rehearsal behind her going straight on a release Naturally, I told her the 'Pop Noir' philosophy and played her some of Ron's work. She picked up the idea very quickly. Like all new band members, I re-christened her and called her Daffodil Lil. (because I believe she was originally from Wales). Sadly she didn't last very long because of a personal problems with a boyfriend and the fact that she was living up in Cambridge at the time.

The final 3 tracks were all solo compositions by me. Although there are 5 co-writes on the album it is a testament to the fact that I practice what I preach and that out of 20 or so songs I had written since the 'Twilight Zone' album I only deemed 3 solo written songs fit to grace this album. But many say they are amongst the best I have written. Although I wouldn't go that far, I would say they are all very good songs indeed.

I Want You All The Time, is perhaps the catchiest song I have ever written. At face value, it seems like a catchy sing-along type song. However, it has some dark parts in the song that portray the real message of what the song is all about, which is that there are too many people around who are jealous and possessive and trying to control or ruin peoples lives. (I suppose you could call this song the daughter of *Think For Yourself*). Musically it has an unusual arrangement for a catchy song and the cello riffs and sixties organ dominate the song. But what makes it one of my best is Misty's vocal. It's a very tricky song to sing and I wanted it sung in a very specific way and Misty mastered this fairly quickly because at least on an artistic level we were still very much in tune. It's hard to imagine anyone else singing this song and along with Louie Louie, these are probably the best vocal performances of Misty's life as far as Box Office Poison goes.

A while after H.B.D came out Ed Ball (formerly of the Mod band The Times) was a main player at Creation Records and was going out with Misty and heard the track and said it was a sure-fire 'number one' if ever he'd heard one. He played it to Alan McGee, head Honcho at Creation who said the same and within minutes they were looking to poach Misty from me but one of the main reasons was they thought Misty had written the track and they wanted the song as well. Misty informed them I had written it and McGee had turned down B.O.P in the past and I didn't really like Alan much when I met him anyway. So Misty said there was no way I'd let the song be recorded for release on Creation, Alan then said he may have got it wrong initially and they would reconsider signing B.O.P but then Creation went out of business when Sony bought them out and Sony just kept Oasis. I doubt I'd have gone with them anyway.

A top influential European fanzine called 'Original Sin' were big Box Office Poison fans and called the next track *All I Want's a Baby,* a classic song and the best song to come out for 10 years. Musically again it's catchy but unusual. I decided I'd put an ultra-catchy backing vocal on it as the main hook of the song. It also has a hypnotic moody bassline and an Indie guitar band type drumbeat that I hadn't used before plus moody organ and arpeggio harpsichord filling it out and Abbie does another great 'Pop Noir' sax on it. Punk cello and brass bring up the rear. Misty again excels at this song. The song was based on my experience with a girl called Teresa, with who I had a one-night stand after splitting with Eleanor and returned to Djing. She wanted a baby with me after that one night. I had also heard that there are girls around known as Sperm Bandits, who are not interested in getting married or the hassle of relationships, they just want a baby and go on one night stands until they get pregnant but never inform the would-be father that they've had the baby. The final song on the album was *Sex On the Internet.* Some said it was like '*My Generation*' but for today. It's catchy but in a strange way, since it has a very unusual arrangement. It has a dance feel to it but it's not really a dance track. It has a very hypnotic high-pitched bass and percussion riff. Bass and cello drive it along and a brass line adds a lot of atmosphere to the track. Having included so many catchy pop songs on this album I thought there must be room for something very experimental and cutting edge and this was it.

Despite its cutting edge it has proven to be one of the most popular tracks on the album. The lyrics especially are popular. My opinion is that most people in the world are voyeurs but if you accuse someone of that they deny it. But I find it quick to prove. Most people watch soap operas, read the newspapers, or even look out of the window and check out what the neighbours are doing. That is all voyeurism in one form or another. It's people's natural instinct to find out what other people are doing via T.V or in the press and the Internet. But people think voyeurism is related to sex. How many people can say that if a sex scene comes on in a film on T.V that they don't watch it and run out of the room including females? It's common knowledge that many girls watch porn on the net these days and most men who say they don't are lying. But it's all voyeurism at the end of the day. So I wanted to write a song about this subject. So I started to cruise the Internet and stumbled on some adult dating sites. So I read a few girls' profiles and I couldn't believe what I was reading. Some said things like I want a shag and I want it now. Others were looking for cybersex and some wanted to exchange naughty photos. There are many millions of peoples on these sites and you don't need me to tell you porn sites are the most visited on the net but how many people would admit to it? So I decided to combine the voyeurism idea and reflecting what was going on in people's lives and in particular on the Internet. I believe most peoples life's have been revolutionised by the net in one way or another and Internet dating and porn are part of tens of millions of peoples lives world-wide whether they like to admit it or not.

I can also reveal exclusively here there is a 16th hidden track on the H.B.D album. It goes with the theme of the album and has caused embarrassment to a few people. All you need to do is leave the CD on after track 15 finishes and it will suddenly come on about 5 minutes later (That's the only way to hear it, you can't select it) I don't want to spoil the surprise so won't say what it is but make sure the vicar is not popping around for tea when it's on as that's what happened to one person and they still haven't forgiven me.

I WANT YOU ALL THE TIME

Fatal attraction, physical attraction, explosive action.

Chemical reaction, intelligent retraction, more and more action

That's us, that's us

I want you, I want you, I want you, I want you, I want you all the time

Everyday and every night

I want you, I want, I want you, want you all the time

I want you I want you I want you, I want you, want you all my life

A sudden movement, a certain look, His body froze and then it shook

He opened me up like a book, a passionate chapter, then the hook.

Possession is aggression Obsession is regression

I want you, I want you, I want you, I want you, I want you all the time

I want you, I want you, I want you, I want you, want you all the time

Possession is aggression Obsession is regression

Kiss goodbye to your mind

I want you, I want you, I want you, I want you, I want you all the time

I want you I want you I want you, want you all my life

I want you …I want you

Surfing on the seedy side, It's something that I cant hide

I slip and I slide but I always enjoy the ride.

You'll always be part of me.

I would later return to the internet for some very interesting adventures but my priority was getting the *Heavy Breathing Decade* album out.

In some ways, I had been surprised that Anne and I had stayed together for so long. But the open relationship is probably what helped its longevity. Anne is still one of my best friends even now. However, I noticed a change come 98 for both of us. We started meeting more people on the side and then a new girl came into my life that I thought had potential on many levels. Her name was Martina, she had long dark curly hair and was an extremely sexy German.

Above the unusual cover (normally in orange) The title is a play on words as I am also an environmentalist. I wanted something to reflect this (hence the gas masks & chemical suits) but of course the album was all about sex and only Misty naked and the title portrayed this. So, effectively it's a thought-provoking sleeve with a message. Although 4 characters appear, I am 3 of them and Anne took those photos, I took the one of Misty. The Instruments also reflect the sounds on the album.

CHAPTER THIRTY

THE NEW MANAGER

With funds running low I was wondering how to promote the Heavy Breathing Decade album. With no touring band and no new videos, apart from reviews and a few bits of airplay, there was not a lot I could do. Since I had significantly raised B.O.P's profile via the recent singles I thought it may be time to try and get a major record deal again, especially as these songs were very catchy. Although no great fan of networking around the music business I always liked to show my face at PRS events, which were usually once a month. It was always good for the odd contact as well as some fresh blood, or should I say fresh female blood. (What can I say I'm a thirsty person). At one such event, I met a lady called Irene who did a songwriter's showcases. At one such event, I had sex in the middle of a club surrounded by hundreds of people with her best friend. I can hear the disbelief emanating from your brain so I'll explain. As Bill Clinton would say 'What is your definition of sex?' Intercourse is the main one. But I think if one of the 2 parties involved cums in some way that is a sex act. At one of Irene's showcases, I met her friend Sue who fancied me. I was wearing my long stylish Matrix-type coat (it could have its own biog) and in the middle of the dancefloor (during a few slow tracks), I wrapped it around both of us. I then kissed her and stuck my hand straight down her knickers and played around until she came right in the middle of a crowd of people. How many people realised what we were up to I don't know, not many I would think. The next time I met Sue was at Irene's Xmas party where we soon found ourselves on Irene's bathroom floor this time going all the way, but that's another story.

The reason I brought up Irene is that I was so exhausted by having to do the plugging, the PR, the producing and numerous other things I was desperate for a new manager and that's when Irene introduced me to a German manager, Martina. I know people always say don't mix business with pleasure but I wanted to mix everything I could with this frauline. However, she was married so I settled for the management. She loved the music so that was a good start but she wasn't that experienced as a manager and this will blow your mind. As I entered her flat for the first time on her bookshelf in pride of place was my 'Music Business Bastards'. book. She had learnt most of her trade from my book. After we laughed about that we agreed on a 6 months trial period to see how we got on and if she could get the sort of results I wanted. Her experiences so far were managing Indie guitar type bands and getting them gigs on what was commonly known as the 'Camden Circuit'. Although she thought gigs were always helpful she felt we were established enough not to have to do these gigs. She was a member of the manager's forum and said she was getting lots of contacts through it. She was impressed that we had a top distributor in Pinnacle and said the priority would be to get behind 'Heavy Breathing Decade' and create a buzz around it then she would try and get a licensing deal where a major label would put a bigger push behind it. Being mister originality and a rebel to boot I decided on a very unorthodox approach and idea to launch the 'Heavy Breathing Decade' album. My ex Ministry of Ska partner Dick had kept in touch from time to time and he had invited me to a launch party for a compilation of new acts he was putting out. He claimed he had lots of media coming as well as major labels. I felt I owed him one for ripping me off previously. So I got to the venue early with Martina and a few friends armed with boxes full of our album, press releases and fact sheets. Whilst the majority of the media were at the bar with Dick we broke into the main room housing Dicks CD's and promotion material. We put his stuff behind ours and effectively hijacked the media for own launch. Later on, there was to be a concert and I knew one of the bands who just happened to owe me a favour and I asked them to make up a story about their equipment going missing. I then saw Dick and told him he had a crisis on his hands and a band wanted to see him urgently. I lead him to the band whilst Martina approached the media and ushered them to the room where our CD's were. I then joined her and we gave out all the CDs and chatted up as many journalists as we could and then left. This resulted in some quite good reviews and a few interested record labels.

Never a person to do only one thing at a time I decided there was a need for a new Cult Themes album to raise funds and keep Pinnacle happy. So I started thinking about acts to appear on 'Cult Themes from the Seventies Vol.2'. One such act was Bellatrix, an Icelandic band who I'd heard on Dick's compilation (just mentioned) and I wanted to see them live at a venue in London. I was thinking about who might like to go with me and then almost telepathically Misty called me.

Whether Misty was manic-depressive I don't know but after the high of recording some great tracks for the H.B.D album, she'd had another breakdown and sectioned herself. She had just come out of the hospital and was in a semi-secure hostel. All her friends had deserted her so she called me to come and get her out of where she was being held. When I turned up it wasn't a pretty sight as her arms were full of recently healed cut marks and she had butchered her hair once again. But she was in high spirits and wanted to go out. She put on a wig and a catsuit and we went off to see Bellatrix in a venue known as the 'Water Rats' near Kings Cross. They were one of the best live acts I had seen in a long time and I immediately offered them a deal to do a Cult Themes track with more to follow if this were successful. However, they wanted to do *A View to a Kill*, The Bond theme (which is 80's') I wanted them to do *Moonraker* instead and they weren't keen. So I pointed out that it had to be 70's but they could choose any theme as long as it was a cult one. They seemed happier about this, but my presence at the venue that night did them a big favour and me none. I was known by many A&R people at other record labels and they always kept an eye on what acts Future Legend was interested in. As soon as Polydor and Fierce Panda saw my interest they both offered Bellatrix a deal and they signed with Fierce Panda soon after meaning that they couldn't do my Cult Themes album or anything else with me. They got a few minor hits singles and had an album release then got dropped about a year later, became disillusioned and split up.

Anyway, at least Misty and I saw a good gig and Misty wasn't long in getting drunk (mixed probably with medication) and threatening to beat up the doorman as we left. I then attempted to drive Misty back to her hostel. However, just before we reached Kings Cross central my car broke down. I called the A.A. to come to fix it.

Whilst we were waiting Misty was dying to go to have a pee and to my surprise she just whipped off her catsuit and stood by the side of the road naked with dozens of people walking by. Then she just pissed on the curb saying to passers-by in a Johnny Rotten style vibe who the fuck are you looking at. I thought at one point she was going to get up and piss over one guy's shoes as he hovered around for the spectacle instead of moving on. She got back into the car and was putting her catsuit back on when the Police arrived and asked us to step out of the car, they then accused Misty of being a prostitute and me being her pimp. When I explained the car break down they checked the car and saw I was telling the truth. Then they apologised and fixed my car and sent us on our way. It was a hysterical incident but it could have easily ended up with a night in the cells.

I finally got Misty back to her abode and went in for a drink. Then not for the first time when she has been drunk she declared that she loved me and that she was sure I was the one she would end up with at the end of the day, so we had a kiss and a cuddle and I left before it went any further as I wasn't keen to get my head scrambled. Besides she was still recovering from a breakdown so I was not sure how serious to take anything she said although she did say similar things long after she recovered but only when drunk.

The other new female in my life Martina further scrambled my head. I knew there was definite chemistry between us but she had kept me at arm's length by being married. But one night she invited me to a party. I got there before her and was busy dancing with a girl I met. Martina arrived at the party and cut in and danced with me. Quite a few drinks later we were in a tight embrace on the dance floor and I asked her why she didn't come with her husband. She said she didn't care for him any more and that it was an arranged marriage to keep him in the country, as he was an Arab. Armed with this new info I went for it and kissed her, she responded by kissing me back a few moments later and so I felt this relationship was going to go somewhere. By the following day, however, she was acting like nothing had happened and when I brought it up she just said I'm still living with my husband but when he moves out we will see what happens but let's just keep things business for now. (that old cliché)

As an innovative record producer, my idol was Joe Meek and I was pleasantly surprised when the Joe Meek Appreciation Society contacted me and offered me an honorary status with the organisation citing me as the nearest thing to Joe Meek and his natural successor. I went to several events and saw a few concerts and was interviewed a few times by their magazine 'Thunderbolt'. At one meeting they were asking me about my next release and I said it would be 'Cult Themes From the 70's Vol.2'. Many of them had all the previous volumes and one said I noticed you changed the format on 'Cult Themes from the 70's Vol.1' and put a previous hit act on in the shape of The Lambretta's instead of just breaking new acts. I said I wanted to keep the idea fresh and do something unexpected. They then said it would be a good idea to get one of Joe's acts out of retirement and produce them on the next themes album since some of those had number one hits and I was supposed to be the new Joe Meek.

I agreed and The Honeycombs sprang to mind as I always loved their number one hit *Have I the Right*. Somebody had the lead singers number and so my next port of call would be to ring him. However, before I left 2 other members piped up saying what about Glenda, she deserves a chance. As a Joe Meek fan, I was familiar with Glenda Collins and I had quite a few of her releases. She was perhaps one of the unluckiest acts in the 60's. I could see why the J.M fans rated her; she had a great voice and made some brilliant records. She had a typical 60's girl singer look and was dark-haired and pretty. Vocally the nearest thing to her was to Lulu. Rumour had it that despite Joe being gay he nearly married Glenda. (Mostly likely it would have been for appearances since homosexuality was still illegal at the time.) Anyway, early in Glenda's career, she was signed to Decca but a series of average singles had failed to make an impression so she was let go in 1963 and Joe picked her up for his label. Her first 2 releases *Gotta Pick a Baby* and the much better *I Lost My Heart At A Fairground* were good but got lost in The

Beatles led Mersey Beat revolution, then because of Joe's leanings towards male acts she had to often wait on the sidelines. He was also putting out a new single every day. This added to Glenda's next release being amongst a stack of releases from Joe at the time and when *Have I the Right* by The Honeycombs hit number one then the focus went on them.

Joe's other favourite Heinz, formerly of the Tornadoes with a hit of his own in *Just like Eddie* was also getting the priority treatment, especially as he was Joe's boyfriend. By the time Glenda's 2 brilliant singles *There's Something I've Got To Tell You* and *It's Hard to Believe* came out in 66 Joe had run out of money and since Payola via Pirate radio was still the order of the day the singles hardly got any airplay. In early 1967, Joe killed himself and his landlady leaving one almighty mess behind for the multitude of artists that remained. Had another bigger company pushed Glenda she would have surely taken off and been known as one of the greatest female singers of the sixties. Devastated by Joe's death and with all the business left in a mess, she found herself without a deal and faded off the scene. It would take a further 20 years for the rights to be sorted out and for Glenda to get her own 'Best of' compilation called '*This Little Girls Gone Rockin*' released in 1997. (which still sells well today) The Joe Meek society gave me details of how to contact her but they were not optimistic about her doing anything since she had not been seen since 1991 and all efforts to coax her out of retirement had failed.

Upon hearing this I decided to also carry on with my other plan to contact The Honeycombs. The band were much more than their number one hit *Have I the Right,* they made quite a few excellent records and in fact, had other hits but hardly anyone except Meek fans remembers them.

Anyway, I was initially expecting one or the other of these former Meek acts to come back to me but to my surprise both got back to me quite quickly. Glenda was keen to do it after hearing a previous themes album and a few of Eleanor's singles. So it looked like I had the right credentials. I decided the track that suited her best was *Avenues and Alleyways* (*The Protectors theme*) I hit it off with Glenda and am still friends with her now.

Next, I met up with Dennis the lead singer of The Honeycombs. The band hadn't played together since 1969 and Dennis was performing in a Blues duo. Often with a lot of these 60's bands doing the rounds, you get one original member, often not even the singer. So, I decided if I were going to produce The Honeycombs, I wanted the original 60's line-up complete with girl drummer, which they were notorious for. Dennis said he had checked out the themes albums and was impressed and keen to do one. He said he talked to the other ex-members and they all liked my production and agreed to reform and wanted to do the Bond theme *Live and Let Die.*

Ironically it turned out their last 60s number one was an instrumental of *Goldfinger* in Japan. It was also their last ever release before they broke up. *Have I the Right* was a number one hit in nearly every country in the world selling a staggering 27 million copies. However they did have a few other number ones after that including 6 in Japan. Even in the UK., they had more top 30 hits with *That's the Way & Is It Because* (the latter as good as *Have I the Right*) Ray Davies of The Kinks also wrote a song especially for The Honeycombs called *Emptiness* as he rated the band highly.

Despite selling such a huge amount of records the band had rarely seen any of the money made from them and had been hit with a huge tax bill for millions and couldn't pay it. This was eventually resolved.

However, I was pleased to see the band were not bitter about this. Dennis attitude was he got to travel the world 6 times, stayed in the best hotels and had lots of girls after him. The alternative was working at Dagenham motors and looking forward to receiving his pension. He said you couldn't put a price on the experience. Of course, now he was older the money would have been nice but there was more to life than money.

(Glenda below from her heyday + Honeycombs)

CHAPTER THIRTY-ONE

THE TRAITOR

I had met a record label called EMG as they wanted to licensed Eleanor's single *You Only Live Twice* for a number one's hits compilation that also featured The Supremes, Dusty Springfield, Fleetwood Mac etc. The man in charge, Gerry also wanted to hire me as a producer. Amongst the productions he heard he said he really liked Box Office Poison, which was music to me ears of course. I told him we were looking for a deal and to endear me to him he told me about a rights fair in Germany, Pop-Kom and said he knew a contact there that would be interested in B.O.P. He added that he would recommend us and set up a meeting. Martina was already going to this rights fair as it was on her home turf giving her an advantage over English speaking labels, so I thought she could do the meeting and at least see what the offer was. She agreed this was a good opportunity. However Martina turned up to the meeting and persuaded the label to sign another band instead of us and we didn't get any sort of deal. Very bizarre!

After her return from Germany Martina kept a low profile for a few weeks and wouldn't return my calls. I finally caught up with her but she would only speak to me through her letterbox saying she no longer wanted to manager Box Office Poison and that's all she wanted to say, no explanation as to what had gone on. I waited for a while outside her place and she finally came out, she saw me and ran off. I think she thought I was going to run her over or something. It was a strange business. I started digging around contacts who had also been at Pop-Kom and who knew Martina. It turned out there was another manager who had been keen to get into her knickers for a long time (I had met the guy and believed it to be true). Martina had finally split from her husband before she went to Germany this other guy put pressure on her to help him instead of us. He promised her joint management of the band he was managing and it appeared they were about to break big by supporting Oasis on a world tour. The deal was she had to be his girlfriend and drop us. So that's what she did and never bothered doing anything for us and betrayed us by getting a deal for this other guys band instead, using the contact I had provided who were very keen to sign one British band to their label. She was frightened of how I would react and thought the best policy was to ignore me and I'd move on. I wasn't happy and even less so as she never returned a thousand pounds worth of stock she had. So that put me off having a manager ever again and we lost our opportunity in Germany at a time it would have been very helpful (I also still had a bit of a following there from Eleanor's loyal fans). I don't take any great satisfaction from other peoples misfortune but when I heard that Oasis had cancelled their world tour a few weeks later and knew that's the only thing Martina's new band had going for them, it looked like she'd be back to square one and I haven't heard anything about her in the music business since then.

I then decided at this point to just throw myself into the new Cult Themes album. First off, I had to dish out a few favours. Mark Aquera who had made our videos had kept to our budget so I promised I'd put his group 'Ambassadors of Om' on the next Cult Themes. They wanted to do the Gerry Anderson show theme *Space 1999.* They were a lazy bunch and initially just wanted to sample the original record and remix it but without paying a royalty for the sample. I soon kicked that into touch. Instead they did it most ly on computer and gave it a dubby feel. They were not the best band in the world but the track sounds=ed interesting and contemporary. It wasn't a great session either and I nearly walked out on it when everybody started smoking dope and kept getting their parts wrong. If it hadn't been a favour I doubt I'd have put the band on the album at all.

Next up was Hareem, he was an Indian lad that had played on Misty's solo tracks. As a thank you, I said I'd put him on the album. He went out under the name of 'Illegal Immigrant' and did *The Rockford Files*. As I was in Joe Meek mode I wanted to try and record a few tracks as Joe would have done via 4 tracks. This was one such track and the reverb was very much to the fore. It turned out to be a very powerful track and nobody believed it was done on a 4-track machine. It had some good psychedelic touches and an interesting arrangement and I got him to use a lot of guitar effects that many musicians never use. With the majority of well-known classic 70's Cult Themes covered on Vol.1, Volume 2 would be both a gamble and a pleasure. Although this album does include some well-known tunes like the 2 tracks already mentioned plus *The Streets of San Francisco* and some Bond Themes the rest of the album would be made up of not so well known tracks but still cult themes. I wanted to concentrate on the lesser-known classics written by the best Cult Themes writers such as John Barry and Lalo Schifrin. (Most famous for Mission Impossible)

Apart from Box Office Poison the band that most people now looked forward to appearing on a Cult Themes album was The Incredibly Strange Film Band. They were big Schifrin fans and wanted to do 2 Schifrin tracks. *Magnum Force* (The theme from Dirty Harry 2) and *Enter the Dragon*. The BBC ended up favouring this version of the track to the original. Pat from I.S.F.B knew his stuff so choosing this track may not have been a coincidence. Both tracks are very funky and jazzy and suit this 10-piece band down to the ground. With my 'Pop Noir' style production I added lashings of atmosphere to both tracks and made both better than the original versions. Pat was a guitarist and also came up with some great guitar sounds on these tracks to give them extra distinction. I added a bit of humour at the beginning of *Dirty Harry* track and got Pat to mimic Clint Eastwood saying 'Do you feel lucky Punk' and echoing it into the start of the track. With *Enter the Dragon* I brought out the oriental flavour more by adding oriental instruments like koto, finger cymbals, gongs and so on to the proceedings. Another big band I came across who also specialised in live theme shows were E.L.B.O.W who had come out of the easy listening scene inspired by the Cult Themes trend, I had a lot of fun with them. They had all learnt *The Streets of San Francisco* but I told them to be aware of each other's parts. When they arrived at the studio I told them all to switch parts and I re-arranged some of the track, the band were certainly put through their paces. But I had also worked out individual parts to let each person shine on their own instrument. By switching say the organ to play the bass line and bass to play guitar and brass to play organ parts it gave the song and distinctive sound and feel from the original version. This album featured 3 Bond themes, which went from one extreme to the other.

Although I had wanted to do a sixties enthused *Live and Let Die,* The Honeycombs had other ideas and wanted to do a more 'Guns and Roses' type version. We ended up somewhere in the middle plus some Ska on top. They also wanted the track to capture their live feel rather than the Joe Meek style. I wasn't over the moon about this but since they had gone to the trouble of reforming I felt I had to compromise. I hit it off particularly well with the drummer Honey who had been famous for being the first ever girl drummer in a band and we flirted a lot together. The session was quite fun because I got to hear a lot of stories about Joe Meek and once again was likened to him but by the end of the session, the band said it was the best recording of their career and 10 times better than any of Joe's productions. Strangely though I disagree. I felt Joe tracks were better than this. That's not to say this track sounded crap because it sounded very good I also added some innovation to the track that really went into Joe Meek territory. I asked the bass player, Honey's brother, John to do some bass overdubs like slides, big notes, and other incidental bits. He said it was unheard of for a bass player to do any overdubs. Maybe so but it wasn't the first time I'd done it. Also, I tried to get Honey to do some drum overdubs on the floor toms to give it an unusual feel and atmosphere but she found it difficult to play another drum track along with her own track as she had not had to do it before. So I did a few bits myself, I then added some timpani and organ to the track and when the album came out it was these unusual parts on the song that people noticed more but Honeycombs fans did seem to like the track overall.The band themselves did extremely well considering the amount of time they hadn't played together. It was also an ambition fulfilled to produce a Joe Meek act with another to follow.

When Glenda turned up at the studio the engineer Jez was shocked to see how old she was. But it's not about age. She was very nervous having not been in a recording studio for over 30 years and found it a bit daunting at first but she had faith in me and I soon got her to relax. Her voice was still as special as it had been and that familiar menace it had really suited the lyric in the song *Avenues and Alleyways* (*The Protectors theme*). It didn't take her many takes either. The only stumbling block came when I asked her to do backing vocals. She said in the 60's specialist backing singers, 'The Ladybirds' came in to do backing vocals unlike a lot of singers today who do their own in the studio. She had a brief go but didn't feel comfortable with doing it so I came up with an alternative idea of keyboard voices. This gave it an unusual feel of menace meets easy listening. There are some nice touches on this track but around this time I'd run very low on money and my studio time was limited and I've never been 100% happy with the drums on the track. But I'm pleased to have worked with a singer I really rated and to let people know that she was SOMEBODY. After the album came out I got her an agent as she was keen to do some concerts but backing band problems meant that it never materialised. (But I also got a nice phone call from the songwriters of the track the famous, Mitch Murray & Peter Callender who'd written many a number one hits, saying how much they loved this version. (Job done!).

I mentioned a lady called Irene Bull before who introduced me to Martina; well she used to put on new talent showcases. I discovered the 2 acts that would do the other 2 Bond themes at these showcases, which would turn out to be both the best Bond theme and the worst. Joan Martin (aka Phoenix. J) was an oriental songbird from Singapore where she had a top 30 album released. She had married an Englishman and come to live in Ross on Wye in Herefordshire and Peter her husband was determined to make her career a successful one in the UK. but they were struggling. Apart from some of the well-known acts already mentioned who I had influenced into doing 'Pop Noir' style tracks, Joan was the first new act I'd met who was doing something similar only she called it Asian Fusion. Of course, I'd been doing it a lot longer but it was nice to find a kindred spirit. She was petite and cute and had a voice that reminded me of one of my favourite singers, 'Diana Ross'. One track I had some great ideas for was The Bond theme *Moonraker.* Shirley Bassey had done the original but unlike *Goldfinger.* (Which was unbeatable. So I didn't even attempt it) and *Diamonds Are Forever,* I felt on this, her third Bond theme she had just gone through the motions. The music was not very inspiring so I felt this was one theme I could really go to town on.

The track was becoming a problem track for me though because I had already offered it to Bellatrix and even asked Anne to do it as her final recording, which she declined. I was beginning to think this track would never get done. But in the end, it turned out Joan was the perfect candidate for it. A lot of bullshit is spoken about having to record in an expensive 48 track studios to get great results. Maybe an incompetent engineer needs this but a good producer can get great results from anything from a 4 track upwards as I proved on the Themes from the 60's albums I'd done and of course Joe Meek had done before me. I had certainly mixed things up by including recordings from 4 tracks to 30 tracks on some themes albums (including this one) and nobody can tell which is which. So it's about what you do and your degree of skill and imagination. Joan had her own 8 track home studio and I felt this adequate to do the job. I had asked Joan to just put together the basic track and I would work on it when I arrived but she decided to try and be clever and do the whole track herself and presented me with a finished version. It was awful and made me cringe. I'm not talking out of tune or anything here. She had done a bland R&B version that had zero atmosphere. I trashed it immediately and started the track from scratch. Unfortunately, Joan was suffering from music business 'Bullshit City'. She was getting turned down everywhere and was advised to just do similar to the recent charts. Desperate to get a deal she threw out her great Asian Fusion approach to try and sound like everybody else around doing bland R n B, which was a real shame. (It still didn't get a deal though and she seemed to be constantly chasing her tail). I decided there would be plenty of Asian instruments in this track. I started it playing a hypnotic koto riff playing a percussion part underpinned with an echoey big-sounding bass drum. Then along came the familiar Bond type strings reminiscent of *You Only Live Twice,* played by Joan, then a moody bass line. I then got Joan to do haunting and dreamy vocal and backing vocals that make the hairs on the back of your neck stand up and sounded very ghostly, atmospheric and haunting and as 'Pop Noir' as it gets. Bits of percussion fly across the track like birds in-flight. I then came up with a new middle 8 for the song, which was to get Joan to play a variation of *You Only Live Twice* on a Chinese flute. It was far and away the best 'Pop Noir' production I did on any track except Box Office Poisons ones at that point. When I played it to Anne she nearly cried saying if she had known I was going to do such a brilliant production and arrangement as that she'd have done the track and was now sorry that she hadn't. She said I was at the top of my game with this track and the album would be worth getting for this alone. Joan also learned a valuable lesson doing this track. She had recorded many tracks at home and had a babysitter for her young twins. The babysitter had never said a word before about Joan's original music but came into the studio when I was mixing *Moonraker,* saying that it was one of the best tracks she had heard in many years and far and away the best thing Joan had ever done. She was raving about it for days after. Joan also had some pre-conceived ideas about recording equipment that did surprise me. She had learnt about producing her own tracks through music business manuals and magazines and when I said I wasn't going to use a compressor on her voice she was shocked. She said it's standard procedure to put compression on vocals when producing them. Standard procedures for morons, maybe but if you put compression on something the sound hits an artificial ceiling and stops the voice from going where it should go. One of the key parts of a haunting vocal is to let it flow in the track and compression would spoil that. Compression for vocals was introduced to stop having drastic level changes in vocals throughout a track and is valid quite a lot of the time but since Joan was such a good singer she didn't need it.

Another coincidence that cropped up when producing Joan was, she had been ripped off for £3,000 by guess who?...Yes, none other than Jane Wallace. They said they were going to sue her but hadn't got around to it yet but were heartened by my result against her. A final coincidence was Joan lived 10 miles from where Joe Meek was born and I had just been invited to an appreciation society weekend at Newent to check out all Joe's related sites and meet his niece. (Good timing)

The other band I had discovered at Irene's showcase was a Mod band called 'The Club'. They were very reminiscent of The Small Faces and the lead singer sang as good as Steve Marriott. The bass player was also like a young cheeky Paul McCartney and they got a great reception to their set especially from girls. Since I had a good Mod track record I had high hopes for this lot. However, come the recording session, it was a disaster. The 2 main attractions of the band, the singer and bass player had left the band but the other band members had neglected to tell me this and just turned up as a three-piece. I should have just sent them packing but I had to pay for the recording session anyway so I thought I'd see what I could do. Because they half expected me to send them away they hadn't really learnt the song so I had to start from scratch. I came up with a very good Jam Mod type arrangement that worked well on the song but the singer wasn't that great and I felt a bit cheated as I had signed one band and effectively got another. So out of 400 tracks, I have produced this is one of the few I am not totally happy with. Strangely, as an instrumental, it sounds as good as most Mod records so it does have some good qualities. It was quite popular in the end so maybe it's just me being overly fussy. It was just that I know how great the track could have been with the original line-up.

Misty was raring to go for her obligatory solo spot and because we were both big Kinks fans she chose to do a fairly obscure Kinks song, *The Way Love Used To Be* (From the film Percy). We recorded it on my home set up and it has some interesting things going on in it. It has lots of moods and atmosphere. The press likened it to a lost Kate Bush treasure upon release so that gives you a flavour of what it was like. It is piano and string-based and for a 4-track recording, it has a massive sound. But the undercurrent of the music has some unusual instruments doing unusual hypnotic riffs then halfway through it turns into nearly a different song making it very filmic sounding. Such was Misty's influence on me, she managed to blag a second track with a new duo she was doing called 'Digital Lemon'. She chose to do *A Clockwork Orange,* which was a good bit of foresight since the film was re-released the following year. It is a very Gary Numan like version and is heavy on the electronica but is excellent and moody. (This track is also known as *The Mass for Queen Mary)* . The intro conjured up the mood of Queen Mary of Scots walking to the gallows with the sound of sharpening knives, ominous drums beating, and menacing sounding bells ringing. I also got the guitarist to play the song's outro with a little bit of *Singing in the Rain* riff to add a bit of humour to it. (If you have seen the film you will know why I did this) Of course Misty was well to the fore on one of the 2 B.O.P tracks as well. With *The Deep,* not many people realise this was written by John Barry and Donna Summer.

Donna Summer came to fame on the back of a banned single called *Love to Love You Baby.* What I could never understand was how the theme from The Deep was not banned as it was equally if not more sexually charged with heavy breathing and from what I could make out the lyrics were a lot stronger, with lines like 'Something warm is coming inside of me'. (Least that's what I thought) Since we had recently recorded tracks for the Heavy Breathing Decade album, which was pretty much a concept album about sex and I had a distinctive sound and vibe in my head this was the ideal choice for us to do as a track for the themes album. Misty's sexy vocal style suits this track down to the ground and my cello playing on this track is amongst my best ever. Not only do I add the atmospheric bits that creates an orgasm to the music I play some raw riffs that any guitarist would be proud of. When I thought up the line-up for B.O.P I made a decision not to include guitars. I felt if we did, we'd be lumped in with The Electric Light Orchestra. (Not that they are bad because they were quite good). The idea was to have a unique line-up not done before. With no guitars, some people were sceptical and felt the music might sound too easy listening. But once I played my punk cello like a saw, sometimes it was as hard as any guitar and it was far from easy listening. The sax too could be quite raucous when it featured on some tracks. I think with the 2 B.O.P tracks here I came of age as a cello player and showed what punk cello could do. Before it had added unusual sounds and lots of atmosphere and was the icing on the cake of a track and something that made it unmistakably our sound and interesting. (Live it is even more impressive sound and makes more of an impact). By the time we arrived at this album we no longer had a sax player so the pressure was all on me to play what both the sax and the cello would improvise and play more upfront riffs as well. I had always loved the Jimi Hendrix record *All Along the Watchtower.* In it he plays about 5 different guitar riffs all with different sounds and for me, this is his finest hour. I always wanted to do something similar so with no sax in my way this was the track where I play 5 different sounding cello sounds doing different things all over the tracks. It was all-upfront and no longer standing in the shadows. The same applies to the other track we did *Madalenna.* If I had asked a composer to write a perfect 'Pop Noir' instrumental this would be it. It was the B-side of an Ennio Morricone record and the film it came from was a flop so hardly anyone has heard this track. Its correct title is *Come, Madalenna.* It's nearly as good as Morricone's masterpieces, *The Good. Bad and Ugly, A Fist Full of Dollars & For a Few Dollars More..* It suits koto and jumpy strings and my punk cello once again dominates the track and sounds like a Wolf, a Dolphin or a Whale and others things. The track also has a couple of brilliant 'Pop Noir' type backing vocals in it that really suited Misty. If we managed to perfect the 'Pop Noir' sound on the previous Cult Themes then this was the one that took it to its ultimate level and would be hard to better. One funny anecdote about this particular recording was, Misty was going out with Ed Ball of The Times pop group and he had beaten her up and thrown her down some stairs and she still bore a few scars so when it came to the backing vocals she would sing 'Ed Ball is a bastard' over and over again and I got to disguise this into just a vocal noise but not exactly what she said. I mixed it with another backing vocal that she excelled at as there were no words to this track it was an instrumental. She kicked Ball into touch not long after this, fortunately only to end up with another Ball, Dave of Soft Cell, another abusive relationship followed. Misty did say her romantic relationships were always shit. (She was definite not on the Ball in these relationships;; ha ha) She was always happy with me though although we never had a conventional relationship.

I must have been quite inspired when doing this Cult Themes album because on reflection it seems a bit like a solo album in many ways. I actually did 2 solo tracks for this album under the pseudonym of 'Uncle'. The first is one of my favourite Cult Themes, *The Adventurer* (which could easily be my theme tune). It's a more obscure John Barry track. If someone asked me to play one track that portrays the sound of a Cult Theme this would be it. The mood is just right and it could be a theme for any show. It actually sounds more in keeping with the 60's shows but came out in 1970 so just missed being on the 60's comps. I decided that with my solo tracks I could afford to be as groundbreaking as I liked. On this track, I felt a harpsichord or koto wasn't quite the right sound. I needed something in between the 2 but couldn't find the right sound, So I messed about with a bass guitar sound on a keyboard and tuned it up to one octave above what a bass guitar can normally play and got just the right sound I was looking for. It sounds so right for this particular track. The track itself is quite catchy. This could not be said about the other track I did. In the next one, I created a new innovative urban soundscape type track. John Carpenter is famous for directing classic horror films like Halloween and The Fog etc but what few people know is, he writes the music for all his films as well and a rare album of all his music is a sought after collector's item in the Cult Themes market. I had always loved the mood of the theme *Assault on Precinct 13,* so now I was going to take his repetitive synth track and turn it into a true representation of what the film is all about. The film was about a down-town Police station cut off from the rest of the world and every villain in the town had got wind of this and were heading towards it to kill the occupants. So my track painted a strong picture of chaos and violence and impending doom. Gunshots become part of the rhythm track. I also created this rolling rhythm with bottles and cans being kicked along the street. A deep menacing timpani plays as well as plenty of eerie punk cello, then people hitting trash cans. I created a lot of sounds by improvising on household goods and furniture. I played the drum track on the back of my sofa amongst other things. I rattled a folk around a glass and a cup and put it through an effects unit then added something I nicknamed stereo travelling to the track. This is where I got lots of different shades of sounds placed at certain places in the mix with various frequencies. This gives the effect that the sounds are spinning all around your head then travelling from one ear across the top of your head and back again. Unfortunately, you only get the full idea of this when wearing headphones. A few years down the line a thing called 5.1 stereo was invented and costs half a million pounds and I was asked to test it out at the famous Abbey Road recording studios and give my opinion. I checked it out and it just sounded similar to my stereo travelling mixes only my investment was a few pounds on my own home equipment. I pointed this out to the people at Abbey Road and they were shocked and disappointed. The major problem with 5.1 is the engineers and technical people who invented it did very uncreative mixes. For example, one mix they played me of The Eurythmics in concert had the front speakers playing the concert in stereo and the back speakers were all crowd noises. Ok, it was supposed to make you feel you were at the concert (big deal. I'd rather go to the concert). Another mix just had a few percussion instruments playing on 5th speaker (Whoopie). Bearing in mind the cost of the venture and the cost to customers who wanted to buy it I couldn't see it taking off to the general consumer excepting through incorporating it into films and DVDs, which is what happened. Anyway Precinct 13 was a groundbreaking production and a sound that I would develop one stage further with *Blade Runner* a few years later, which many people loved but others also said it sounded like it was recorded 'Off World' on a mixing desk from an Alien planet. I can live with that! It is a new style of urban music and one step beyond 'Pop Noir'. (Urban Pop Noir I guess) The 'Pop Noir' element is still there because it is filmic and conjures up the whole film from just hearing the track and not seeing the movie, punk cello is there along with some minimal music but the more melodic sounds and instruments are scarce. I doubt many people could listen to a whole album of such tracks. But the odd track here and there does sound refreshingly original and different.

Finally, what many people don't know about this album is there is a secret track on it (I do like a secret track). So for those taking the CD out of the player after track 15 you have been missing out all these years. As many will know my other part-time band was Ministry of Ska. You may also have read we recorded the track *The First Time Ever I Saw Your Face*. But Dick and I had fallen out. He wanted to take 3 days to get a drum sound in the studio (very boring) and I am more spontaneous and improvisational. I was a more successful producer than Dick but he always wanted equal say and his opinion started to become the opposite to mine, add to this Kirsty McCall not doing 'First Time' as a duet with us that could have made it a hit and he had lost his enthusiasm for the project and wanted to call it a day. So because of this, he didn't want this track released. I thought it was a great track and should be released. So because the song was featured in the Cult film 'Play Misty For Me' I thought I'd put it on the Cult Themes album but because Dick didn't want it out I had to hide it as a secret track. (He is still none the wiser) However, he did relent some years later and agreed to have a slightly different version it on The Best of Ministry of Ska album. As I had founded and thought up the band name and still wanted to do more Ska I put out one final M.O.S track on my own, *Ska Surfin,* which proved popular but then I got too busy to carry on with M.O.S (but I may revive it next year, so watch this space)

With the themes album completed, we were heading towards the end of the year and not a good time for a new release so the album was scheduled for release in early 99 instead.

(Joan Martin AKA Phoenix J) is below along with B/W version of Themes album cover.

CHAPTER THIRTY-TW0

FERGAL HAS JOINED THE ENEMY

I became fixated on getting a big deal for B.O.P because I felt my labels lack of decent promotion money was holding us back and this is where a major always had the edge. Although I had managed to come up with some innovative marketing that became famous it's not always possible to do this for every single release.

Suddenly it looked like our time had come as I got an unexpected phone call from a recent famous acquaintance. I had often gone to Indie seminars; usually to speak on panels and at one such gathering I met 'Fergal Sharkey' formerly the lead singer with the excellent Irish band 'The Undertones'. He had also had a solo number one hit after leaving them. We hit it off straight away and at a second chance meeting, I gave him some of B.O.P music.

It had been several months since I'd seen Fergal but his voice was unmistakable on the other end of the phone. He said 'Guess what? I've joined the enemy'. He went on to say that he had been made head of A&R at Polydor Records as the label had started to get a boring reputation and been made to look stupid by dropping Paul Weller, who went on to sell huge quantities of solo records. His brief was to spice things up and sign some new cutting edge bands and B.O.P was the first band he thought of. So could I come and see him. I went Polydor's offices and met with Fergal. I played some new B.O.P music he hadn't heard before and he was convinced we were the act to spearhead the new cutting edge Polydor release schedule. We agreed on a basic deal and he told me nothing would get done this side of Xmas, so I should come back in January to collect my contract and get my lawyer to have a look at it. Then hopefully we could have a release out in the first half of 1999. One thing that is important in any record deal is to have your A&R person 100% behind you otherwise at the first sign of sales dropping you are out of the door. So I was pleased Fergal would be our A&R man.

Come January, I phoned Polydor to check the appointment I made with Fergal was still on and I was told that Fergal no longer worked there. I phoned him at home and he told me that he played half a dozen innovative acts to the head of Polydor of which we were one, saying he wanted to make these his first signings. The head of Polydor freaked out and said when we said new cutting edge acts, he meant more of the same old thing but with a slightly new twist. It was too frightening to sign such innovative acts. So, Fergal said what's the point of him being there and resigned and along with it went our chance of a major release.

CHAPTER THIRTY-THREE

PINNACLE

Just prior to the release of volume 2 of 'Cult Themes from the 70's' I got some bad news from Pinnacle. My label manager Stuart called me to say, he was leaving and that I should consider doing the same. It turned out that 'Zomba' had taken over Pinnacle and their priorities would be Britney Spears and Steps and Indie labels would be a low priority. Pinnacle had been our best distributor because they specialised in Indie labels and had reps actually going into the shops to sell our releases as opposed to only selling via phone sales. This made a big difference. It sounded now like we would be lucky to get a mention. Since our contract was up for renewal anyway it would all be down to how well 'Cult Themes from the 70's volume 2' did for both parties. Because I had focussed on cult composers on this album only half the tracks would be well known to the public, so it was always going to be a bit of a risky release. But I pulled out all the stops. First up was a series of gigs. The main one was a launch gig at Madame Jo Jo's in Soho, London that would feature 7 of the acts, which was ambitious.

Leading up to this gig there was a series of smaller gigs by some of the bands including one I did with Joan Martin (Who did the Moonraker track) with me playing the bongos.

Jo' Jo's was a sell-out and that wasn't easy on a Thursday night. Box Office Poison and The Honeycombs were to be joint headliners. This was the first time The Honeycombs original line-up had played together since about 1969. It would be the youngest audience many of them had played to since then. Although I would be performing with B.O.P, as the record label boss and promoter I also had to deal with all the hassle as usual. I couldn't believe some of the attitudes on display that night. It turned out there was a good reason why The Honeycombs had split up. The guitarist Peter was very temperamental and he wasn't interested in waiting to go on last (But that's what headliners do!). He threatened to walk out if they didn't go on soon. (I guess he needed to be tucked up in bed with his coco). So I had to put them on earlier and switch someone else to later and chose 'Ambassadors of Om'. You always get one bunch of toe-rags on each album and this band were the winners of the toe=rag award for this album. Apart from the fact that they had a bit of an attitude problem anyway, they didn't want to be moved from their slot because they told people they would be on at a certain time. (Well performance times nearly always change, it's common). One guy said he had to get up early the next day for work. This person plus another band member then threatened not to play at all if they didn't keep their original spot. I told them if they didn't go on at the new time and didn't like it they could leave and not play or get paid.

First on were the 10-piece easy listening and Cult Themes band E.L.B.O.W, who got the crowd warmed up to the vibe of the night and went down well. Joan Martin then performed a few acoustic numbers including a version of *Moonraker.* She went down Ok but not as good as I thought she would since I had seen her go down very well at other gigs. The Honeycombs got their earlier spot and went down very well. They were very pleased about this, as they were very nervous about it. It was also a buzz for me to hear *Have I the Right* by the original band live. There was then a brief break with DJ' James Karminsky playing Cult Themes. The second half opened with those other specialist Cult Themes boys and girls 'The Incredibly Strange Film Band' who naturally went down well. Misty then had a solo spot to do her track, *The Way Love Used To Be* and some of her own new songs she'd recently written. Her performance was eccentric and memorable and people wouldn't forget her in a hurry. Ambassadors of Om were next and the worst act of the night, no doubt partly brought about by their attitude and change of performance time. Finally, it was the headliners, which were effectively just me and Misty and a backing track (The minimum B.O.P line-up). With time running short we ended up doing only 3 numbers but many said we were the best act of the night and the tracks were very memorable. *The Deep* is a track that stands out especially the way we do it and my original song *I Want You All The Time,* is instantly memorable and to finish, *Mysteries* is always a show stopper. I'm sure most people never thought a cello player could move around so much since cello players are normally quite static. I attempted to play whilst walking across the stage, hanging it off a chair and leaning into the audience etc. Misty was also on fine form.

Both the album and the gigs got good reviews. Next, I played to my strengths, doing interviews with radio, press and T.V. The highlight for me was being on the same BBC radio show with John Barry. The BBC had finally caught on to the Cult Themes phenomena just as it was about to die and did a special on it. After acknowledging me as the catalyst for the trend and asking me to explain the philosophy behind it John Barry then joined us saying he was grateful to people like me for reawakening interest in his work, not just the Bond themes but many other tracks he had written. His back catalogue was enjoying a big renascence. He added that T.V. & film themes were as much a backdrop to peoples lives as The Beatles. Theme tunes like Bond, the Gerry Anderson shows and others triggered memories of growing up and many were classic tunes in their own right. After the show, John Barry told me he liked what I'd done with The Bond themes and thought *Moonraker* was even better than the original. He admitted Shirley Bassey had just gone through the motions because she as a late replacement doing it as a favour to him. I asked who was supposed to do it but he wouldn't tell me, although he hinted it may have been the only time two singers from the same family had done a Bond theme. (In recent years I learned that John had wanted Frank Sinatra but he turned it down but a bigger revelation was Kate Bush was down to do it down but she dropped out late when her only UK tour was extended). John was also a big fan of *You Only Live Twice* and thought Eleanor was a brilliant and distinctive singer and better than Nancy Sinatra, although he did like Nancy's very commercial tones as well. He went on to give me a bit of insight into that Bond theme, saying although musically his was better overall he had been given the title before the film was made and having just done the *Midnight Cowboy* theme he was fond of the harmonica and put this on *You Only Live Twice*

and I had been clever and put koto's & other Japanese instruments on it which suited the track better as I had the hindsight of seeing the film first. He also really liked my version of his track *The Persuaders* , saying I always brought something new to the table with all the themes I produced. He also confirmed that he had heard about me from his agent George who I met in New York and had agreed with him that I could have been good back up to take up some of his work and told me it was a scary time for him but he was Ok now. He'd already got *You Only Live Twice* of course and after that, he had followed my career and got most of my releases especially the Cult Themes which he thought was a great idea. His final mark of respect was to give me 2 complimentary tickets to his show at The Royal Albert Hall. As you could imagine I was buzzing.On the radio front, we also got a big result worldwide. A new digital radio company called 'Music Choice' tracked me down and said they had lots of specialist channels and that The F.L.R. Cult Themes featured heavily on the soundtrack channel and that our releases were the most requested. (They were like a forerunner to Spotify). The most unusual radio show I did was at XFM, the top Independent radio station in London with a cool reputation for playing Indie stuff. We had got lots of airplay through them. They were doing a special show on condoms & safe sex. Because of my legendary condom marketing campaign & having a track with that name on the Ministry of Ska album I was asked to participate in the show and got to mention my new B.O.P album, which tied in well because of the track-listing and I got a few tracks played from it. I got paid with a year's supply of condoms. (Nearly 400 of the buggers). I immediately put them to good use but not in the way you are thinking. I covered a naked Misty in them (below) as a promo shot, which eventually ended up on a single for 'Condoms' by Ministry of Ska.

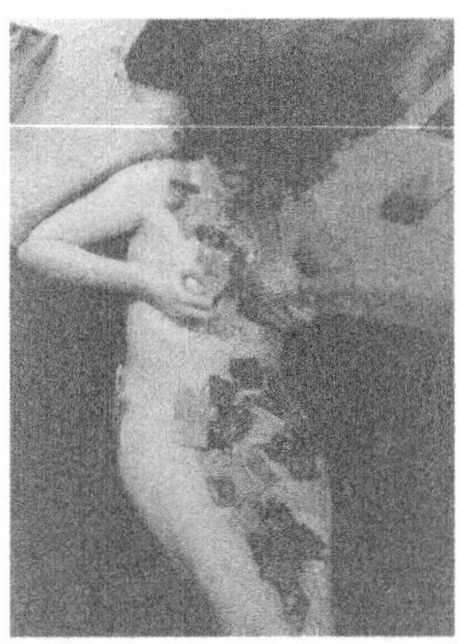

The Cult Themes trend was in decline but luckily the new 70's trend was still going, which made the release viable. Pinnacles new owners introduced lots of new costs meaning we only just made a profit so we parted company with them. I then teamed up with some new Internet distributors to make the release worthwhile. 1999 was also a year of recognition. A book came out on the history of I.D Magazine and I featured in it as an Ace face of the Mod movement and Eleanor featured as a music and Mod icon. The Victoria and Albert had a new youth exhibition where my fanzine Dedicated Follower featured (for a 2nd time, the first being at a V & A Mod exhibition in the previous decade). Scootering International magazine, which sold more than N.M.E and Melody Maker did a Mod Legend series and did a 2-page special on me. Many websites went up either about me, or including me on them including the top 20 most innovative record producers of all time. So, on a creative level, it was a good year. I seemed to always be relevant over the years, even now

CHAPTER THRITY FOUR

FAMOUS IN THE PHILIPPINES

Box Office Poison's reputation had spread worldwide and as if to confirm this, I got an e-mail from a model in the Philippines called ‘Amour’. (real name Maria). She was hot if her photo was anything to go by. She said she had come across Box Office Poison's music on a website and loved it and then saw a photo of me and I really appealed to her as well, so I wrote back to her. We hit it off via e-mail. She then called me to show she was real. The talk turned to how adventurous I was and how much she wanted to make love to me. She said several overseas guys had chatted her up before and said they were adventurous but it turned out to be all talk, she hoped I would be different. So to test me, the next thing she said even shocked me, “If you fancy a sex with me get on the next plane to the Philippines. That’s if you are as adventurous as you say”. I can never resist a challenge so the next day there I was in the Philippines. Everyone I knew said I was crazy, effectively going on what was a 7,000 blind date and anything could happen and we might not even hit it off in person but the adventurer in me went into overdrive and I ignored all advice. Within half an hour of arriving back from the airport, we were back at Amour’s tiny flat in Manila. The double bed dominated the room. She turned to me and said ‘It’s the moment of truth’. I said ‘let’s go for it. It was electrifying, she was as passionate as I'd hoped and sexy and we didn't hold back, it was definitely a memorable encounter. She had however been a little economical with the truth in one area. She had told me the Typhoon season had finished but it hadn’t. This led to a comical romantic dinner where she had made rice and prawns but the prawns weren't cooked, she thought they came out of the sea already cooked. Well, she was a model! (I later found out a maid normally cooked for her, oh and she was very intelligent and even beat me in one game of Chess). To add to proceedings whilst on her balcony we were lashed by rain and the wind kept blowing out the romantic candles. (I had to laugh). Because of the Typhoons, we ended up spending 3 days in bed because the weather was too awful to go out in. So at least we got to know each other very well in those 3 days.

I have to confess that I did have a small back up plan had everything gone pear-shaped on arrival. Six months before a Filipino record company had written to me about licensing some of the F.L.R releases and in particular Box Office Poison. We hadn’t seen eye to eye on a price and they were also keen for me to come out and do some promotion for the releases first but I said that's the wrong way around. You put the record out first then promote it. They said it was done differently there for new artists. I thought whilst I was there I’d look them up as there is nothing like the personal touch. I met them and agreed on a deal. However, because I was in Box Office Poison and already in the Philippines, they asked me to do some radio interviews first before they would ratify the deal. Amour came to the meeting and impressed by what was going on took me out that night to meet all her friends at various clubs and restaurants. I then found out what it was like to be a bimbo. I was literally there as some sort of ornament or prize on her arm. As she hit each table she said, “Hi this is my new boyfriend he’s an English pop star’. Before I could get a conversation going I was dragged off to the next table and so it went. Eventually, we ended up at a nice restaurant called ‘Havana’ but nearly ended the night getting arrested. This was a restaurant frequented by local celebrities and off from the main part of the restaurant was a little alcove part for celebs. It had little portholes with tinted glass to look through and see the rest of the restaurant who couldn’t see us.

Whether it was the occasion or the Sangria that got to me I don't know but I often get a cheeky mood on and go a little wild. Once the waiter had taken our order I got under the table and relieved Amour of her knickers and started giving her oral sex. At some point, the waiter came back but I just carried on. Later on, she was returning the favour and the waiter came back along with some other new celebrity customers. A complaint was made and the manager threatened to call the Police at first but then just asked us to leave.
It turned out that Amour was fairly well connected to the entertainment industry and said she may be able to get me a better record deal than what I had been offered. She then introduced me to Star Records who also owned radio stations and a film company. They were interested and asked if I could also produce the Philippines number one act 'Martin Nievera'. I was asked to go to see him in concert and meet with him afterwards. It turned out he had heard some Box Office Poison music given to him by a contact and was very impressed and wanted me to produce his next album. As an enticement, he asked me to appear on his number one rated T.V show a few days later to do an interview. (It was the equivalent of going on the Jonathan Ross show in the UK). The interview went down very well. They had also asked me to bring a backing tape with me but said it was mainly the interview they wanted and only if time allowed would I have to sing. I had an album of instrumental tracks and Mysteries, B.O.P's most popular song was on it and it happens to be one of the few that I actually sing lead on so that was the logical choice. I certainly lived up to the Jazz/Punk attitude that night.Things got slightly hilarious later on after the show. After having a few drinks with Martin we came out of the T.V. studio (minus Martin) and there were lots of metal barriers with screaming girls and other assorted characters waving autographs books in our direction. Amour turned to me and said ' As I'm a famous model I might have to stop and sign a few autographs, do you mind?' I shook my head and said no problem. However before we reached the barriers they were opened for some reason and a section of the crowd ran in our direction as Amour looked in her handbag to grab a pen they all pushed past her and surrounded me shoving their, pen paper & books in my face saying autograph, please. To be honest I was a bit surprised but then realised they must have seen me performing and being interviewed on Martins show and I was now some sort of international celebrity. As I signed everything in sight including a girl's T-shirt that caused her nipples to become prominent, Amour just stood there with a long face. The next day I had a meeting with Star films about writing the soundtrack for a James Bond type film as they were impressed with the versions of James Bond themes I had produced. It then seemed like various people wanted time to make decisions based on what I was asking for. This seemed an ideal time to see more of the Philippines. So I said to Amour lets have an adventure somewhere and that's just what we did. The adventure was wild and I was fast becoming a film noir character that I loved watching in those type of films but it nearly got me killed but that's a long story, not B.O.P related so you'll have to get my full biog to read about that.
However, there were 2 episodes later in my trip that were music-related that caused a stir. Amour usually accompanied me everywhere in cabs so that I didn't get ripped off. She had a modelling assignment and I went with her to watch but the client wasn't happy about me being there so she then asked the cab driver to take me home. The next thing I know the taxi driver locked all the doors telling me we were going through a dangerous area. But I wondered if I was being kidnapped. However, the next thing I know is he's playing me all these songs and asking for my opinion. It turned out he was also a songwriter. I assumed he knew who I was and had seen me on the T.V. show so I gave

him some decent feedback but he wanted more and I then found myself going in the opposite direction to where I was living. He wanted to take me back to his place and play me even more music and meet his family. It was a bit disconcerting especially as he kept calling me John Lennon. I kept telling him I wasn't John Lennon and Lennon was dead (and I was hoping I wouldn't be joining him). I have been mistaken for Paul McCartney quite a few times, especially abroad and I think he had gotten the 2 Beatles mixed up. Still a bit concerned I pointed out that I had an important appointment with a music publisher at a hotel near where Amour lived and if he got me there double quick I would recommend his music to one of them. I then got taken home at breakneck speed narrowly missing several other cars on the way.
The 2nd incident happened when we went to cabaret club and a singer came on stage and totally and unexpectedly blew me away. I have always been good at spotting star quality and this girl had it. Although she was nice looking and came across like a Filipino Rita Hayworth. I was purely looking at her from a professional point of view because I needed a 2nd singer for Box Office Poison now Annie had quit and duly offered her the post. But all I heard for the rest of the night from Amour was I must but madly in love with this girl who was called Mai. But it wasn't true. The jealous streak didn't endear me to Amour and I decided it was time to go home. Sadly it was way too tricky and expensive to get Mai to the UK so she never became the new B.O.P singer. I went with the Star record deal in the end and although we did sell reasonably well in the Philippines they sold albums for only 99p and once our royalties were calculated it barely covered the expenses of the trip. I decided the Bond-type film wasn't good so didn't do musice for it.
*As a footnote to this adventure. On another day out with Amour, I encountered a lot of very poor people with plastic cups and duly filled them with as much money as I could. Amour said I was wasting my money, as these poor urchins would be dead by the next day. I was shocked. he strange thing was, not long after I returned to the UK I got a letter from a nun, Sister Michaela asking for funds to help feed children and build schools for their education. The place was the Philippines. Now there is no way she could have known of my visit but because I had seen things first hand it had made all the difference, so I wanted to help. An interactive version of Music Business Bastards had just done very well so I gave them all the money from that to help build a school and I have been contributing to them ever since. Part of any B.O.P profits always go there but it's not something I broadcast too often. As is sometimes said 'God works in mysterious ways'.
Another sting in the tale was Amour turned out to be a Royal Princess, a fact she had hidden from me. She tours the world now as royalty helping save the planet and get this, helping Filipino Children as well. So it appeared I left my mark on her after all in a very positive way and we became friends again. (Amour left mai right below)

CHAPTER THIRTY-FIVE

THE POET

After my Filipino trip, I was very much in adventurer mode but still trying to get results on Box Office Poison and this next adventure once again gave me both avenues. I had often heard the urban myth about someone sticking a pin in a map and then going to that place to see what happens. I have never met anybody who has done this, not even seen a book on it and wondered if it was just a myth. . So at the start of 2000 I stuck a pin in a world map and it hit Florida, U.S.A. So I grabbed myself a cheap flight to Florida, hired a car and let the pin do the talking and I did the walking, (well driving mostly to be precise). The pin hit the map and I headed for the location, a place called Clearwater near Tampa. Once there I stopped at the nearest phone booth and put the pin in the phone book in the paged marked hotels. After booking in at the weather beaten hotel I wandered along to the nearest café for a Cappuccino whilst keeping my eyes peeled for the local free paper. Finding one I sat drinking my caffeine hit and opened the newssheet at a random page to see what grabbed my attention and one thing jumped out at me straight away 'NAKED POETRY'. That was most definitely the place for me! The question was, would this be a literal interpretation or fancy ways of saying get something off your chest. Either way, it seemed like an interesting night out. The place was located in downtown Tampa and to be honest it was a bit of a seedy establishment. As the proceedings started it appeared only one person had taken the words on the poster seriously and stood there stark naked on stage to impart their words wisdom via their poetry. The theme of most poetry was erotic or sexual and being comfortable with my sexuality I was enjoying every minute of this experience. Although I tend to stand out from the crowd because of the stylish or distinctive way I dress, quite a few people at this establishment were dressed in a very individual style so I thought I might well blend in. After a while, a sexy looking girl wearing a lot of pink decided to join me at my table. She had recognised me from one of my Box Office Poison releases and after confirming it was me, asked to share my table. After a bit of heavy flirting and a cocktail or two, she hit me with a challenge. Since I wrote songs, lyrics are another form of poetry so I should be up on stage doing a turn not hiding away in a corner. Although I perform with B.O.P of course and write the songs I am by no means the front person. So to get up on my own and read poetry was a bit nerve-racking. But ever one to push my limits I decided to go for it. Luckily 'Heavy Breathing Decade' album had not long been released and the subject matter was just right for the evening's proceedings. The lyric I decided to do are below.

Sex On the Internet

Sexy girl seeks sexy boy, Sexy boy seeks sexy girl

Purpose......... Swap Fantasies

Sexy boy meets sexy girl, Sexy girl meets sexy boy

Purpose.......Danger with a stranger

Chorus

Sex on the Internet

It keeps you warm it keeps you wet

Sex on the Internet, Its up to you what you get

Cyber girl seeks Cyber boy, Cyber boy seeks cyber girl

Purpose.........Cyber sex

Sex on the internet, sex on the internet

Submit hear have no fear

You're so far and yet so near

Sex on the Internet, Sex on the internet

Boy seeks boy, Girl seeks girl

The Internet is a different world

Purpose....To be somebody else

Sex on the internet

I want it here, I want it now

Sex on the internet

Watch out girls here it comes

Sex on the internet

Wipe the screen and keep it clean

Outro

E-mail me your ultimate fantasy

Don't hold back, don't keep it clean

Swap sexy photos over the net

It's an experience you won't forget

We are all voyeurs

We just don't like to admit it

We're all voyeurs

We're all in it!

I needn't have worried. After I finished my performance I got a standing ovation. Before I knew it I was surrounded by other poets telling me they loved my Beatnik delivery and the humour of the lyrics and one particular Goth girl, who turned out to be a journalist said would I go back to her place to do an interview. I agreed to go and everybody else tagged along. At the gathering afterwards, the nice blonde-chic dressed in pink whose name was Laura turned out to have a boyfriend in tow who kept giving me dagger stares repeatedly. (I could almost hear the 'Psycho' music playing in my head). She then stuck her bands' CD on and asked for my opinion. I always give an honest opinion and if people don't want honest opinions they shouldn't ask. (Don't ask me what I think of it because I might well say it's shit!)

The CD wasn't shit but neither was it anything out of the ordinary. I tried to be diplomatic and said, 'Although a good CD the band needed to become more distinctive sounding before a label would sign them up. I felt it had potential but a better production was needed'. The blonde didn't look too happy and then cooled on me like a cocktail with too much ice. I felt that she was used to being the centre of attention and I was taking this away from her, which also didn't endear me to her.

The heavyweight Goth girl suddenly wanted people to vacate the premises so that she could interview me for her magazine and then shag my brains out. The majority of people then started giving me CD's or Poetry books and quoting their work to me before they departed and it looked like Laura had a change of heart at the last minute and handed me her card and asked me to call her the next day to meet up for coffee once her boyfriend was out of earshot.

Before I met up with Laura, a freaky thing happened. I decided to have a look around the shops in Clearwater and spotted a modern junkshop with lots of curious things insides but one curio I wasn't expecting was a gig flyer for Box Office Poison concert staring back at me from the wall. It was the flyer from our first ever gig (Night of the Living Dudes). Just what were the chances of this? I could be anywhere in the world but stumbled into one shop selling a 4-year-old flyer of a small B.O.P gig for $10. I asked the owner how he came by it and he told me his girlfriend had been to the gig when in London. I then decided to tell him who I was and he asked me to sign it. I duly did on the understanding he'd buy a few B.O.P CDs from me (Ever one to help fund a trip & promote B.O.P). He agreed and I took them in the next day and met his girlfriend who wanted a photo with me. So I duly obliged along with a kiss. But I was still scratching my head about this million to one shot regarding the flyer as I approached the coffee bar, which turned out to be attached to a recording studio. Laura was pleased to see me and a lot more friendly and flirty without her boyfriend in tow. She said although she hadn't liked a few of my comments about her music she agreed with some others. She added that her boyfriend was holding her back by insisting on producing the band's music and she knew it wasn't up to scratch. It had been done initially out of necessity because they couldn't afford a producer but once they had been in a better financial position she wanted to hire a producer but the boyfriend wouldn't hear of it and claimed he knew what was right for the bands sound. They had had many rows about it and things had become strained in their relationship lately. She then wanted to show me some new photos of her and the band to get my opinion and as I leaned over to check them out, it was one of those occasions where our lips were in close proximity and I could also feel a certain vibe coming from her so grabbed a cheeky kiss on the lips. It was only a quick one but to my surprise once it stopped she returned my kiss with a longer one and a quick taste of her tongue before exiting and acting all embarrassed. We tried to ignore what had just happened and I started to look at her photos and comment on them positively although I know I could have probably taken better ones.

I then put my hand on her leg and stroked it and she didn't take it away but mirrored my action by grabbing my leg and squeezing it. We then looked into each other's eyes and I wondered where this was all leading then she broke the vibe by saying she was taking me into the recording studio. That was certainly a change of direction. She had chosen to meet at the recording studio café because she had recorded a new song that was as yet unmixed and wanted to get my opinion. We left the café and ventured through a games room with a pool table adjoined to the studio control room. She was dressed very sexily, with a t-shirt that clearly had no bra underneath and a tight-fitting pair of jeans that screamed Camel toe, I was finding it hard to restrain myself so before we reached the door I turned her around and slowly pushed her against the wall near the door and kissed her as my hand slid up inside her T-shirt and played with her already hard nipple as I did so. Things were feeling very passionate and I was getting carried away but so was she and she grabbed my bum and squeezed it thrusting it towards her body. I then thought I'd go for the jackpot and stick my hand down her tight jeans just about feeling her clitoris but then she pulled my hand out and said 'Not here, Not now, later.' We then ventured into the control room where she introduced me to the engineer, Jack and asked him to play her tape. There was only one spare chair and so I sat on it and she sat on my lap as we listened back to her track. I don't know what part of my body I was thinking with but I was very complimentary about the track saying it was better than what I had previously heard and with the right mix it could be a contender. Her eyes lit up and she asked if I could do a mix for her the next day. Before I could answer, her now very animated and jealous boyfriend entered the studio and went ballistic at both of us looking very cosy on the chair together. We both jumped up and she grabbed him and told me I better go. The Clash '*Should I Stay or Should I go*' was spinning in my head. I hesitated and he took a swing at me. The engineer (who was bigger than both of us) then intervened and stood in between us and told him nothing was going on, it was a case of there being only one chair available in the control room and that's why we were sitting together. I decided leaving was the best policy on this occasion.

Before my pin determined my next destination I decided to call Laura to see if she was Ok. She confirmed she was but then imparted that she felt she was caught in a trap and couldn't walk out. She wasn't the best at getting gigs and couldn't afford to pay for every recording and the boyfriend had ticked all those boxes. She had foolishly moved in with him some months before, more to save on the rent than because of any passionate affair and everything would be in turmoil if he quit the band. So in effect, she didn't want to lose all that security but at the same time she was very ambitious and wanted to get to the next level and that meant a decent producer and a record deal. What was my advice? If I was staying in town longer maybe a way for me to produce the band could be found and if that worked out I could put them out on my label. However, things between the boyfriend and me were tense enough and I thought it would take a while to calm the situation down and since I was on an adventure and not hanging around or looking for work the timing wasn't right. The best I could do was tell her to stay in touch as she had my e-mail address.

I continued with my pin journey and had some interesting adventures and met some interesting people that went on to make the basis of the novel 'Adventures of a Dark Duke: The Pin (so if you want the full story that paperback should be your next port of call) But for now I will just relate any stories that have a B.O.P angle to them as It's the Box Office Poison Story.

MIAMI

I had been to Miami before but it had gone downhill a lot. It looked very sleazy and run down and those were the good hotels. (Just joking!). But it did have an air of danger about it that's for sure. I did the usual and put the pin in the phone book to select a hotel. However, the place it fell on was the sort of place where the vibe tempted you to make out your last will and testament. If you didn't die of a disease, the chances were you'd be robbed and murdered before sunrise. I thought, common-sense rules over the pin on this occasion. I drove around till I found a more suitable place to stay and then hit the streets in search of the local free paper. That achieved I headed for the nearest café once more. As I was drinking my coffee and about to open the paper to find out where I would be going that night I noticed a cute girl, looking like a young Chrissy Hynde, walking past my table and she had accidentally dropped some money from her pocket and not noticed. I pointed this out to her and she thanked me. It turned out that she was also English, so I asked her to join me. She had only been over from the UK for about a week or so and was doing a spot of lap dancing. Now believe it or not an adventurer like me had never actually been to a lap-dancing club before. As a thank you for being honest about the money she offered to get me into the club for free and give me a dance or 2 into the bargain. Since I liked to experience most things in life at least once it seemed too good an offer to pass up. Then came the sting in the tail.

First, I have to say the club was an interesting experience. Louise, the English lap dancer gave me a few dances as promised then I noticed that a lot of girls took men off to a side room and I asked what happened there so she offered to show me. I ventured into this semi-private room and she contorted her body around mine in a provocative manner. She then stopped and sat on my lap and said, 'So what would The News of the World make of this?' (The News of the World was a tabloid newspaper noted for exposes but is now no longer going). I said I don't understand what you mean. She then informed me that she had one of my music releases and suggested I was a big pop star. First, I would point out that although I am in a band and have had a few releases and was not totally unknown, neither was I a household name and certainly not 'News of the World' fodder. I informed her that since my band's last album was called 'Heavy Breathing Decade' and all the songs were of a sexual nature her expose would be most welcome. She smiled and said 'Shame, but you can't blame a girl for trying.' Whether this was some sort of a shakedown or just a bit of a joke I wasn't sure. She did ask me to go back to her place after work, but since she wasn't finished till 6 am and I got bored by 3 am I decided not to take her up on the offer, but we agreed to meet the next day. So I left the club, but the night did not end there. Just as I pulled up outside my hotel I noticed a girl in a flimsy nightdress hanging off a first-floor balcony opposite my hotel. As I got out of the car she shouted 'Please help me'. Just as I was wondering what to do she jumped and started running towards me. As I moved towards her an overweight Cuban looking guy ran around the corner from the building she had jumped from waving a gun at me shouting 'stay out of it'. I then asked what was going on and took a few steps towards him. He stood still and aimed the gun at me. I quickly dived behind a car. A black dude then appeared, saying, forget about him and they ran off in the direction the girl had headed.I went back to my room but kept an eye out of the window for a while. About half an hour later the 2 men returned without the girl. Hopefully, she got away. Whether it was a domestic, she was a hooker or a kidnap victim, who knows. Hopefully, me momentarily distracting the guy with the gun may have given her just enough time to getaway.

The next day I went around to see Louise as promised and we had what I would call a normal sexual encountered and I then decided it was time to move on. She did ask me to stay but she was going to be working most of the time and what I'd seen of Miami so far didn't appeal to me at all. She also told me her life story which was quite interesting but this is my biog, not hers so you will have to check out '*Adventures of a Dark Duke The Pin*' to learn more about that.

There were a few more incidents during this pin experience but none relevant to B.O.P and at the very end of the trip I abandoned the pin and met up with an old friend of mine who does having some bearing on B.O.P.

THE LEGENDARY STEVE ROWLAND

I had known Steve since the 80's when he used to promote special club nights for new acts. But he had a very colourful past himself. He grew up in California, the son of a famous film producer father and started off as an actor and appeared in some high profile films like 'Battle of the Bulge' etc. He was a very good friend of James Dean and they used to go racing together. He also hung out with Elvis Presley and lots of other well-known actors and actresses, even going out with the likes of Natalie Wood. Whilst filming in Spain in the 60's he visited England on his way back to America and fell for an English girl. In order to stay in the UK, he managed to blag a job as a record producer at Fontana Records. Everyone was learning their trade back then and somehow he managed to get away with it. He produced The Heard with Peter Frampton, also The Pretty Things but his biggest success were Dave Dee, Dozy, Beaky Mick and Titch who had lots of big UK hits including the number one *The Legend of Xanadu.* He also had a few big hits with his own band 'Family Dog'. *The Way of Life* being the biggest. Apart from Joe Meek I rated Steve's production better than most other producers around, even over the more well-known ones like Mickey Most and George Martin. To know what I mean you'd have to check out those Dave Dee records. Often done on 4 or 8 track they had whole orchestras, multiple percussion and dozens of other instruments, not to mention all the vocals. He got such a big sound you wondered how the hell did he get all that on 4 tracks and the singles still sound good today. They also had an atmosphere that influenced me when I came to do 'Pop Noir'. After his heyday in the sixties, he became a record company executive at Hansa Records. Steve discovered the likes of Japan, The Cure, Thompson Twins, (everyone's allowed one mistake!) and Mel & Kim who he recommended to another label (PWL). But his biggest hit in those days as a producer was Sarah Brightman and Hot Gossip's *I lost My Heart to a Starship Trooper.* The '80s saw him drift into dance music and then club promotions, which is where I'd met him. He was one of the many who said I was the greatest producer of my generation and the only cutting edge record producer pushing the boundaries rather than playing safe like all the others. I later did a version of *The Legend of Xanadu* with Box Office Poison, which he rated highly. All the talk was of how the whip sound had been achieved. Steve had noticed that when he tried to record a real whip crack it didn't sound like a whip so he improvised with a block of wood sliding along the control panel so he wanted to know how I'd achieved my whip sound. It was my trusty old cello once again. I slid my finger along one string quickly and added an effect to it.

Anyway, I linked up with Steve in Palm Beach. It was a totally different flavour of Florida altogether, mostly rich people. I met some of these influential people like Brooke Shields and the Mayor of the city and hit some nice restaurants and clubs but it wasn't really my scene or so I thought. It appeared lots of famous former Hollywood types were now living out there away from the glare of the spotlight. They had very unusual and outrageous parties, one of which Steve got me invited to. Discretion dictates that I can't say more about what happened at these parties or who was at them but if you read my novel '*Adventures of A Dark Duke: The Pin*' you will get a better flavour of what went on at these parties but remember that's a fiction novel and so I can't confirm what was based on real events and what is not!

This was the last stop on my adventure and it was time to return to England. So that was my adventure and the novel just mentioned was inspired by it.

Above Steve and me (looking like a refugee from The Ramone's but in Mod attire)

Plus the novel this experience generated.

Left Steve with his other mate James Dean (It was always impressive to enter his flat and this is the first thing you see on the wall).

CHAPTER THIRTY-SIX

THE NEW MILLENUM

As mentioned previously our deal with Pinnacle had ended and various new internet entities came along but didn't prove worthwhile in the end, so to keep the buzz going I did a series of very limited edition CDs in 2000 and amongst these were 3 Box office Poison releases.

Our version of Popcorn was very good and we had missed out twice, first, through the hit records going bust then by majors turning us down and seeing The Crazy Frog proving us right and getting a big hit with it. So we finally released it on CD for fans with the B-side being the Sex mix of *Checkmate* that was previously exclusive to the 12" vinyl of that release. It got another release years later when we did a download deal with Itunes and I did a very good video for it.

Although I love my original songs I do like to do the occasional cover version and one of my favourite covers was *The Legend of Xanadu.* Misty was rightly getting a lot of attention but I felt a bit sorry for Anne so when she said she was leaving the band I asked her to do one last recording with me and this B.O.P track was exclusive with her. I also love the production on this and Mouse's voice on this track most of all. Another important thing about this track is I did a vocal part in it and it was the first time I ever actually liked my voice on a recording. Although I did Mysteries it's a stylised vocal that suits the song but I neither love it nor hate it but do love the song & production. Because I liked my voice for the first time I decided to do lead vocals on another song I liked, *A Day Without Love,* formerly by The Love Affair. Anne's backing vocals on this were also excellent and very 60s sounding. I also wrote and sung a new track, *Skag Kids* but this was more of a raw demo but interesting. After also doing extra mixes of *Xanadu,* it got released as a limited edition CD in 2000. (8 tracks in all). The icing on the cake as I mentioned is that original producer Steve Rowland really rated this version. It proved reasonably popular but we had strayed from Pop Noir music to pop. When released as a download it did prove very popular in recent years. I also released *A Day Without Love* on download recently as it apparently influenced Billie Eilish singing style. The other Ltd edition CD release was a The Best of Box Office Poison called 'Themes, Dreams and Schemes.

THIS TIME NEXT YEAR WE'LL BE MILLIONAIRES: THE DOT COM REVOLUTION

In 2000, with the labels future up in the air and no physical distribution to shops, I got an unexpected invite to a big party in the financial district of London called 'First Tuesday'. The Dot-Com revolution was at its height with a new millionaire being made every other day (probably twice on Tuesdays!). First Tuesday was an organisation that put entrepreneurs together with investors over cocktails. Although I wasn't actively looking for investors it seemed like it might be worth checking out as both B.O.P and the record label were at a bit of a crossroads. To my surprise, it was packed out. I could smell the desperation in the room from the entrepreneurs as they hunted down the outnumbered investors 5-1 and I could see many of the investors were getting off on this power trip. Since I wasn't that interested I just made use of the free drinks and chatted up any good-looking girls. But one of the girls I chatted up started introducing me to investors and it turned out I was exactly the sort of company they were looking to invest in.

Future Legend Records had built up a great reputation as an Independent record label. It was a trendsetter, it was considered a very cool label and it was one of the few independent record labels that had stayed in business after 5 years. However, more importantly, where these people were concerned we had a strong internet presence. So I could see why F.L.R may be of interest. Being a person with foresight I had already started to get interested in the Internet around about 1994 and joined forces with people like Cerberus Internet Jukebox, where we became the first record label in the world to have its tracks downloaded. The tracks were Box Office Poison ones *Checkmate & 1995,* plus a couple of cult themes. However Cerberus were a bit too early in the scheme of things as broadband still ruled, so it took half a day to download a track but I both learned and earned a little bit from our liaison with them.

It wasn't until 1995 that F.L.R got its own website and presence. This was still early days for the Internet and the real Internet explosion was still a few years off. But what I discovered straight away was, if any record company was born to be on the net, it was us. After porn, the next most visited websites were those dealing with Cult T.V and films. Because of our Cult Themes album releases we were perfect for these sites to do links with. Sites like James Bond, The Prisoner, Gerry Anderson and much more. So early on lots of traffic was coming our way with no advertising costs involved. The other sort of site people wanted to visit were cool sites. Ones with different designs on the site rather than the bog-standard templates the boring major records companies used. People also liked cult artists like Eleanor Rigby, Box Office Poison and the Ministry of Ska. Although we had decent sales we were still a secret from the mainstream by and large, which made us cool (The keyword on the internet!).

Part of the fun of the Internet in those days was stumbling on sites where you could learn about things that most people didn't know about. It was like you were in on a big secret. Also, our site was not full of advertising either. Getting on the Internet early meant I could learn all about it and see what worked and what didn't. This is where the major record companies fell down. They ignored the Internet at first feeling it was just a fad and not a threat but once they realised it was important they jumped on the bandwagon and were taken to the cleaners in many ways because of their lack of knowledge.

Anyway back at First Tuesday once the investors checked out the F.L.R. site via their laptops and heard more about the label I found myself surrounded by potential investors. I was asked half a dozen times how much money I wanted. I didn't have the first clue.

I knew about normal investments and profit and loss via conventional means but I.P.O investment was a whole new ballgame for me. In short, the crux of the game was investors would put a lot of money into your company, build up your brand name and Web presence, get a lot of advertisers interested and then launch the company on the stock market. Then the investors sell their shares and make a lot of money. That's the theory anyway. The key to my labels appeal was all the links & webrings (which were big back then). As I said we had all the cult T.V. and film sites linked to us that generated hundreds of thousands of fans to come to our site. I was told it's all about eyeballs and that was what the investment was all about. I was ill-prepared at this first meeting and so when a few of these people asked how much I wanted I plucked a figure out of the air that had a nice ring to it. One million pounds but when one of these chaps asked if that would be enough money, I suddenly realised I better start treating the whole thing a bit more seriously. I collected the business cards on offer and attended another one of these parties the next month and got the same interest. The main thing I couldn't get my head around was that I didn't have to make a penny profit to make all this money. I started to read about all these other companies earning millions and to me, these other Internet companies had nothing much to sell, not even any stock and I referred to them as 'fresh Air Dot- Coms'. I thought people were mad investing in these companies and surely it would all crash in the not too distant future. At least my company stood to make a profit and was well placed in both the Internet and the bricks and mortar world to do well. Although I can be good at business, I was mostly a creative person, I never felt that comfortable talking with money people, as I didn't really speak their language. So I figured the smart thing to do was to get myself a financial Wizard who knew how the whole I.P.O and Dot-Com thing worked. I advertised and got nearly 100 replies. I met a few people but as soon as I met Stephan, a French financier with a top investment house. He understood me straight away and he spoke to me about the whole thing in a way that made it easy to understand. At our first meeting, he said he thought my company and website were hot property and we'd probably be beating people off with a stick. As well as the website I mentioned one other project I had in mind. Stephan looked like he had just had the equivalent of a financial orgasm. He said he thought we'd do so well because of this further idea we could pick the cream of the crop of investors and be in a strong position to call the shots. The idea was a virtual pop star based on Eleanor Rigby. People had been talking for a while about having the first virtual pop star but the idea hadn't worked because most people came at it from the wrong angle. They had designed the mannequin/Avatar, and then got a session singer and jobbing songwriters to do the music, meaning there was no real personality. It was the equivalent of a Eurovision song contest entry but without the mass audience. Because Eleanor had long since disappeared I had lost out on many licensing deals because record companies wanted her to come and tour to promote the releases. So, I came up initially with the idea of making her into a cartoon character that put out records (like The Archies), I then switched to the idea of making Eleanor a virtual act like Max Headroom that toured and promoted via the net. The reason why she would work where others had failed was that she had a track record and an interesting story to start with. She also had the material recorded already, plus her image really suited the virtual thing because in real life she was already considered the pop singing version of Lara Croft. If you remember Cubbi Broccoli had wanted her as a female James Bond or Modesty Blaise and this element could also be incorporated to make her more than just a pop singer. I also spoke with him about Box Office Poison and Stephan said the money I earned from this deal would help me break B.O.P much bigger. He put together a business plan and estimated that we could get a 3 million pounds investment for the company.

He wanted a percentage of course and was already looking at yachts he wanted to buy he was that confident. He got quite a few people interested and I did a presentation with many other Internet entrepreneurs at some flash establishment just off the Tottenham Court Road. Everyone came up to me afterwards saying mine was the best presentation by far. However I was taken with one person in particular who praised me since I'd actually fancied her from afar and never met her. Her name was Nanette and she was related to actress Diana Rigg who I was also a big fan of. She had held some top positions in the music business and her photo often appeared in Music Week and each time I saw it I thought I'd love to meet her. She was shocked to find out that I knew who she was and I soon asked her out.

Meanwhile, Stephan had acquired some offers in the form of free premises and use of staff from people like Stellios at 'Easy Jet' as just a teaser to see them first before others and presents were sent to us by other companies plus a few initial cash offers. But Stephan felt none were right and we could do a lot better. So, I started going to a lot of meetings with him. I don't remember all the names but I think Tamara Beckworth's father was someone we saw. The future looked bright and the whole thing was a bit of a buzz, Stephan even said we were closing in on some big deals and I should go and pick out a house I wanted to buy that had lots of additional space to have a recording studio and offices as well to give us some tax relief. I looked at a few at around half a million mark but then it all went pear-shaped. Stephan got very ill for a while so nothing got done whilst he was in the hospital and by the time he came out the Dot Com bubble had burst as I predicted. So it was back to doing things the traditional way.

Above one of a few Eleanor cartoon images:

CHAPTER THIRTY-SEVEN

CULT THEMES FROM THE 80s

With no new B.O.P material and in need of a new distributor I thought I'd return to the releases the label was best known for, although it has to said I was very reluctant at first as I didn't think the 80s was cult enough at this point, so to get me into it, I decided to be very ambitious with this album. Plus of course it would mean at least two new releases for Box Office Poison via two tracks as we feature on ALL the cult themes albums, so this gave me some incentive.

Having got some kudos of working with Glenda Collins & The Honeycombs I thought let's go up a further level with some bigger hit acts from more recent times and who were actually associated with the 80's. So with this album, I went for three acts that ticked that box. First up was Blondie. Since *Call Me* was one of the tracks I wanted to do I thought it might be nice to do a new version with the original band who also happened to be one of my all-time favourite bands. But to keep the originality of the album also get them to do another track not associated with them, *Absolute Beginners* (a Bowie track) which I intended to produce in a Walker Brothers style. Although Blondie had made a big comeback with the number one hit *Maria* in 1999 and a good selling album 'No Exit' they had once again faded from the scene and I had heard the label that put those releases out had either folded or dropped them, so I thought it might be possible to get them. So through a music contact, I spoke with Debbie Harry about the project and she said the band were up for the challenge and had heard some of the previous albums and liked them but a few weeks later Debbie called back to say they had been offered a new deal with a new label which meant they were contractually not able to do the themes album but she had an off the wall suggestion for me. I asked what it was and she said when Blondie is not touring many tribute bands do well and they officially recommend 'Once More Into The Bleach' as the tribute band to go and see. Debbie gave me the lead singer, Sam's number and said give her a call and go and see them and see what you think. It's a bit left-field but it could work and it's the nearest thing to having us on the album. My initial instinct was 'A tribute band... I don't think so' but as Debbie had gone to the trouble of recommending them I phoned Sam and went to see them in The Midlands the following week as I was up that way to watch an Athletics meeting anyway. I was very impressed with them and thought what the hell, let's give it a go. I told them what to learn for *Absolute Beginners* and they obviously knew *Call Me* like the back of their hand but I had a unique idea for that one as well. On arriving at the recording studio the backing band were still practising the arrangement I had given them so the singer Sam and I went into another room for a drink. There was instant chemistry between us and we were quick to embrace and have a snog followed by a bit of heavy petting. We were looking to go further when a band member popped his head around the corner and said they were ready to start recording. I then produced an excellent version of *Absolute Beginners,* which everybody was over the moon about. The idea was to then spend the night in the spare room at the studio in sleeping bags and record the second track the next day. Sam and I shared a sleeping bag with just our underwear on and our hands were all over each other but just when it was time for the underwear to get ditched another band member came into the room and started making noises and throwing things at us which put off proceedings. He then came and said he needed a word with Sam. She got up and went off with him for a few minutes. When she came back she said now wasn't the right time or place to have sex and we should meet in London once the albumcame out and celebrate it at my place. I reluctantly agreed and the next day we did *Call Me,* which I arranged to sound a bit like the Dr Who theme as it had a similar feel to it.

Many months later once the album was out Samantha & I met in London and went to see Debbie Harry together when she was in the Jazz Passengers. We then went backstage to see her and gave her a copy of The Cult Themes album. She said she was happy it had all worked out and it was a shame Blondie couldn't have done it, especially after she played *Absolute Beginners*, which she said was fabulous, adding she knew David Bowie very well and thought he'd really like that version and he certainly did after I got a copy to him. So two tracks were done and it was time for another big name. I had always been a big fan of Siouxsie and the Banshees and in the 80's I was trying to get a model friend of mine, Debbie a record deal and she took me out quite a lot and one night we went to a London club called Legends and at the bar introduced me to Siouxsie as she knew her. We had a drink and I asked her out as I really fancied her up close and personal. She had just had a throat nodule operation and was recovering from it so not touring or recording at the time so she agreed to spend the odd bit of time with me. She was probably one of the most intelligent and interesting girls I ever met and I hoped something might happen but she had to go off and do a promotional tour after being given the all-clear to continue her career because at one point it was touch and go. The reason I mention her is I was going over my track-listing and had earmarked another David Bowie film theme *Cat People* as one of the album tracks and I thought It would suit Siouxsie a lot. I knew the Banshees had split up at the time (they were always having a problem with guitarists). So I contacted Siouxsie. I wasn't thinking about anything personal as she had married Budgie (The great drummer of The Banshees, I still have part of his drum kit from when I knew Sioux the first time around). Anyway she was very interested in doing the track as she was always a big Bowie fan but said although the Banshees were not going at the time she was reactivating her side project, The Creatures and they were waiting on a deal to put out some new recordings but if it didn't go through she'd do *Cat People*. It was like Deja vu. The Creatures deal went through so no Siouxsie on the album. Then a strange thing happened. I got a CD from a band called 'Phosphoric' looking for a deal. I listened to it and the girl in this duo sounded a lot like Siouxsie, although she looked nothing like her, being blonde and Scandinavian. The music too was a pleasant surprise as I had this koto and percussion idea in my head for the arrangement along with cat noises to act like guitars. The guy in the band played a Persian version of a koto. It was obviously meant to be. The track came out brilliantly and exactly how I would have done it with Siouxsie and it sounds like it. (In fact a lot of people asked if it was Siouxsie recording under an assumed name)

The final name I was looking to resurrect was Hazel O'Connor as Breaking Glass soundtrack was a great 80's film & album and I fancied doing a new version of *Will You* in a reggae vein plus get her to do a Bond theme *The Living Daylights,* which I thought would suit her voice. Strangely as I was thinking about her I learned she was doing a concert not far from where I lived in a few weeks so I went to see her in concert. She was in fine form and went backstage afterwards. We hit it off very well and she agreed to do the themes. We then had a few more meetings and she started to learn the Bond theme. I quickly asked if she had any potential record deals pending to which she replies 'NO' so I was relieved. But would you believe it, a month later I had the studio booked to record her tracks and I got a call from her saying she couldn't make it as she wasn't well. She got

back to me a week later with more bad news. She said she still wanted to do the album but had a new manager who had committed her to many lucrative concerts in Europe and there was no way she could now record until the following year, which was far too late as I need the album out in 2001. So I had to forget about the idea of having famous acts I liked on the new cult themes album and decided I would stick with going back to the original ethic of helping to break new acts. Obviously Box Office Poison and The Incredibly Strange film band had to feature of as would Misty Woods.The Incredibly Strange Film Band wanted to do a combination of *Hill Street Blues* and *The A-Team* and this was quickly polished off. I then set about sorting out the two Box Office Poison tracks. My old mucker Mr Bowie was having a major influence on this album, mainly because he had done so many film themes in the 80's. With *Absolute Beginners* and *Cat People* already done the final song of his I wanted to do was, *This is Not American (The Falcon & The Snowman).* It went out as a solo track by Misty but effectively it was me and her (so B.O.P). This was done on my home 4 track again and was very cutting edge with raw drums and her doing a couple of different vocal styles. Then there was one random strummed acoustic guitar chord with echo moving randomly around the track. Misty then added some interesting synth sounds. Random was definitely the brief for this track and it ended up with a sample of an advert for Iceland (the country). Mr Jones liked this radical interpretation of it a lot. He loved the production on *Absolute Beginners* and said *Cat People* suited the film even more than the version he did with Giorgio Moroder.
The Bowie connection wasn't finished there as I was a massive fan of the theme *Merry Christmas Mr Lawrence* (which David starred in). I was keen to do this as a B.O.P track (which was effectively me & Misty again) It contains some of my best punk cello playing and is a very hypnotic track. In fact, my punk cello got quite an outing on this album. Most times I like to concentrate on just the production and often people ask me to play on their track and I'm not keen but with this album, I played on most tracks. My punk cello is very good on *Cat People* in particular. The other track B.O.P did was *Blade Runner* and it featured a lot of innovation including playing the rhythm track on an old typewriter and additional drums on a baking tray and like *Precinct 13* it features many household items again but only a synth as far as a musical instrument goes if you don't include my punk cello. Misty's evocative backing vocals were superb as usual doing a counter melody.
This was fast becoming one of my most innovative albums, as the next track would show. I had gone to yet another a new songwriter showcase by my friend Irene and discovered some more great acts, the top one being 'Celebrate the Sun' from Sweden. They were a very talented 3 piece and reminded me a lot of the supergroup 'Cream' (that featured Eric Clapton). This was one act I thought had a very bright future so nabbed them quickly. The other band I liked was called 'Toon but spelt 2oon. Celebrate The Sun were big fans of Prince and when they looked at the track-listing I had chosen there was only one track for them, *When Doves Cry (From Purple Rain).* They turned up to the studio looking to just copy the original. Their singer actually sounded a lot like Prince, so I couldn't do my usual trick of having someone from the opposite sex do the vocal so I went to town on a very innovative arrangement instead which blew the band away and although they didn't quite understand it at first they loved it by the end. There were 4 main innovations in this track. First, my punk cello, which I made sound like an actual Dove crying. Secondly, I also flicked the cello bow thru the air a lot then slowed down the recording of it and it acts as the intro and sounds like Doves flying around the room especially the way I panned the end mix, Thirdly, I translated the drum rhythm of the original to a guitar rhythm on this

version. However, the guitarist had a problem doing the hypnotic guitar effect I wanted so I ended up for the first and only time playing the guitar on an album (I used to only play a bit previously when writing songs for Eleanor but never played in the band or live preferring to play the percussion before I became a cello and koto player). Anyway, this guitar riff and effect worked to very well indeed (You have to hear the track to get what I mean)

Finally, the next innovation was some of the drum parts. I wanted a Fleetwood Mac Albatross vibe and the drummer didn't have the pom-pom sticks to play this and as I was trying to teach him what I wanted on the toms I decided to improvise further and I took my socks off and told him to do the same and we wrapped them around our hands and played them like pom-pom sticks together and I got the effect I was after. Lots of people really rate this cover of the song and I heard through a third party I knew in the music biz that Prince liked it a lot (Although I didn't hear from the purple persona myself). I thought it would be hard to compete with such a great original but we managed it. Sadly Celebrate the Sun didn't shine on and split up not that long after the album came out but they could have made it big in my opinion.

Next up were Toon and I wanted them to do *For Your Eyes Only.* Straight away it was going to be different with a male vocalist instead of the female original by Sheena Easton but the production and arrangement of the original version is a bit basic so I thought this is one Bond theme I could really go to town on like I'd done with *Moonraker* previously. You may recall Madonna was influenced by my Pop Noir style music and in particular Mysteries and this was very evident in the single *Frozen*. Although influencing this track, the producer William Orbit added some great production ideas to it and it's one of Madonna's best tracks lyrically and production-wise, in my opinion, and her best ever song. So I thought a similar production to Frozen would work on *For Your Eyes Only* and it did. I liked the band a lot as they had shown me a lot of respect and had also been checking out my photography and wanted to hire me to do a promo shoot for their original material and I did just that getting some great shots. A while later when the band split up (as they all do) the lead singer Phil, a bit of a Simon Le Bon look alike wanted to become an actor and again wanted to hire me to do his promo shots and the transformation I did was nothing short of miraculous (The results are in my book 'Music Business Bastards').

This ties in nicely with the next artist to grace the cult themes, one Carmel Morris, an Australian multi-talent. She was a published author as well as musician and inventor and she had put out a great album of music dedicated to the TV show The Prisoner of which we were both big fans. She wanted to license her album to a UK label for distribution and since I loved it I agreed (We had in some ways come full circle). Here I was about to do the latest cult Themes album and one of the first tracks on the first Themes from the 60s Vol.1 album was *The Prisoner Theme* and my first B.O.P single *Checkmate* was a Prisoner tribute. So we had a lot in common. However, although I loved the music on Carmel's album 'Another Number' the CD presentation left a lot to be desired with her looking very mumsy on the cover and when she came to England to see me I could see she could look a lot better and did some new photos transforming her (which again is featured in the book Music Business Bastards) and these made a big difference between not a lot of interest of her CD to suddenly lots of interviews and even a licensing deal to another label of one of her tracks. We hit it off big time and the sensuality just crackled between us and we spent a great few days between the sheets as well as doing some raunchy photos, not for publication. This girl had a real edge to her that I liked and she

was very intelligent which also turned me on and it didn't surprise me to learn she had once been Michael Hutchens of INXS girlfriend. Things could have gone to a whole new level between us as the chemistry was there but she was staying with another admirer who was covering the cost of her trip and so it didn't seem quite fair to continue with this brief affair so we ended it. (Although we are still mates). Anyway, with Hazel O'Connor having dropped out of doing the Bond Theme, *The Living Daylight's,* I got Carmel to do it instead and it's a very good version. It was time for the final 2 tracks to be produced. Another CD I had been impressed with was by 'A Girl Called Max' So, I went to see her live at a lesbian club, for she was a proud lesbian. I agreed for her to go on the album and luckily for me she was a big fan of the film *Pretty in Pink* and this was one of the last tracks on my list to do. Unfortunately, the record label was running out of funds because of what happened in 2000 and so the deals we did with the artist were, if we covered the recording the royalty was lower and there would be deductions. But if the artists had recording equipment or access to a studio of their choice there were no deductions and they got a higher royalty. Max chose the latter but upon recording the track, her equipment wasn't the best and although it came out quite good it's not as good as it could have been.
The final track had already been decided a while back, *The Blues Brothers.* This came about from a guy called Darren who was previously with ELBOW who appeared on the previous cult themes album and he had formed a new band, The Soul Detectives doing soul covers and cult themes and because he had done a great job promoting the last album I gave his new band a shot to do a track. However, the band would be put through their paces as I got them all to learn each other parts and kept them on their toes. I again swapped the rhythms around the guitar to drum and it's a very interesting version of *The Blues Brothers*. The final pleasing thing about doing this album was the respect I got from many of the bands as I was now very established with a big reputation. None more so than when I produced this band with two members saying to me it's a buzz to work with such a legend. At long last, I had arrived as a record producer at the top of my game.

There was to be a quick footnote, however. I got a final CD thru that I was blown away with by a Rockabilly act from Switzerland called coincidently Max. He was a fan of my production, Eleanor and Themes and was desperate to do a cult theme but they had all be allocated and the album was finished but he pleaded with me so I agreed he could do a track but didn't know what track. He wanted to do *Dynasty* but I wasn't sure it was cult enough, he assured me it was. I was supposed to fly out to Switzerland to record it but my plane was cancelled and I couldn't reschedule it and with the album release deadline looming I took the unusual step of letting him produce it himself as I liked his production anyway. However, I would remix the track slightly once he sent me the tape so that I was still effectively part producer. This was done and the album was finally finished. (In hindsight it was a mistake as this track never seems to sell, so it was not cult after all. I shouldn't have taken his word but was pushed for time). Oh and by the way I slipped our original track *Alien* on the album as well. Although Alien is a cult film it never had a decent tune. I was just being cheeky trying to get some promotion for one of my favourite songs and some might have even thought it suited the film very well and might have been in it.
As for the album sleeve, this was one of my first Alien type photo-art attempts. It features Misty wrapped in netting and turned into an Alien egg floating in space with other planets around her.

I felt the album had some of my best ever productions so was pleased in a way that I'd done it. This was also confirmed when I was nominated for UK record producer of the year for it once it came out. (Although in my opinion I would go one better with the Psykick Holiday 'Forever Pop Noir' as far as production and arrangements go). But the road ahead for this 80's album would be very rocky and nearly finish the label off. The Cult Themes from the '80s was a tricky customer in many ways. It was a great album production-wise and creativity wise. It was even full of acts from all around the world not just the UK but Sweden Australia, Switzerland, Demark. But I was still deliberating about whether the 80s was a cult period yet. The daunting thing now would be to find a new decent distributor for it. (below what might have been + sleeve for release)

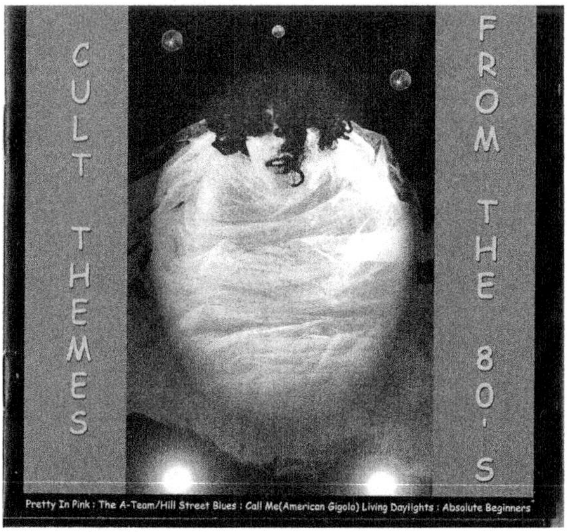

SIOUXSIE

CHAPTER THIRTY-EIGHT

JANE

2000 had pretty much been my year as an adventurer but in 2001 despite saying I wasn't keen on another manager after the Martina incident with things slowing down I felt a new manager might give us new emphasis. I also needed more help at the record label. Everybody remembers where they were when the twin towers came down on September the 11th 2001. I remember it clearly. I was with my new manager, a dusky sexy blonde newsreader type called Jane. Sadly I hadn't learnt my lesson about business and pleasure I was wondering how I could relieve my new mangers of her knickers at the earliest opportunity I had met her some months before at an X-factor type affair when she managed one of the bands on the bill. It was a bizarre event where I sat on the panel book-ended by a Marilyn Monroe and Princess Diana look-alike. What they knew about singing talent I wasn't sure but this set the tone for the new millennium of Z-list celebrities. There was a queue of these Z-listers both on the panel and performing in between the new starry-eyed talent. It was reminiscent of the Showbiz Eleven I was involved with that you will have read in an earlier chapter. The word 'WHO' was constantly stuck in my mouth as they were introduced to the crowd. Lee McDonald of Grange Hill fame was the biggest celebrity there, so that tells you all you need to know. He was a lovely chap though and better than Z-list material. However, I had bigger fish to fry though. The Princess Diana look-alike came across as extremely sexy and I was looking to be her Prince for the night. I felt I definitely deserved something for my troubles as I felt I'd been conned by an ex-agent to take part in one thing but got another. I was used to judging The Battle of the Bands type contests and quite enjoyed those but most people on this bill were like Karaoke artists except for one Irie White, a wannabe white reggae singer and it was his manager that accosted me during the interval offering to buy me a drink. Was this a bribe I wondered? I didn't care because I'd already decided he was the best on the bill so it was music to my ears when Jane asked to make an appointment to see me as she had found out I ran a record label and was a record producer. She was all business but all I could think of was, I want to do other business with her! I had seen her a few times since our first meeting and persuaded her that I was altogether a better bet to manage than the current crop she had. She was loyal to her other charges but agreed I was a bigger fish. With the new Cult Themes album in full swing, her entrance to my life was very timely. She had come over to my place to discuss the forthcoming big concert to promote it and September 11th cemented our relationship in more ways than one and she agreed to manage B.O.P and continued with me for many years even after B.O.P. She really believed in me and the band's talent and was very good at networking and a few other things, however, she rarely knew many of the very top people in the industry and our main goal was to get with a bigger label. (That's not a criticism, just the way it was). I'm still close to her now and she does bits and pieces for me on a non-exclusive basis. So as she is part of The B.O.P story thought I'd give her a mention.

CHAPTER THIRTY-NINE

THE FINAL CONCERT

I finally managed to get a new distribution deal. It was with a major company, Universal. Being a positive and optimistic person I decided to do the biggest concert we had ever done to launch Cult Themes from the 80s, plus a few smaller gigs as well.

One of the other bands on the album, The Soul Detectives were playing a gig in Southend to promote the album and asked me to D.J at it. Toon were supposed to be the support act but dropped out at the last minute and the S.D asked me to fill in and do a solo spot. Me playing Avant-garde punk cello doing Pop Noir music at a soul concert to a mainstream audience It would be a challenge and I thought I'd be lucky not to get bottled off. I nearly did and lots of the audience were scratching their heads but then they started to respect my nerve and by the end, I converted a large selection of the crowd who at least gave me a decent ovation. Most people would need to wear their brown trousers to do something like this but I took it all in my stride. (I lived Pop-Noir)

Madame Jo's maximum capacity was about 500 at a push and we always filled it so I looked for a bigger venue and someone recommended the Subterranea, close to the famous Portobello road, Notting Hill. It held 1500 people. The Mean Fiddler Group owned it and so I went to see them.

I felt we were famous enough by now not to do a door money split or even hire a venue but have them pay us a set fee and they take the door money and bar takings. . With our good reputation and having six acts on the bill it was a good deal for them. The promoter had also recently seen The Incredibly Strange Film Band pack out The Jazz Cafe so they agreed to it my terms. We got £1500. At the last Jo Jo's gig the bands all got paid about £50 each. I decided the headline acts should get £300 and the smaller acts £50 each plus free drinks and a guest list. This seemed like a good deal for all concerned as most bands were still on door money shares for other concerts and in the case of the new acts even paying to play. I also persuaded the venue to do some advertising and foot the bill for 5,000 quality flyers. Bands would also get a rider, which is FREE drinks. This is something that acts on big labels get. Even without the concerts, most acts did well in raising their profile from appearing on a Cult Themes album and that was the whole point of the exercise, helping bands get to the next level. As well as getting a good deal for the venue, I also got an additional sponsor for more free drinks and an advertiser to put freebies in doggie bags for fans (which my new manager Jane had sorted this out as her first big result)

.It was looking like this release would be the make or break for the label .Then came the bad news. Pre-sales of the album through Universal were only 350 initially, most other themes albums sold a minimum of 1,000 and usually in more than one format. Although this was CD only it was disappointing as that barely covered our costs. I suppose I should be used to the incompetence of big distributors. I phoned my label manager at Universal, a girl called Lesley (Who used to be in the hit band The Belle Stars) to see what happened and she said it was a hard to sell as The Cult Themes trend I started was long gone and unlike the last album, it didn't feature any former million-selling acts on it and record shops were sceptical about the 80's decade being cult. The release timing also wasn't great. It was being sold into the shops in September/October with an early

November release and I should know as a former record shop manager all the big-name acts albums are sold in at this time with a view to Xmas sales.

I did know this of course and I had planned the release initially for the start of September but waiting on decisions from name acts, especially Hazel had delayed things a lot, hence the November release. Lesley had said the big concert should shift the CD's easily enough and create a buzz and we'd be fine. She also thought the album was great and loved the production, track-listing and most of the acts. So much so she would recommend it to a few influential people and someone at the trade paper Music Week and also give it to Jonathan Ross. Universal may have been crap but Lesley was actually very good and the album got a great review in Music Week and elsewhere. The influential chat-show host Jonathan Ross also started playing *Absolute Beginners* on his radio show and loved it. He said it was such a unique idea to get a Blondie tribute band to do a Bowie track and it was a great version but that it could have been even better had the real Blondie done it, but that aside it was a great cover anyway. (If only he knew) So it wasn't all bad news.

On the night of the big gig at the Subtariania, we were expecting a great night and a large turnout. The Incredibly Strange Film Band normally get a crowd of about 500 and promised to bring their normal crowd, Once More Into the Bleach said they always got a similar number and many people had been asking them to play London for a long time as they rarely played there. Misty was doing 3 spots, solo, Box Office Poison and with her new band The Ju Ju Babies and she could always drag in around 100. But I was less optimistic about Phosphoric as they hadn't done many gigs and thought 50 might be a good result and A Girl Called Max had about 100 people last time I saw her, so I figured if half those turned up that would be good. As for Box Office Poison, we had somewhat of a unique following. We regularly had about 3,000 fans buy our original records in the Uk and about 2,000 outside the UK. Some bought the themes some didn't. The good news was they were scattered in every major town in the UK and many rural areas and there were few corners of the UK where we did not have a fan. This was good news to try and get a chart hit as lots of people only buying in one area looked suspicious and because of this records were sometimes thrown out of the charts. But the bad news was because the vast majority lived outside London (quite a lot in Scotland for some reason) with it also being midweek many were not going to make the effort to travel to London for this gig, so I thought at a push 300-500 might make the effort. I was relying on my new manager Jane to get the fans interested and get advertisers for the goody bags, She did well with the latter but struggled to get the buzz going with the fans managing only one postal mailout as the Internet was still in its infancy back then. I had more than enough to concentrate on dealing with all the acts, the venue and the Mean Fiddler promoter and I would also be D.J on the night. I had hired a compare for the event but that was the first downer of the night when he didn't show up and I was stuck doing that as well. The good news was all the acts performed brilliantly and it was one of the best concerts I went to but the bad news was the sparse crowd. The place held 1500 and even previous themes gigs had about 500 but it looked like less than 300 turned up (Ok for a small club but in a big venue it looked bad). Also, the free drink for the acts had gone missing and the venue's promoter was nowhere to be found. A lot of frantic phone calls and liasing with the venue manager finally got all the drinks sorted out but too late for some who had been moaning for an hour or more. I was supposed to be D.J, and it was also a sad night for me as well because Misty had told me she was leaving B.O.P and this would be our last ever concert, So I decided that would be the end for B.O.P. without her. So all I needed was more shit going down. It was still coming my way when the night ended with the bands looking for their payment and the promoter on the missing list still. He was supposed to be bringing the balance of payment with him to pay me. Fortunately, I had the foresight to get half in advance and a combination of this and my writing a few cheques quelled the situation. But did the bands deserve to get paid at all? The inquest started on the night. It looked like most acts had brought a handful of people and the biggest parts of the crowd were there to see Misty's new band and B.O.P. The excuses were flowing thick and fast. It was because it was midweek, it was because it was a hard venue to get to but Misty did a bit of digging and found that because all bands were guaranteed to get paid certain bands decided to hold back their fan base for another gig where they were on a share of the door money. I wasn't happy. Although it was a good gig to watch it was a crying shame not many people had come to see it. The highlight and lowlight for me was Misty and me performing as Box Office Poison for the last time that night and we excelled.

Because of the low turn out only about 100 CDs were sold on the night and sales still hadn't picked up via Universal. We then had to hammer the Internet to double our sales so the album did make a small profit and not a loss in the end. I was exhausted and despondent about the whole episode and started to reflect on my future. (below BW version of colour flyer for concert).

80s THEMES CONCERT

Me & Misty and below Incredibly Strange Film Band, Pat McGarvey & Once More into the Bleach

CHAPTER FORTY

THE END WAS NIGH

Many people had said over the years I was a talented songwriter as well as a record producer and I should have pushed my own career more rather than helping so many others. So at this point it would have been a good time to concentrate on Box Office Poison but sadly that too had come to an end. One big sting in the tail of proceedings was Music Week nominated me for UK record producer of the year for Cult Themes from the 80s along with my track record for innovation.
Before the Cult Themes release because B.O.P had been just me & Misty the idea was that we start to co-write the next B.O.P album together. We wrote one track called *Oh Captain* (It was a madcap catchy pop song). Misty then suggested a songwriting session purposely drinking a bottle of Absinthe to see what happened (This was the drink that made Van Gough cut off his ear apparently). It was illegal to buy and considered slightly dangerous. I decided what the hell let's give it a try. But it did nothing to me I didn't even get drunk on it and Misty ended up doing a whole lot of primal screaming onto tape but nothing coherent so we abandoned that Idea.

Misty had also met a French keyboard player called Yan & oriental guitarist called Karen (picture bottom left) when I had my year off as an adventurer in 2000. I felt I she needed her freedom to do her own stuff and that's what she did calling the trio 'Molotova'. However, she did want me involved in one way and asked me to do some promo photos for her band, which I did upon a return from one trip. She released a low-key album and did some gigs including one at in The City that Tony Wilson ran that I had been to some years before as a panellist with Peter Hook of New Order/Joy Division. However, she confided in me that it was a lot harder than expected to be the main driving force in the band and she now had double respect for me because when you are the driving force in the band you tend to organise and get things done and her other band members despite her asking for help did nothing and were lazy so in the end, she called time on this project and we did the Themes tracks for B.O.P and her solo tracks and I thought she would continue with B.O.P but her contract with the label and B.O.P was about to run out and she didn't want to renew it and said the Cult Themes concert would be our last performance together as B.O.P but she wanted to carry on seeing me as we had such a strong bond. Also far from giving up after the bad taste left by her first band she quickly got together a new one called The Ju Ju Babies and asked if they could play the Themes concert. I agreed of course and this band did a bit better than her first band going off to do a residency in IBIZA and releasing a good EP *Electro Trash (pictured below)*. But I knew Misty and me were not finished and she'd be back, the only thing was I didn't realise quite what that was going to involve. With Misty now out of the country doing her new band, B.O.P now dead and the Cult Themes project at an end. I decided to dissolve my contract with Universal and take a much-needed break from doing the record label and go on another new adventure out of the country.

WOULD I LIKE TO PRODUCE ONE OF THE MOST SUCCESS ACTS EVER?

Sadly I didn't win the record producer of the year in 2002. I came third. Had I won, would that have led to bigger things? Well even before the result I was offered bigger things. I got a call from a publishing & management company called Windswept Pacific. They wanted to see me about producing some big hit chart acts. Once at their offices if was dumbfounded to learn it was. **Westlife**. This band were the most successful act in the country with numerous number one hits, 14 in all and not far behind even The Beatles. They had shifted over 50 million records. Why was I not jumping for joy? Well if you asked me to sum up the band and their music the word 'Bland' springs to mind. The question was, why did the blandest band in The UK, if not the world want one of the leading cutting edge producers producing them, it made no sense. After I got over the shock I put this question to their representatives at Windswept, adding, were they looking to go in a whole new direction and shock people with some exciting cutting edge music? The answer came back 'NO' they just want more of the same. I was even more confused 'What gives?,' They offered a 5-figure sum to produce their album. I asked had the band actually heard anything I had produced? Why me? It turned out they had read about me being nominated in Music Week and said we want this guy to produce our next album. They had fallen out with a previous producer and didn't know much about producers but had a say in who produced them because of their clout, so were flexing their muscles and thought as I was nominated and it was thought I had a good chance of winning I must be really good and the go-to producer. I can't say it was an easy decision. On one hand, there was no way I wanted to produce such bland music and spoil my reputation of many years. But on the other hand, I needed money at the time and tens of thousands of pounds plus add-ons would end up being a big cheque in anyone's language. The lads at Windswept were very surprised at my reaction and the fact I didn't jump at the opportunity. So they asked me to let it sink in and have a think about it and in the meantime, they had another act they thought more suited to my talents that needed producing, 'Atomic Kitten' This was another manufactured band but this time they were all female which is more my speciality but again they leant towards bland records. It was also unfortunate that the main one 'Kerry Katona' was in the press most days for dodgy tabloid stories. I wasn't thrilled about the prospect of producing a band with her in it. The meeting ended with them giving me two days to think about it. I decided to turn down the Westlife opportunity as my producer reputation was hard-fought and meant a lot to me and I didn't want it ruined. Also, as a producer, I needed to get a creative buzz from each project I do and it looked like none here at all. I asked for a bit more time to think about the other job as I was busy promoting the cult themes. Unfortunately, I didn't do my homework properly because every time I started to check out Atomic Kitten lots of stuff kept coming up about Kerry and it was off-putting. I should have persevered a bit more as later on I finally got to hear more of the other singer in the band Natasha Hamilton and she was a brilliant singer and sexy as well. I was thinking of turning this this down as well but was then told the band were on the verge of splitting up now anyway.

As a footnote to this story: During 2002 I was hired by several cutting edge acts and the recordings were far more rewarding artistically. Also, when I mentioned to a few of the acts about the Westlife deal they all said if that had been on my C.V they would never have hired me in a million years. I still regret not producing Natasha Hamilton though but that's life. Although there were a few highs like the nomination and I was therefore getting some long overdue recognition I took time off to reflect on my situation overall.

CHAPTER FORTY-ONE

AFTERMATH

Although B.O.P were dead the creativity lived on in a different form. Once Misty's two other bands had let her down and folded she came to me saying she now wanted to give modelling a go and asked me to take some photos because I had always taken good one of her. This resulted in a number of both raunchy and creative photos. We spoke about doing music again but it was a case of the door isn't totally closed but it was highly unlikely. When I finally got the successor to B.O.P, Psykick Holiday I asked her to be the singer in this band but she declined and said something that would become prophetic. She said although you prefer girl singers to sing your songs you should sing more and front the band yourself. Despite doing the odd vocal I was always very reluctant. She was always getting me to do bits and pieces of vocals with B.O.P and on the themes. For some reason, I felt fine being lead singer with Ministry of Ska but not beyond that despite Mysteries being well received. But she proved to be right in the end as when I did do lead vocals they proved to be the most popular tracks for Psykick Holiday.

Misty and I remained friends for quite a while till she went off the radar to concentrate on politics and union stuff and it was only recently that we met up again and still got on very well and now there is an outside chance of us writing a song for Psykick Holiday.

As for Ron, he still plays live with various bands although he also has a full-time job as a tree surgeon. However, there was a B.O.P reunion of sorts when we teamed up to do a very innovative version of the X-Files on Cult Themes Forever album in 2019. (Ron doing multiple sax parts, me on multiple percussion and production). I put it out as just Ron Howe though. (Psykick Holiday are also on the album doing 2 Bond Themes). Ron also features in the group Shame About the Girl doing Beat Girl (both instrumental & sung version by my new P.H vocalist Maiko)

Both Louise & Jo briefly contacted me in the preceding years saying they hadn't fulfilled their ambitions and that B.O.P now stood as the nearest thing to making it and being famous and they looked back on it with fond memories.

Nothing is known about sax players Dave (Bowler) or Abbey but I can exclusively reveal Solfried's backing vocals did end up on Mysteries. I also briefly teamed up with Avril again when she became my publisher for the reissue of Music Business Bastards book in 2013 (she also featured in the Eleanor Rigby Story Documentary)

I am still best friends with Anne and she is still the major owner of Future Legend Records. I gave her the opportunity to make a comeback doing a one-off track for 'Cult Themes Forever' album but she declined. Ironically, after feeling overshadowed by Misty in the B.O.P period she has gone on to outsell Misty with her solo version of *All the Young Girls Love Alice* which became a lesbian anthem in recent years and her album 'Mirror Image' still sells most weeks and she is contemplating doing an anniversary deluxe release of it on CD. People still get Misty's solo tracks as well and once again to my surprise my solo tracks are quite popular, in particular, The Adventurer (which is on the CD 'Cult Themes From the 70s Vol.2' or on the download album 'A Tribute to John Barry'.)

However, our influence has lived on and we are being discovered all the time. Apparently, I influenced Billie Eilish with my whispery style vocal so my solo track (that was really a B.O.P track) *A Day Without Love,* was re-released recently on download and Spotify. In truth, it was basically a demo but it has a certain charm and isn't too bad so in a way, this was a final B.O.P release. It features Anne/Mouse as well.

Prior to that, we emptied the vaults and made one of our first-ever recordings *Lazer Love* a download single. So that is the last one to come out with the B.O.P name on it. However those getting the early batch of this biog got an MP3 of the unreleased B.O.P track *This Gun's For Hire*. The lyrics were featured in a B.O.P zine and people wondered why this track was never released. It is a good song and innovative music but I noticed after I recorded it that the chorus had a similarity to a Bruce Springsteen song so not wanting to be sued I decided against releasing it officially. It's from B.O.P mark 1 and features Jo singing lead vocals on it.

As I mentioned elsewhere I am involved in many charities and Titus House homeless charity wanted me to do a new version of *Backstreet Boulevard* with Ed Sheeran no less but it never happened in the end so I re-released Box Office Poison's original version in 2019 instead to raise money for the homeless and did a one-off solo performance of it for Centerpoint homeless charity. So this was the last official release by Box Office Poison, so our legacy lives on and new people are discovering us all the time.

BACKSTREET BOULEVARD

Stroll on stroll on down the street

Electricity flows through your feet

Down and outs are all you meet

Huddled together for body heat

Chorus

You've got to be so hard. on backstreet boulevard

All weakness is barred, On backstreet boulevard

My god love you look a terrible sight

So would you, if you'd been open all night

Junkie, flunkie, why take dope?

Because without it there's no hope

Junkies, wino's, pimps and hookers

You're nothing to them except onlookers

They crave and kroner, ten pence or a dime

The outstretched hand is the same world mime.

Chorus again

LEGACY

If you miss B.O.P and want more then Psykick Holiday is your next destination as we carry on where B.O.P left off. We fly the flag for the Pop Noir music genre, and it's still the only place you can hear punk cello. I obviously do the songwriting & production. Some have even said it's B.O.P mark 3 but I feel we have taken Pop Noir music to another level and the **Forever Pop Noir** album by PH is the definitive Pop Noir style album. PH itself has gone thru many changes but the consistency is present because the punk cello and I are still there.

There is also a possible B.O.P mark 4. I have another long-term project, The Alien Orchestra UK. It's like Ennio Morricone meets Alien sounds. We have released two songs already. Unsurprising an instrumental version of the B.O.P track *Alien* (therefore a big link to B.O.P) The 2nd track was *Chi Mai* , a cover of a Morricone single (that was a no.1 hit) It's on 'Cult Themes Forever CD album and is definitely worth checking out. This outfit will be like a classical orchestral version of B.O.P . *(Below: A few less X-rated photos done of Misty after B.O.P's demise & Psykick Holiday Cd Sleeve)*

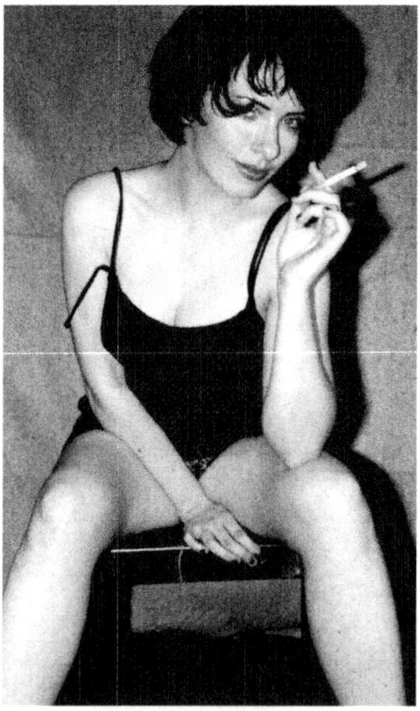

CHAPTER FORTY-ONE

PUNK CELLO

As Punk Cello is such and important part of Box Office Poison and people always ask about it or are fascinated by it I decided to give it it's own chapter.

I do many things but often put musician at the back of the queue as I consider this my least important skill. I am purely an improvisational musician and can just about play enough of a few instruments to be able to write a song. My chosen instrument was originally drums and my first band The Ice Age (Aged just 13) was where I developed this on cardboard boxes & biscuit tins.
But then life took many other turns away from music until I finally became songwriter & producer for Eleanor Rigby.
Fast forward to Box Office Poison in the 90s and it was here punk cello was born. Again I started as the drummer but after struggling to get a cello player who could improvise (most can only read music & play what is written as most are classically trained) I thought it would be quicker to learn to play the cello than find the right person to do what I wanted. I learnt the basics and then improvised. Although I came up with some great cello riffs in songs like *Alien* & *Think For Yourself* playing more conventional cello it was creating an atmosphere and getting a different sound out of the cello that interested me more. I made it sound like various animals or punky like a saw (Hence the punk reference sound wise but just doing it was the other punk ethic at play). The final two ingredients to it are the way I play it, also adding different effects to it (mostly a delay effect)
I started off playing a conventional cello but using an electric pick up but now I have an electric cello more suited to the task. On top of this, I discovered another first, which was that I could play cello lines on a keyboard (using a cello sound) that were physically impossible for a classical cello player to play because their fingers couldn't reach and therefore creating classical cello bits never done before because classical composers would never write such parts as they would be impossible to play.
Although when I play live people often comment on the punk cello sound making the band distinctive it also makes the recorded tracks different and special but it's often subtle. Good examples of this atmosphere & sound can by found on *Merry Christmas Mr Lawrence* & *Cat People* on Cult Themes from the 80s'. It's also interesting to note what I did on *When Doves Cry* (as detailed in the Cult Themes from the 80s album). On the Cult Themes albums I prefer to just produce and arrange the tracks but am often asked to play as well. I am always reluctant but made an exception on Cult Themes from the 80s in particular although on the B.O.P tracks I was obviously required to play as an integral part of the bands sound and what sets us apart.

Because the Pop Noir bands like Box Office Poison and its successor Psykick Holiday don't use guitars they need other instruments that can drive the track but also give it a raw edge a guitar might normally contribute (Otherwise a band might start sounding like a string quartet), so this raw hypnotic element of punk cello can be found to good effect on tracks like *The Deep* by B.O.P on Cult Themes From the 70s Vol.2 and *Dark Horse* on Psykick Holiday's 'Forever Pop Noir' album (which also has what sounds like horse sounds on the intro but is in fact punk cello playing these bits making it sound like a horse).

So how many punk cellists are currently out there? I consider myself probably the only one and am definitely the inventor of it but whilst recording 'Forever Pop Noir' album another cellist came to the session and tried to replicate what I was doing for his band Stereo Art. He got some elements but struggled to get others bits of the concept as he thought in a too conventional way. So you could safely I am the worlds leading punk cellist and it keeps my current music with Psykick Holiday standing out from the crowd. I may be doing less of it in Psykick Holiday recording to concentrate on trumpet & koto and my newfound popularity as a vocalist. However, I will continue to develop punk cello more in my future band The Alien Orchestra UK.
I also did do one solo track *Mixing with The Unknown* (the title of a book I wrote) that features just punk cello & vocals and this is rare but on Itunes. It will be redone when the film of the book is made. So that is a quick insight into punk cello.

Russ with original cello & above exclusively his new electric cello with his current muse Maiko doing a sort of homage to Misty.

SONG

Although I haven't put all my song lyrics in this book I put what I considered the most relevant ones, but it seems fitting to put this last lyric at the end as this was our first ever single.

1995

It was a violent country, when the ice age came
The war was over, but the world was the same
The eyes were upon us in search of a name
Nothing was answered and the questions remain

Will anyone survive in 95, in 1995
Anyone alive in 95 in 1995

The blackness erupted from the burning snow
The people were running, but with nowhere to go
The heat came down like a sledgehammer blow
It happened so fast and I was too slow

Will anyone survive in 95, in 1995
Anyone alive in 95 in 1995
Will anyone survive in 95, in 1995
Anyone alive in 95 in 1995

The sky cleared of mist all around
The sea was frozen and as hard as the ground
We lay for a moment void of all sound
The world was in fragments, where it once had been round

Will anyone survive in 95, in 1995
Anyone alive in 95 in 1995
Will anyone survive in 95, in 1995
Anyone alive in 95 in 1995
Now we're into atomic override
Who wants to be a radiation bride?

DISCOGRAPHY

Singles

1995/Checkmate on 7", 12 Vinyl, CD & Cassette single (features two different versions of each track on CD & cassette) and on 12" a French version along with special sex mix & of English track + 1995. (*1993*)

Mysteries on CD & 12" vinyl (12" features French & Spanish versions & special bongo mix & normal version). CD features Getting Thru the day (dance mix) instead of bongo mix of Mysteries (*1994*)

Alien/Teenage Sex CD-EP : Bonus tracks 16 Year Old (new version featuring Mouse) + Psycho City (featuring Russell) (*1997*)

Think For Yourself/Lady Grinning Soul CD-EP : Bonus tracks Louie Louie + Nightmare on Elm Street (*1997*)

Popcorn (limited edition CD) (*2000*) bonus track Checkmate rave mix (download release *2009*)

The Legend of Xanadu (limited edition CD-EP) (*2000*) features 4 different mixes of Xanadu + 1. A Day Without Love 2. Skag Kids 3. Department.S 4. General Vibe (download released in *2009*) B-side Skag Kids.

I Want to Sleep with You (Pt.2)/Merry Christmas Mr Lawrence (Download only or on demand CD: *2013*)

Lazer Love (download & limited on demand CD) (*2017*) *Also appeared on a white label.

Magic (download and on ltd on demand CD) (*2018* **)**

Backstreet Boulevard (download only or on demand CD) (*2019*)

There was a 5 track 7" vinyl white label promo EP: featuring Think For Yourself (album version) 1995, 16 year Old, Sad World + Lazer Love (done for record labels) (*1991*)

There was a one sided 7" vinyl white label single for promo of final mix of Popcorn (*1992*)

There was a 7" & 12" yellow label provisional mixes of Popcorn promo (*1992*)

All the above promos did escape to the collectors market.

*** Special deal to celebrate the release of this book & B.O.P's 30th anniversary we are doing thirty 7" vinyl copies of the debut single '1995/Checkmate' for just £1 + P&P. Just email december.books@yahoo.com to get your copy (If you want it signed as well just say so)

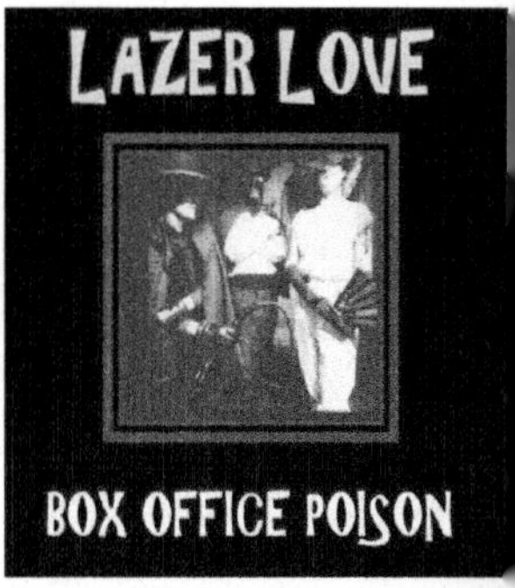

ALBUMS

Beyond The Twilight Zone : *1. Think For Yourself* * *2. Checkmate 3.Mysteries 4.Magic 5. Love on the Phone 6. Cry Out the Pain 7. Sad World 8.1995 9. Backstreet Boulevard 10. 16 Year Old 11. We're All Insane 12. Alien* * *13. We Are the Future*. (released *1995*) CD

* denotes original version: They were redone in 1997 as singles with Misty singing.

Heavy Breathing Decade : *1. Come With Me (pt.1) 2. I Want to Sleep With You (pt.2)3.Don't Sleep With Him 4. Take Me Up to Heaven and Back 5. Strip Show 6.All the Young Girls Love Alice 7. I Want You All the Time 8. Making Love to the General Vibe 9 Is It Sex You Seek 10. For the Video 11. All I Want's a Baby 12. Penicillin Passion 13.Teenage Sex 14. Sex On the Internet 15. Come With Me (Pt.2)* (released *1998*) CD

Themes, Dreams, Nightmares & Schemes (The Best of Box Office Poison)
1.Mission Impossible 2. Checkmate 3. 1995 4. Mysteries 5. Alien 6. Teenage Sex 7.Think For Yourself 8.Lady Grinning Soul 9.Louie Louie 10. Nightmare on Elm Street 11.Popcorn 12The Legend of Xanadu 13. Merry Christmas Mr Lawrence 14. I Want to Sleep with You (Pt.2) 15. Department-S 16 From Russian With Love 17. The Deep 18 Bladerunner 19. Madelena 20. Man in A Suitcase. (Released *2000* Ltd edition CD) download *2016.*

<u>Album Tracks</u>

Mission Impossible, Man in a Suitcase & The Prisoner Theme: **Themes from the 60s Vol.1** *1993*
All Too Much (Yellow Submarine) & The Ipcress File : **Themes from the 60s Vol.2** *1994*
Department-S & For a Few Dollars More : **Themes From the 60s Vol.3** *1995*
The Persuaders & The Chase (Midnight Express): **Cult Themes From the 70s Vol.1** *1997*
The Deep & Madellena : **Cult Themes from the 70s Vol.2** *1999*
Bladerunner & Merry Christmas Mr Lawrence: **Cult Themes From the 80s** *2001*
Louie Louie : **Generation to Generation** Dr Martens *1997*

That Instrumental Vibe album. Instrumental versions of B.O.P tracks
1.*Think For Yourself* 2.*Mysteries* 3.*The Legend of Xanadu* 4.*Louie Louie* 5.*Teenage Sex* 6.*Alien* 7.*Lady Grinning Soul* 8.*General Vibe* 9. *Sex on the Internet* 10. *1995* 11. *From Russia with Love* 12. *Nobody Does it Better* 13. *Popcorn* (on demand CD in *2000*)
Download 2010 :

From Russia With Love: **The Themes Bond..James Bond (Alternative Bond themes)** (*2007*) (Ltd Edition CD & Download)
B.O.P also featured on The compilations: ***Mod Tunes (3 Button Legacy), The Future Legend Records Singles, Kick Ass Crime Fighters, 20 Shades of Erotica & Femme Fatales of Music***

LOOKING BACK

After writing this in-depth biography I thought it would be interesting to look back in hindsight about our career, our ups & downs and our legacy. Like most bands, we set out to be successful and get to number one and appear on Top of the Pops. Well, we didn't get a national number one, we didn't appear on Top of The Pops and success is down to how you interpreted it?
We did hit number one in the college charts and top 10 in the dance charts. Our releases all made a profit although not a big one. We did appear on mainstream radio & TV and in the major press but it was the fanzine community that embraced us most as did cabel TV. We did make a dent in music influencing other bands. We even played some unique gigs that were much talked about.
We came very close on a couple of occasions to breaking through very big. If you add our singles sales to those of the compilations we appeared on we sat in over 100,000 peoples homes. In the digital age we now live in many more as all our tracks still sell weekly and get played daily, be it only on Spotify. Many bands can't say that.
I would say our career was a quite a good one and I and the Pop Noir genre do live on in my new band Psykick Holiday.
I have read many bands biogs and they are all full of the same type of thing. Record an album then tour it to death, then do the same thing again and again and it becomes like a 9-5 job. Then come the many rows between band members who mostly hate each other because of this lifestyle so the drugs and drink enter into the equation and things get worse for the band experience but also the person. Then many find they have done all that work and earned very little if anything. Not a very happy existence or outcome.
I had a taste of the above with Eleanor Rigby, so purposely decided I would not go on that treadmill of, record - tour - record - tour Etc. We could have sold more records by touring for sure and I'd like to have done a few more gigs than we actually did but it kept them unique. I'm sure when playing every single day the novelty wears off after a while.
Although I wanted a regular band initially I was aware of the pitfalls so decided I would have a fluid line up from the start.
I have always been anti-drugs and the mental stress of having to deal with that in other band members would have tainted the whole experience. (it did with Eleanor)

I did have a number one hit with Eleanor and it was strange because I never felt that elated about it. (So maybe it's not all it's cracked up to be). As for Top Of The Pops, nobody has been able to do that for many years and being number one seems a whole lot less exciting in this millennium. But at least we were in the 90s and that was the last hurrah for having the buzz of being in the thick of the music business with 7" vinyl singles out competing with others and it was the heyday for the Indie label pioneers. The new millennium brought us homogenised pop songs, acts and productions and as far as aiming for the charts, that lost its visibility after TOTP disappeared and not so many people are aware of what is in the top 20 these days. Once the powers that be mixed up all the different digital sales from downloads and streaming and one person (ED Sheeran) had all the top 10 places it ceased to be credible not to mention hard to earn from (IE: Spotify)

So I did take a break from it all and didn't miss it but got that buzz again with my new band, Psykick Holiday and the buzz was mainly about making great music but mostly about being a music pioneer. Whilst today's acts seem interchangeable I have managed to remain relevant. Even as I write this book I had recently been on the front cover of songwriting magazine, been interviewed by popular DJs on the radio such as Paul Ross regarding being a music pioneer and James Whale about my take on the music biz today and pioneering the Cult Themes productions and I was just in record collector about my producing as well a few weeks ago.

Then, of course, I do many other arts as well. I am still a record producer of others. I have had 12 books out including a best seller 'Memories Are Made Of This' (The Ultimate Retro Pop quiz) 50s to the 90s. I am a Photographer-Artist who has had a big solo exhibition in Mayfair London (the heart of the art world). I was then signed by Saatchi Art who called me an artist of some significance.

But one of the biggest buzzes musically is, every day I wake up I can check my music stats via my distributor and without fail, a dozen or more of my productions or songs are being played each day somewhere in the world including Box Office Poison and most weeks at least one CD or vinyl of B.O.P sells. So new people are still discovering us all the time.

I have already mention Bowie, Madonna & John Barry but one of the biggest buzzes was learning Brian Wilson of the Beach Boys loved the production on the Cult Themes albums and he especially liked Box Office Poison (after hearing our Cds via another producer contact Andy Paley), so much so he put me on the guest list of his first-ever solo concert in London earlier in this Millennium and there was talk of us working together, which could still happen.

The hardest part for any artist is to break through and make your name. Hit acts have it slightly easier having big labels money to break them but they hit the lifestyle mentioned earlier and hate each other then split up but they underestimate how hard it is to make your name in any art form. Many ex-band members carry on doing music but make no dent at all so that's when you get the reunion tour to capitalise on the name (they all still hate each other but they need the money)

Being on an Indie label, we didn't have the big bucks to make us instantly known, so it was hard graft to make your name. But we did it and so the reward is still being bought and played 30 years on although it's unlikely there will be a reunion tour. I am a still friends with all B.O.P members but I am very much into Psykick Holiday and in some way, it's like B.O.P Mk.3.

So if you are missing our music and haven't got **Forever Pop Noir** by Psykick Holiday on CD, that should be your first port of call. Alternatively, I hoped you have enjoyed reliving B.O.P memories with us via this book and discovering many things you may not have known about.Talking of which, here are a few bits of B.O.P trivia. B.O.P had its own fanzine 'Metropolis' for its ten years existence. I ended up doing a few solo gigs that were initially supposed to have been B.O.P gigs. An American hardrock band stole our name at one point so, never gets suckered into thinking that was us............Love Russell

Rare photo of my solo spot in Southend supporting the Soul Detectives for Cult Themes from the 80's

Mouse Russ & Misty Including many rare never seen photos

More rare band shots from an early session

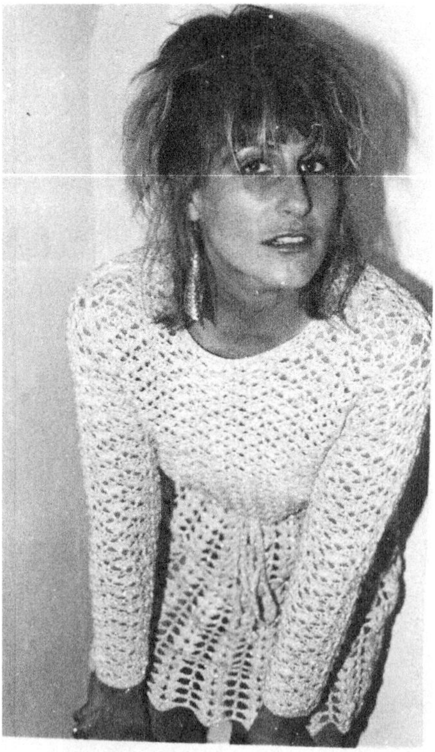

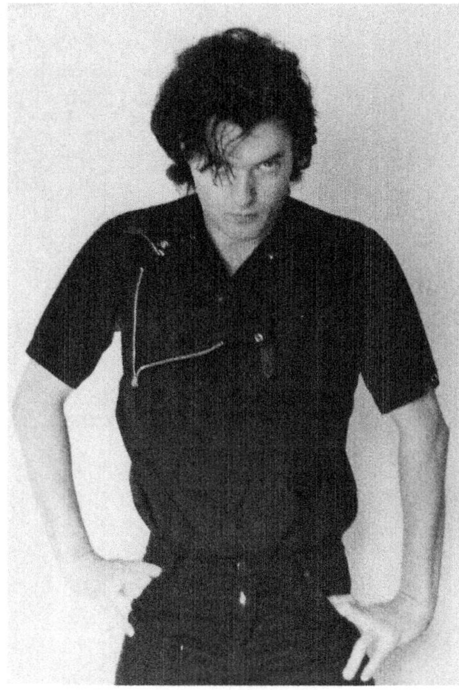

RUSS RARE UNUSED PHOTOS

Mysteries & 1995 stills

Photos of Misty in Moltova as duo taken by Russell

Alternative sleeves & rare concert shots of Mouse with Lynus & Misty with Bruce Li Foundation

Misty from after B.O.P By Russell

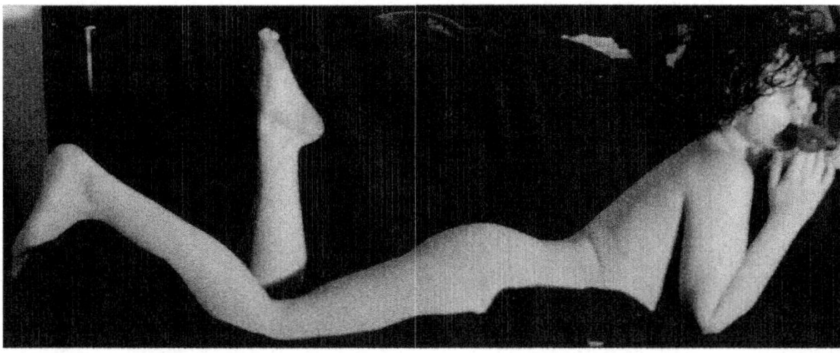

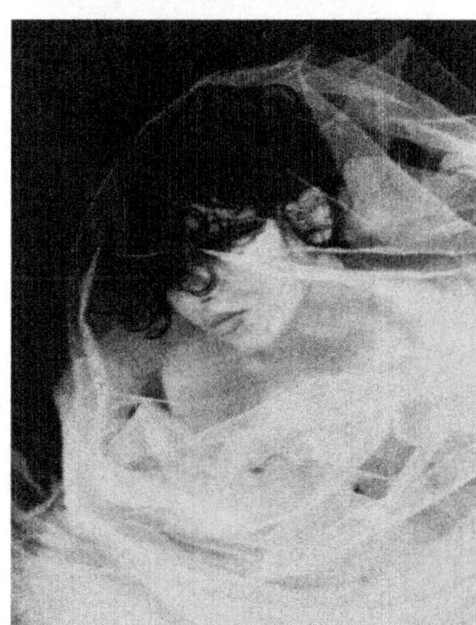

Very rare graphic image of Russ by Mouse plus early session outtake & me as a model for Hi-tek still and Russell's famous coat

OTHER BOOKS OF INTEREST

Although the limited edition books, The Definitive Eleanor Rigby Story, The Eleanor Rigby Picture book & Voyeurs Welcome Vol.1 have all sold out and been deleted the following books are available via Amazon. We are doing two special half price deals on two books that relate to Box Office Poison Direct from us : Those books are Voyeurs Welcome Vol.2 & Adventures of a Dark Duke: The Pin, just email for more details december.books@yahoo.com

Music Business Bastards (How to do well in the music business without getting ripped off) (3rd edition) *Many have said It's the definitive music biz manual.*

Voyeurs Welcome Vol.2 (More photos and lyrics of Russell C. Brennan) Limited edition

Adventures of a Dark Duke: The Pin (novel) *About an indie Rock-star who sticks a pin in a map and has the adventure of a lifetime (Set in Florida, Cuba & Mexico)*

Kidnapping Time (novel) *An erotic sci-fi conspiracy thriller featuring Marilyn Monroe, Frank Sinatra, Cleopatra, Jane Fonda, Bridget Bardot, The Kennedy's, Princess Diana, Queen Elizabeth 1st and many more icons from history. (history will never fell the same after you read this)*

Beyond the Painted Smile (Kindle Only) *(mini biog on road to being a Geisha)*

Memories are Made of This (The Ultimate Retro Pop Quiz) Vol.1 (50s, 60s, 70s, 80s, 90s)

Memories are Made of This (The Ultimate Retro Pop Quiz) Vol.2 (50s, 60s, 70s, 80s, 90s)

Mod Memories are Made of This (The Ultimate Mod Trivia Quiz)

Mixing with the Unknown (novel) *Traditional Horror meets Pulp Fiction with new twists*

Over and Over (novel) A Music Business revenge noir story

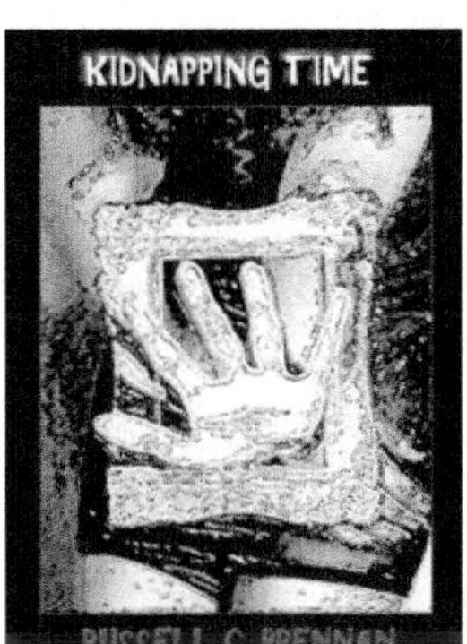

Printed in Great Britain
by Amazon

83301848R00113